W9-AGI-905

Greater Baltimore Urban League
512 Orchard Street
Baltimore, MD 21201

ISBN 978-0-615-65960-2

Layout & Cover Design:
Brown Hornet Design
brownhornetdesign.com

Image:
Copyright: Jon Bilous
Old Town Mall, Baltimore, Maryland.
Courtesy of Shutterstock, Inc.

CONTENTS

Part III: Leadership: Reclaiming Black Power & Looking Forward

ACKNOWLEDGEMENTS

Lilly

Institute for Urban Research, Morgan State University
Evelyn Smith
Rev. Marcus Garvey Wood

Editor's Introduction

On a dreary, cold, rainy morning, in February 2014, J. Howard Henderson, CEO of the Greater Baltimore Urban League (GBUL) and I drove the short journey from the headquarters of the GBUL, the 177-year-old Orchard Street United Methodist Church and Underground Railroad stop, to Providence Baptist Church. At Providence, we met with Rev. Marcus Garvey Wood, one of the most pivotal surviving members of the Civil Rights Movement in Baltimore, and Dr. Martin Luther King, Jr.'s only surviving classmate from Crozer Theological Seminary in Chester, Pennsylvania. Professionally, I envisioned that the interview would help frame the State of Black Baltimore 2015 by revealing the progresses and failures since the 1960s. I entered with an admitted naiveté of perceiving the interview with high hopes for signs of progress that I had somehow been unable to see. Personally, having born witness as a young child to the fires that burned out sections of Baltimore along North Avenue and elsewhere following the 1968 assassination of Dr. Martin Luther King, Jr., I'd hoped the interview would shed light upon questions that have perplexed many: What happened? How and why is Baltimore different from other cities with high levels of chronic poverty? How is it that so much of what was burned out in the 1960s following the assassination of Martin Luther King, Jr., continues to bear the scars of dilapidation, remains un- or underdevelopment? How is it that so much of what was underdeveloped in the 1960s remains further underdeveloped and in an even more advanced state of decay today? How is it that the gap between the haves and have-nots appears to have broadened over the last 50 years? How much of the 1950s and 1960s accounts for what one sees in the lives of the City's most marginalized residents where we bear witness to the effects of "weathering", where sorrow and trauma are worn like armor to shield one from the elusive elements of hope and faith?

We sat and talked with Rev. Wood for almost three hours as he told the story of his life from childhood, arriving in Baltimore from rural, Gloucester, Virginia, tracing the years of life throughout the American South and mid-Atlantic. After a circuitous journey infused with local and national civil rights leaders—across space from Virginia to Maryland, to Pennsylvania, and time from the 1940s to 2013, at the end, Rev. Woods closed with a framing of the past and the present that I had not quite expected. He described how people in Baltimore engaged in protest—how folks demanded, fought, marched, and sat-in; yet, at the end, gained freedom, but only in the sense of how Blacks are free to move around space. While there is now legally sanctioned access to schools and neighborhoods, at the end of the day, the city's public schools remain largely segregated, employment opportunities for many of the City's locals are lacking, and the lack of access to capital for Blacks and in Black neighborhoods continue to inform a neighborhood's economic vitality. For decades, Black Baltimoreans could not really live where they wanted to because of systematic and government sanctioned denial of Blacks to be able to move into certain neighborhoods even if they had the means to do so. The practice of redlining deliberately stifled housing investments in Black neighborhoods and continues to have a tremendous adverse impact.

In the end, we left the meeting with Rev. Woods with many more questions than answers, and certainly not answers we anticipated leaving with just three hours prior when we arrived. Multiple narratives co-exist, sometimes in alignment, sometimes in conflict, and sometimes in muted silence. The narrative that emerged from our meeting was confirmation that in many ways the Civil Rights Movement (CRM) in Baltimore came to a stuttering stop before it fully gained traction and remains incomplete today. The CRM in Baltimore afforded the growth of a concept of equal access and opportunity in education, housing and employment, yet when one looks around today it seems that the imagining of the concept exceeded true and authentic access to these opportunities.

In August, 2013, the Greater Baltimore Urban League of (GBUL) issued a call to invite submissions for this edited volume, The State of Black Baltimore 2014. Similar to the National Urban League's State of Black America, which aims to illuminate pressing issues and pose solutions from a national vantage point, the State of Black Baltimore focuses on some of the most challenging issues to Baltimore. This year's theme, "Baltimore: Calling for a Social Revolution, 50 Years Later" looks back at the March on Washington (MoW) 50 years ago, and related events in history that changed the experiences of African Americans across the U.S., and what that legacy has left us here today in 2014. Among these events are court cases including Brown v. Board of Education of Topeka (1954), Heart of Atlanta Motel, Inc. v. United States (1964), Loving v. Virginia (1967); the passage of acts including the Civil Rights Acts of 1957, 1960, 1964 and 1968, the Economic Opportunity Act of 1964 and the Voting Rights Act of 1965; the passage of the Twenty-fourth Amendment to the United States Constitution (1964) which outlawed mandatory polling and other taxes which prevented many African Americans from voting, the issuance of several Executive Orders related to employment, housing and the armed forces; and the establishment of the Civil Rights Commission (1957), the Civil Rights Division in the Department of Justice, and the Equal Employment Opportunity Commission (1964).

The year 2013 marked the 50th anniversary of the March on Washington for Jobs and Freedom (MoW), where more than 250,000 people gathered in the nation's capitol to demand change and equal rights. Led by a coalition of leaders representing civil rights, social justice, economic justice, labor and religious organizations the issues of the historic 1963 MoW were focused on a core platform which demanded equality and access in education, employment, housing, and police protection. It is these issues that authors of chapters in this volume were invited to grapple, explore, and evaluate.

While the historic march as part of the broader social movement led to legislative victories, in 2013, most of the MoW's demands remain unmet. While some of the language has changed, racial inequities persist in areas that include access to: quality and decent housing, adequate and integrated schools, employment hiring and promotion practices, and police protection. Similarly, unequal access persists in banking, health care, grocery stores, insurance, employment, housing, technology, and transportation. Authors were invited to submit articles focused on the issues raised in the demands of the MoW in the context of Baltimore, in 1963 and in 2013. Authors were also invited to illuminate new barriers to freedom and jobs in Baltimore, and nationally, that have emerged since 1963. We welcomed papers from different disciplinary backgrounds, voices, and communities, and asked that all papers reflect innovative, actionable, programmatic, practice and/or policy-relevant strategies in Baltimore. What follows is a collection of chapters that shed light upon some of the substantial issues for Black Baltimore and Black America: housing, home ownership, employment, health, criminal justice, incarceration, education, and leadership. Most, if not all, of these issues were raised in some form on the Mall in Washington DC on that hot day in August 1963, when Dr. King and so many others spoke of their frustrations and their dreams for fairness, justice and equality.

This volume is divided into three parts. And, in these three parts, the authors describe the state of Black Baltimore in 2014 as one in which Blacks are more likely to reside in high poverty, resource-poor communities with less access to adequate food, housing, education, transportation, and police protection. Perhaps the legacy of decades of unequal opportunity is most profound in the extraordinary burden of illness and premature death faced by many in Baltimore. As in other high poverty areas across the U.S., the ultimate cost of being Black in Baltimore is a shortened life, far too often filled with poorer health status from birth until death. Chapters in the first part illuminate the social, economic and geographic contexts of the 1960s and the present by investigating issues of employment, education, housing, neighborhoods and politics. The second part examines the explosion of public health related issues that have emerged since the 1960s. The third part, authors examine critical issues of Black power and leadership. Each section concludes with a list of recommended resources the authors hope will inspire the volume's readers to become catalysts for change by taking action—by learning more, by exploring and joining forces with existing local resources to mold change and equality by being part of a movement to create change.

The year 2013 also marked the passing of Dr. Homer Favor, economist, Civil Rights activist, and founder of the Urban Studies Institute at Morgan State University. In the 1950s and 1960s, Dr. Favor, along with other members of the "Goon Squad" focused on the issues of the day—substandard housing, suppressed property values, unemployment and suppressed wages, and daily economic challenges for Baltimore's Black population. While many of the challenges we face today are the legacy of decades of systemic oppression and inequality, the work advanced in this volume is intended to create new conversations and actions in response to persistent dilemmas with the hope that you as a reader will share in carrying the torch for justice, equality and progress.

Tracy R. Rone, Ph.D.
Institute for Urban Research
Morgan State University
Baltimore, MD

State of Black Baltimore 2015:
Still Separate, Still Unequal
President's Message

J. Howard Henderson

The Baltimore Urban League is profoundly grateful to the local community activists, scholars, writers and thinkers who contributed their time, scholarship, perspective and vision to examining the state of Black Baltimore and its progress over five decades in healthcare, housing, education, and economic, social and criminal justice.

Our report's title, **"The State of Black Baltimore 2015: Still Separate, Still Unequal"** reflects disappointment in the progress of the 50 years since the watershed events that resulted in civil rights victories for Black Americans. We would love to have another, more uplifting story to tell but regrettably the data does not support that picture. In this report, we look at the decades since the iconic 1963 March on Washington for Jobs and Freedom that led to the historic passage of the 1964 Civil Rights Act. We conclude with acknowledgement of the 50th anniversary of "Bloody Sunday," when a peaceful voting rights demonstration in Selma, AL was met violently with teargas and billy clubs wielded by state troopers.

Yes we can claim improvement over the 50 years since we memorialized our rights in landmark civil rights legislation. But every few steps forward have been accompanied by backslides. To this day, headline after headline continues to reveal that we remain challenged by official policies and practices that neuter civil rights gains. The violent death of teenager Michael Brown in August 2014 at the hands of the police echoed throughout the world. It shed awful insight on what it means for many Blacks living in America and put Ferguson, MO center stage, making that St. Louis suburb the archetype for the continued abuse of civil rights for African Americans. A subsequent report by the U.S. Justice Department in 2015 found that the city's criminal justice system used the Black community as a cash register, applying excessive fines and fees that generated nearly a quarter of its $13.3 million budget for the 2015 fiscal year.

No, Baltimore is not Ferguson, but what happened there is a sober reminder that we cannot fall asleep at the wheel at any time, anywhere. We must pay attention to the practices within our city's police department, courts, housing, employment and be aware of all of those official acts that subtly strip citizens of their rights. Remaining silent is not an option. It also is critical that we engage in meaningful discussions about race, not just among ourselves but with the Baltimore community at large. The failure to understand impacts us all. We cannot allow indifference to become a silent partner in our lives.

As one of the youth leaders for the NAACP in my home state of West Virginia in the 1960's, I was well aware of the goal of Dr. Martin Luther King, Jr of achieving equal justice in the context of a multiracial community. He believed in the concept of a "beloved community."

He became the symbol not only of the civil rights movement but of America itself: A symbol of a land of freedom where people of all races, creeds, and nationalities could live together as a "beloved community". We must also pay tribute to a number of gallant Americans who refused to be compromised by the forces of racism and injustice. Today, I challenge all of us to look toward the next years with renewed determination to dismantle the lingering vestiges of institutionalized discrimination that still remain deeply embedded in the social fabric of our society.

Unless we find the political will to eradicate racial inequity and exploitation, this society will perpetually mired in tragedies. Today, the quest for equal justice must be viewed in terms of multiracial—multicultural—and multilingual layers if we are to transform our society.

With the unemployment rate for Black America over 18 percent and the number of the long-term unemployed at a 25-year high, we must empower our communities. Too many people have moved from well-paying jobs to lesser-paying jobs to no jobs at all. America's cities are hurting when over 60 percent of young black men are out of school and out of work.

Since the mid-1990s and continuing today, politicians and a number of grass-roots organizations have launched new assaults on affirmative action and voting rights. People died for the right to vote. We must use those rights lest we lose them.

The effects of poverty have taken its devastating toll on the citizens left in these inner city neighborhoods. They are the people whose lives are in the direct line of fire of the urban violence surrounding them twenty-four seven. We need a chance at saving the lives of those of our young people. The headline of a Sunday, October 6, 1985, New York Times article read, "Baltimoreans Mounting Drive to Fight Violence." Sadly, this article could be dated today, nearly 30 years later. The failed measure of the past 30 years to address the murder rate has had a crippling effect on the health and stability of our neighborhoods. Our forward progress will be severely impeded—unless we make reform of the educational system.

School reform alone cannot substantially raise performance of the poorest African-American students unless we also improve the conditions that leave too many children unprepared to take advantage of what schools have to offer. Social and economic disadvantages depress student performance. Concentrating disadvantaged students in racially and economically homogeneous schools depresses it further. Schools that most disadvantaged black children attend today are located in segregated neighborhoods far distant from middle-class students.

As we embark on the next fifty years, the Greater Baltimore Urban League continues to seek equality. We are compelled to close the gaps between the limitless potential of our youth and their achievement. We can do this.

In 1963, Whitney M. Young, Jr, then President of the Nation Urban League, spoke at the March on Washington and warned that "The hour is late. The gap in resources and opportunities between Blacks and whites is widening…" The alarms that were sounded then, which have been repeated by many since, are unfortunately repeated in this year's *State of Black Baltimore*. We must activate the goals and vision of those seminal civil rights leaders who preceded us. Join with us as we advance the work of bringing about equality in Baltimore and among all Baltimoreans.

Part One:
Getting to the Current Context: Jobs, Education, Housing, and Neighborhoods

Editor's Introduction

The historic 1950s and 1960s U.S. Civil Rights Movement was driven largely by the quest to gain equal access to quality education and equal opportunities for employment, hiring, promotion, and fair wages. Indeed, it was the labor sector that emerged as a champion for worker rights and helped to orchestrate employment and wages as the center of the platform for the 1963 March on Washington. In 2014, Baltimore City attempts to navigate the challenging landscape of:

- an annual unemployment rate of 9.8% to 10.9% since 2009

- marked disparities between a highly skilled and educated workforce and a poorly skilled and uneducated workforce;

- a disparate wealth gap between the City's wealthiest and most economically impoverished residents;

- the predominance of African-American residents in hypersegregated, low-resource neighborhoods

- disparate Pre-Kindergarten to 12th grade schooling options, in which an under-resourced public school system is populated overwhelming by students who are African American and/or low-income, and an elaborate network of well-funded elite, independent schools populated overwhelmingly by the wealthy, white students

- the environmental and health impact of thousands of lead-laden homes, many in some state of abandonment or dilapidation;

- a lack of affordable, quality, safe housing; and

- displacement and gentrification under the guise of urban renewal and development.

The authors in this section offer keen historical insight into some of the underlying root causes of today's neighborhood and wealth disparities. They describe the disturbing legacy of racist practices and policies and the implications for Black Baltimoreans today in housing, education, employment, community resources, and health.

Understanding the Importance of The Civil Rights Movement in Baltimore by Exploring Jobs and Education

Linda Loubert & Jeanetta Churchill

Abstract

One of the main components of Civil Rights Movement that stemmed from The March on Washington in 1964 was jobs. Indeed, Martin Luther King, Jr.' life ended during his struggle to bring justice for the sanitation workers in Memphis, Tennessee. Because education and jobs are highly correlated, this study explores the educational levels and job types. The time period from 1960 to 2010 are used to capture what changes occurred during that 50 year span and what that implicates for this quinquagenary. Among other important policy prescriptions for the March on Washington was the "dream" for changes in the lives of poor, African Americans as articulated by Dr. Martin Luther King, Jr.

The location of education attainment and job types are explored spatially by U.S. Census Tract decadal data for Baltimore City. Baltimore's racial makeup flipped from predominately white (65%) in 1960 to predominately black (64%) by 2010, yet it stills exhibit a high degree of poverty during those times. With these changes in demographics, we examine whether or not the Civil Rights Era of policy reform for jobs on a federal level play a significant role in putting African Americans to work and out of poverty in a city such as Baltimore, MD. Our study indicates that although some things changed, much stayed the same, particularly the percent of those below the poverty line.

Introduction

One of the main components of Civil Rights Movement that stemmed from The March on Washington in 1963 was jobs. Indeed, Martin Luther King, Jr.'s life ended during his struggle to bring justice for the sanitation workers in Memphis, Tennessee. Because education and jobs are highly correlated, this chapter explores educational levels and job types. The time period from 1960 to 2010 are used to capture what changes occurred during that 50-year span and what that implicates for this quinquagenary. The location of education attainment and job types are explored spatially by using U.S. Census Tract decadal data for Baltimore City, Maryland. Baltimore's racial makeup flipped from predominantly white (65%) in 1960 to predominately black (64%) by 2010, yet it still exhibited a high degree of poverty in 1960 and as well by 2010 (see Table 1). With these changes in demographics we try to answer the question of whether or not the Civil Rights Era of policy reform for jobs on a federal level played a significant role in employment for African Americans in a town such as Baltimore.

TABLE 1: Demographic characteristics of Baltimore City, MD in 1960 and 2010

	1960		2010	
CHARACTERISTIC	**NUMBER**	**PERCENT**	**NUMBER**	**PERCENT**
White	610,608	65%	183,830	30%
Black	325,589	35%	395,781	64%
Other Category	2,827	0%	41,350	7%
Male	452,606	48%	292,249	47%
Female	486,418	52%	328,712	53%
Age under 18	315,584	34%	133,560	22%
Age 18 to 34	200,406	21%	181,674	29%
Age 35 to 64	338,167	36%	232,915	38%
Age 65 and over	84,867	9%	72,812	12%
Percent below poverty line	212,154	23%	Not available	23%
Total Population	**939,024**	**100%**	**620,961**	**100%**

SOURCE: U.S. Census Data, www.socialexplorer.com, New York City, NY: Social Explorer 2014.

Education in Baltimore

Beginning with the history of education in Baltimore, we see it was not unlike most Eastern cities in the early 18th and 19th centuries. Clergy were the overseers of the early schools. Colleges like Morgan College (now known as Morgan State University) were established under religious entities. Philanthropists also contributed to schools for the poor. Public education which started around 1830 in Baltimore did not come easy for it was beset with an indifferent citizenry for public schooling. The board of commissioners of Public Schools, however, was diligent in seeing it come into fruition. Funding for public schools came from tuition fees, a city tax, the State school fund, and from dividends on bank stock and rents (BCPSS, 2007).

During the period of 1860 to 1900 the population of the city doubled and its growth advanced the importance of education and culture. The city began to be known for its universities, colleges, and medical and professional schools. This also marked the period for the beginning of the "colored" schools. Culturally, it was the norm to establish separate schools for nonwhites at that time. In 1883 the "Colored High and

16

Training School" was the first high school for African Americans and later acquired the name of Frederick Douglass High School. It was first located on East Saratoga Street near St. Paul Street but moved slowly west to different locations before it settled at its the present location on Gwynn Falls Parkway on the west side of Baltimore. One of the most notable alumni was Supreme Court Justice Thurgood Marshall, a graduate of the class of 1926. Interestingly, Paul Laurence Dunbar High School, which opened its doors as a high school in 1937, settled right off Orleans Street to accommodate the community of African Americans on the east side of town. Douglass and Dunbar high schools became the two important institutions for educating African Americans in the city. Their location in the city served as a focal point on the east and west side for African American households. Geographic Information Systems (GIS) serves as a useful tool to emphasize characteristics of these neighborhoods and to explain the changes in education and jobs for citizens in Baltimore. Knowing that large numbers of African Americans were clustered in US Census tracts around these schools during the 1960s provides robustness to the analyses that follow (**Map 1**).

In 1960, education for a small number of black middle-class helped show the affluence that was possible. McKay (2007) found that upper middle-class women in Baltimore's African American community exhibited labor force characteristics seen mostly with white women in 2000. That is to say, a large percentage of the women worked rather than stay-at-home. These women were a part of the "Lads and Lassie Intensive Study Sample" done by the University of Maryland Medical School. Even though the study only had 169 men and 169 women which represented 0.1% of the total black population, it did offer a glimmer of what was possible for African Americans as well as a reality check that very few were well-off during that time. Most of these women (82%) were employed in professional occupations and 91% of them had a college degree , (McKay 2007). The study showed that as many women as men held positions in professional and managerial occupations which was unusual since that phenomenon was not seen until 2000 for white women.

In 1960 the overall percent of African Americans receiving a high school diploma or more was 45 and increased to 76 by 2010 which indicates that more were graduating at least from high school. We also know that the number of African Americans almost doubled in the city during that same period. Using a spatial crosstab analysis (**Map 1**), we can show the pattern of those neighborhoods that were predominately African American with a high school diploma or more moving farther away from the center of the city into the county by 2010. Sadly, the inner east and west side now have predominately Black neighborhoods with high numbers of residents without high school diploma.

MAP 1: Variability of completion of a high school diploma or higher by African-American residence (among African Americans aged 25 and up), by census tract; Baltimore City, MD, 1960 – 2010.

1960:

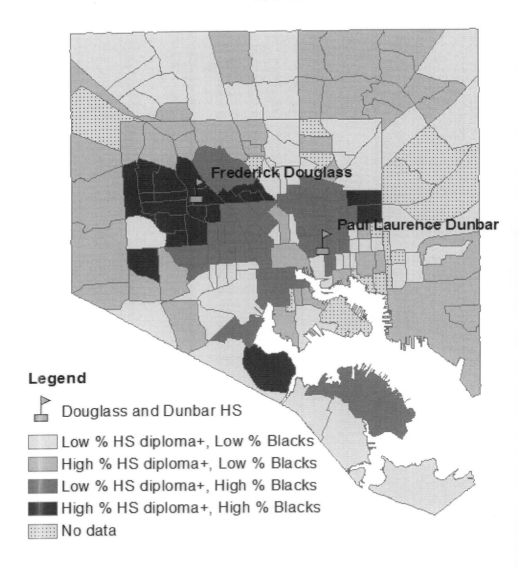

Legend

⚑ Douglass and Dunbar HS

▨ Low % HS diploma+, Low % Blacks
▨ High % HS diploma+, Low % Blacks
▨ Low % HS diploma+, High % Blacks
■ High % HS diploma+, High % Blacks
▨ No data

2006-2010:

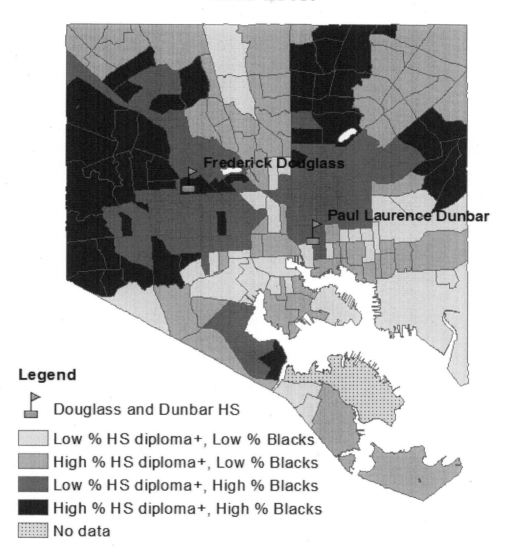

Legend

⚑ Douglass and Dunbar HS

Low % HS diploma+, Low % Blacks
High % HS diploma+, Low % Blacks
Low % HS diploma+, High % Blacks
High % HS diploma+, High % Blacks
No data

SOURCE: Raw data from 1960 Decennial Census Data, www.socialexplorer.com, New York City, NY: Social Explorer 2013. Raw data from U.S. Census Bureau, 2006-2010 American Community Survey.

Neighborhoods which were predominately black in 1960 like Forest Park, Walbrook, and Sandtown-Winchester had more than 50% of their residents aged 25 and over with a high school diploma or more level of education. Neighborhoods like Ashburton, which was commonly known as the "Gold Coast" due to its stately homes, was 22% black, and had over 80% of its black residents with a high school or more degree.

Another one of the goals of the March on Washington was to desegregate schools but, even though the city was not predominately black, by 1960 the Baltimore City Public School System became predominately black. White flight had started picking up its pace, making segregated schools the reality. Dot density maps (**Maps 2-7**) indicate the decadal changes for African American residence inside and around the city, and shows the locations of where the city became predominately black. The maps, also, show that the west side of Baltimore has the greatest migration out of the city using Liberty Road as a quasi "freedom" passage from segregated neighborhoods without realizing that newly segregated neighborhoods would soon be created even within the county. *De facto* segregation that occurred in the neighborhoods worked its way to racial segregation in the schools, leaving Baltimore with large numbers of poor residents and students with lower than average expectation for school success and consequently, less chances for better paying job success.

MAPS 2-7: Dot-density maps of African-American residential patterns; Baltimore, MD 1960-2010.

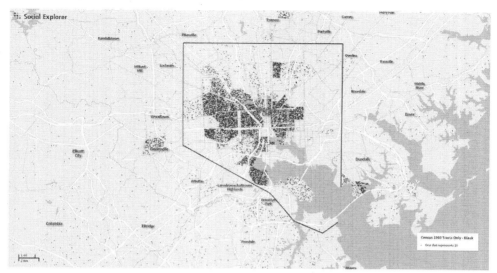

MAP 2: 1960

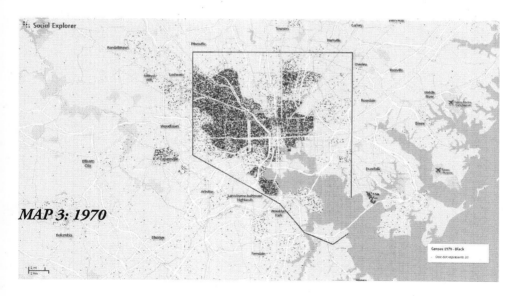

MAP 3: 1970

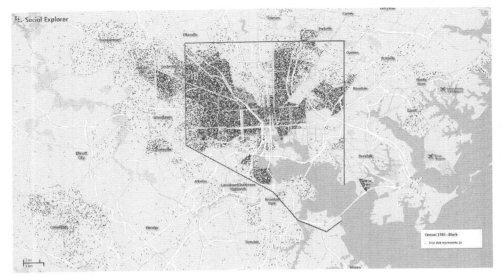

MAP 4: 1980

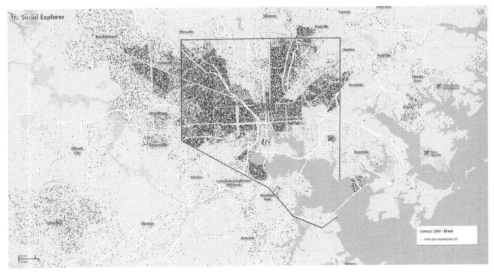

MAP 5: 1990

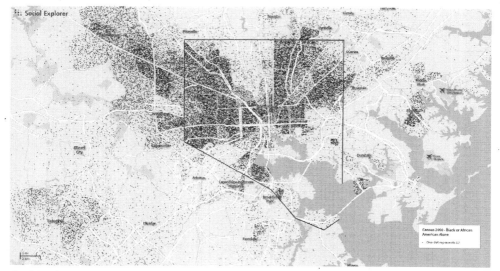

MAP 6: 2000

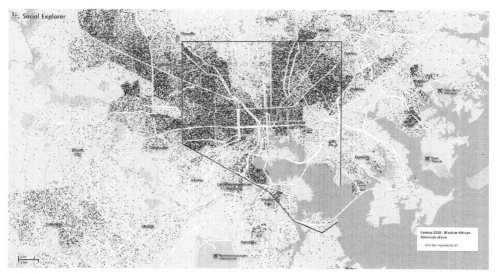

MAP 7: 2010

SOURCE: U.S. Census Data, www.socialexplorer.com, New York City, NY: Social Explorer 2013.

The following chloropleth **(maps 8 - 9)** present the starkness of that predominately westward migration of African Americans from the city. Areas spreading west, as well as east, represent a greater than 70% concentration of African Americans.

MAPS 8: African-American residential patterns by census tract; Baltimore metropolitan area, MD, 1960-2010.

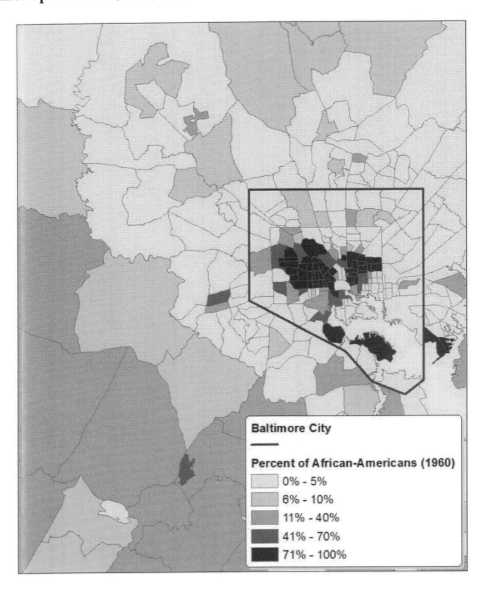

Baltimore City

Percent of African-Americans (1960)

- 0% - 5%
- 6% - 10%
- 11% - 40%
- 41% - 70%
- 71% - 100%

SOURCE: Data: U.S. Census Data, www.socialexplorer.com, New York City, NY: Social Explorer 2014. Shapefiles: Minnesota Population Center. National Historical Geographic Information System: Version 2.0. Minneapolis, MN: University of Minnesota 2011

MAPS 9: African-American residential patterns by census tract; Baltimore metropolitan area, MD, 1960-2010.

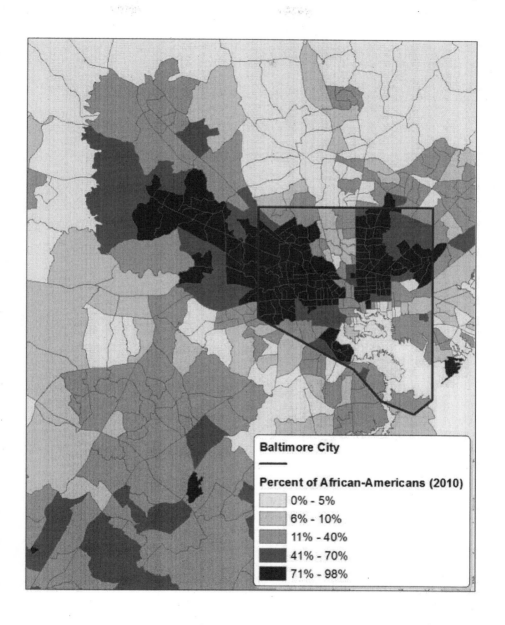

Baltimore City

Percent of African-Americans (2010)

- 0% - 5%
- 6% - 10%
- 11% - 40%
- 41% - 70%
- 71% - 98%

Occupations among African Americans

Data from the 1960 U.S. Census records indicate the primary occupation from which the person in the labor force earns the most money. The main categories are listed in Figure 1 and it presents the percent of African Americans working in the major occupational classes. The Sales category includes any job from peddler to newsboy, insurance agent or sales clerk. Clerical workers such as secretaries, receptionists, attendants in medical offices, or bookkeepers fall into the Service category of occupations. The Management category ranges from floor and building managers to officials in administration. This also includes business, science and arts occupations. The Production category can be seen in transportation and material moving occupations like truck drivers. The Construction category includes jobs utilizing natural resources to maintenance. Some examples of jobs in this category are laundry and dry cleaning operatives, bus drivers, asbestos and insulation workers or furnacemen and smeltermen. Figure 1 shows that in 1960, two-thirds of African Americans worked in service, construction, and production categories.

FIGURE 1: Percent of employed African-Americans by major occupational class, Baltimore City, MD; 1960 – 2010.

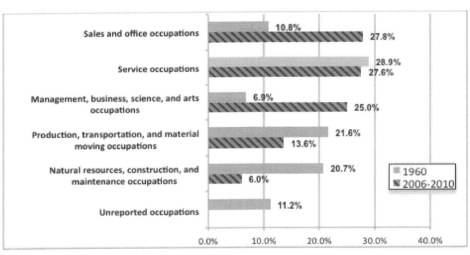

SOURCE: *1960 Decennial Census Data, www.socialexplorer.com, New York City, NY: Social Explorer 2013. U.S. Census Bureau, 2006-2010 American Community Survey.*

Although not shown as a category in the figure, the Classified Index of Occupations and Industries of the 1960 Decennial Census of Population indicates that 11% of nonwhites ages 14 and older were employed as private household workers. (Social Explorer, 2013). The representation in Map 10 indicates where most of these household workers were employed. These areas were white but employed black household workers.

MAP 10: Percent of African-American females aged 14 and over employed as domestic household workers by census tract; Baltimore City, MD, 1960.

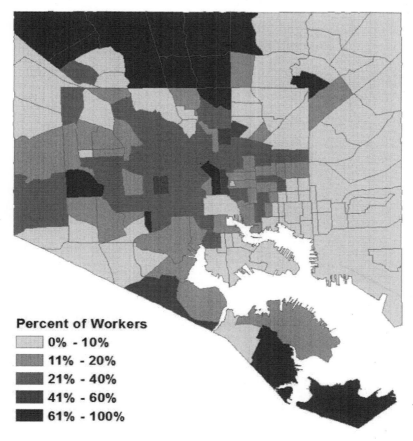

Percent of Workers
- 0% - 10%
- 11% - 20%
- 21% - 40%
- 41% - 60%
- 61% - 100%

SOURCE: 1960 Decennial Census Data, Minnesota Population Center. National Historical Geographic Information System: Version 2.0. Minneapolis, MN: University of Minnesota 2011.

By 2010, many more African Americans worked in the sales and office and management occupations even though about the same percentage (28%) worked in service occupations. The data seem to indicate that labor improvements were in progress. A more detailed examination is necessary to validate these changes in the percentages. Therefore, we use the rigor of spatial analysis (**Map 11**) to uncover concentrated areas in the city whose workers were employed in the occupational categories of service, management, construction, and sales. The clusters of neighborhoods for sales workers are used to illustrate migration of categories of workers moved out of the city The legend in the map shows clusters of areas that have higher levels of people in sales which are surrounded by other census tracts with high percentages in sales and it gives those clusters a label of "High-High". The label "High-Low" means that there are a significant amount of workers in sales but they are not surrounded by tracts that have a significant amount of workers in the sales category. This means there were some scattered pockets in the city where there were a significant amount of residents who worked in the sales occupation category. Similarly, the Low-High category means that there were few residents in that Census tract working in sales, and those tracts were surrounded by tracts that had high numbers of sales workers. The Low-Low category simply indicates that there were few workers in sales in that tract or in the surrounding tracts. This type of spatial analysis helps to cement the notion that those with "good" jobs were moving out of the city by 2010. All of the other categories showed the same movement; African Americans with jobs moved away from the city center by 2010.

MAP 11: Clustering of African-Americans working in Sales and Office occupations, by census tract; Baltimore City, MD, 1960 – 2010.

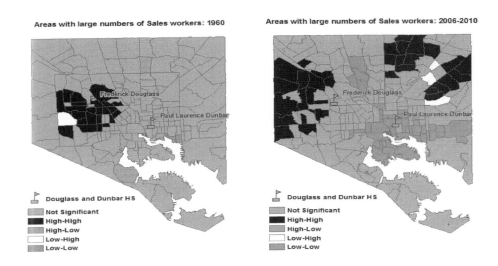

SOURCE: *Raw data from 1960 Decennial Census, www.socialexplorer.com, New York City, NY: Social Explorer 2013. U.S. Census Bureau, 2006-2010 American Community Survey.*

The Unemployment map from 2010 (**Map 12**) presents a "telling tale" on the idea of poverty in the city. Although unemployment data for 1960 are not shown, areas with 10% up to 23% of unemployment are similar to the areas with the low education rates in 1960 as shown in Map 1 which stands as a great proxy to indicate the location of those low unemployment rates. Those areas are closely aligned with the same areas in Map 12. This could then solidify the reality of a "poorer" and "worse off" Baltimore. This, of course, was not the "dream" based on the March on Washington in 1963. Policy prescriptions following the March on Washington like the Civil Rights Act of 1964 failed in many aspects when the patterns of unemployment over the years are closely observed.

MAP 12: Percent unemployed among labor force aged 16+, by census tract; Baltimore, MD metro area, 2006-2010.

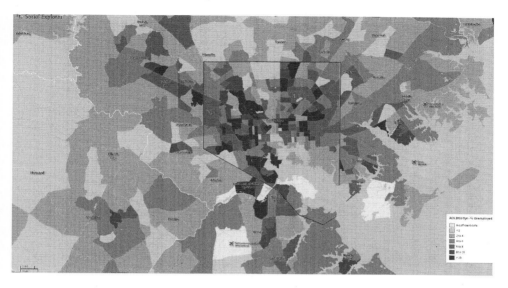

SOURCE: U.S. Census Data, www.socialexplorer.com, New York City, NY: Social Explorer 2013.

The evaluation of education and labor is seen on one hand as two improvements for African Americans from 1960 to 2010. Indeed, improvements in the percentages receiving a high school diploma or higher did occur and movement into more management type occupations occurred. Yet, a closer examination of the data using GIS, we can see that the migration of African Americans out of Baltimore City and the growth of unemployment within the city suggest that the best outcomes did not occur as a result of the "dream" for African American. The best contemporary policy prescription would be to improve access to higher quality education, occupations and employment in higher earning categories, thereby, reducing the poverty levels and unemployment that exists today for the State of Black Baltimore.

References

Baltimore City Public Schools, Early Schools http://thomasghayes.baltimorecityschools.org/About/History/Early_Schools.asp   Retrieved January 9, 2014.

McKay, Ruth, 2007, *Monthly Labor Review*, vol 130 n 2, February 2007 p.3-8

www.socialexplorer.com. New York City, NY: Social Explorer 2014.

U.S. Census Bureau, 2006-2010 American Community Survey.

A Tale of Two Baltimore Neighborhoods: Redlining in 2014

Samuel L. Brown

Abstract

After 50 years of legal civil rights, African Americans in Baltimore City are still on a quest for substantive equality. In the context of a changing global political economy, with all of the legal and policy changes extending procedural rights to African Americans since the 1950s and 60s, how can the persistent social, political and economic inequalities in Baltimore be explained? The puzzle of the persistent racial inequalities in Baltimore can be traced to law, policy, and the habits of the actors in the housing market. This paper explores the persistent effects of housing segregation, as a source of the contemporary patterns of the social, political, and economic and health disparities for Black Baltimore.

Introduction

In the 50 years since the 1963 March on Washington for Jobs and Freedom's call for a Social Revolution, the persistent effects of housing segregation remain in Black Baltimore. Indeed, this city has a long history of housing and financing policies that provided the context for the historic March on Washington in 1963. It has been over a century since the City of Baltimore passed the West Ordinance of 1910—a law which prohibited the transfer of ownership of homes in major white communities to black residents—however, the legacy of thoughts and the institutionalized habits of public and private actors became the substitutes for the instrument of law. The racial segregation in housing that we see in contemporary Baltimore can be linked to law, public policy, and the actions of landlords, homeowners, bankers, realtors, and government officials. The aim of this chapter is to explore how social and economic racial inequities are produced, reproduced, and maintained within Baltimore's communities. As such, it attempts to move beyond explanations that rely solely on the acts of individuals to reflect more broadly on the effects of policies and of governmental and private actors.

The Production of Homeowner Communities in Baltimore

At the federal level, the National Housing Act of 1934 established the Federal Housing Administration (FHA) to rebuild the housing market after the Great Depression. To implement its operations at the local level, FHA created the Home Owners' Loan Corporation (HOLC). The HOLC functioned as a risk-appraiser of mortgage markets and created a series of neighborhood-specific risk assessments of all U.S. cities with populations greater than 40,000. Residential Security maps were developed for over 200 cities across the United States, including Atlanta, Baltimore, Boston, Chicago, Detroit, Los Angeles, New Orleans, Oakland, Philadelphia, Pittsburgh, Richmond and Washington, D.C. using colors to indicate the range of risk in specific neighborhoods. The common name for these maps is "redlining" because high risk areas appeared in the color red. The lower risk categories were shaded with the colors blue and green. Race played a significant role in determining the level of risk assigned to communities since "non-white population" was an explicit factor in determining HOLC high-risk classification. This institutional practice worked effectively to marginalize communities on the basis of their racial composition. In addition, FHA rules were implemented in ways that excluded inner city row homes from eligibility for home loans. When the effects of FHA and HOLA rules are combined, the result was a significant increase in available credit in suburbs to foster the development of homes that were sold almost exclusively to white residents. The long term effect of this institutionalized behavior was to expand opportunities for financially accessible homeownership to white suburban residents while suppressing the growth of homeowner communities in inner cities like Baltimore.

During suburbanization of the 1950s many families left cities in favor of suburbs as space was made available outside cities for people who wanted to own their own home. The FHA provided mortgages to these families; however, blacks and other nonwhite groups were consistently denied loans, despite having the purchasing power to repay them. This type of institutionalized behavior has been practiced since the early founding of this nation and it continues to shape the patterns and practices of bureaucratic and market behavior into the modern day.

While the discriminatory practices used by HOLC and FHA have been outlawed at the federal level, racial disparities in access to home loan remain problematic. It appears that banks and creditors apply different approaches to evaluating risk for nonwhite groups as opposed to whites. For example, though a black family may have more than sufficient funds to secure down payment for a house, a black family will often pay a higher interest (or higher price for the home entirely) for the ability to claim ownership. In contrast, whites do not go through the same standard operating procedures of discrimination; if a white family was to provide more than sufficient evidence of funds to secure a home, the white family is not intensively deemed a non-repayment flight risk.

This paper will explore a descriptive analysis as a case study of one historically redlined and one non-redlined community in Baltimore to highlight the contemporary nature of home ownership and community distress. The aim is to highlight the difference between a redlined and non-redlined community in terms of persistent segregation, poverty, education and economic development and the corresponding impacts on community health outcomes.

The literature on effects of homeownership has the following subtopics: (1) proponents argue for low-income homeownership as an asset building strategy for home equity accumulation (Retsinas and Belsky, 2002); as substitute for financial investments (e.g., individual retirement accounts, stocks and mutual funds; as a spontaneous savings program; and as a source of predictable housing costs; (2) Researchers' impressions are that social and behavioral changes might occur because of homeownership (Rohe et al. 2002; Rohe and Stegman 1994a, 1994b); increases in life satisfaction, civic participation, and improved physical and psychological health (Dietz and Haurin, 2003); (3) Evidence that low-income homeownership improves cognitive and behavioral function in children that result in reduced juvenile delinquency and improved school performance (Haurin et al, 2002); and (4) At the neighborhood level, the differences highlighted above translate into positive spillover effects (Rohe et al, 2002a, Rohe and Stewart, 1996; Haurin et al, 2003).

There is growing body of literature suggesting an intertwined relationship between housing quality and health. Population health is argued to be shaped by policies and community conditions. Homeownership has been considered a key motivating factor for building stable communities thereby reproducing neighborhood advantages. As a result, some theories of homeownership suggest that well-maintained and reliable housing play an important role in the social determinants of physical health. From a sociological perspective, compelling evidence shows that certain external factors such as homeownership play a significant role in shaping the mental health of individuals (Manturuk, 2012).

At the individual level, health status has been linked to housing conditions. Some research suggests that ownership seems to link to higher social status, better physical and psychological health and larger life satisfaction (Page-Adams & Sherraden, 1997; Spilerman, 2000). Some studies sought a positive correlation between homeownership and human health, finding that homeowners, in general, possess better health, both physically and mentally than the renters (Connolly et al., 2010). However, it is unclear whether those findings could be generalized to all local areas such as Baltimore City. Therefore, this chapter will examine whether the homeownership is associated with the social and economic conditions of two communities of Baltimore City, Maryland.

Data Source
Community Statistical Areas (CSAs) were used to assess homeownership rates in a historically redlined and non-redlined community in Baltimore City. All of the analysis is conducted at the ecological level, and as a result no inferences will be drawn about the effects of homeownership on individuals and families. The data are from the Baltimore Neighborhood Indicators Alliance (BNIA), a local affiliate of the National Neighborhood Indicator Partnership (NNIP), and is geographically-based on Community Statistical Areas aggregated from Census track data. While the City of Baltimore recognizes two hundred and fifty neighborhoods, BNIA combined similar neighborhood tracts together based on demographic and social-economic data to achieve statistical consistency with Census tract boundaries. The result is a data set of one hundred outcome variables for fifty-six neighborhoods. Of the fifty-six neighborhoods, a descriptive analysis was conducted to compare the neighborhood with the highest rate of homeownership to the neighborhood with the lowest rate of homeownership based on the social indicators identified from relevant theories on the community impacts of homeownership.

Baltimore City, as the largest city in Maryland and 24th largest city in the US, has more recently been challenged with a high concentration of poverty. Maryland is one of eight states in the U.S. that has more than 70 percent of the poor concentrated in one city (Maryland State, 1998). The population of Baltimore is approximately 621,342 according to Census data in 2012, with 0.3 percent increase from the last record. In 2014, 23.4 percent of Baltimore residents live below poverty level, more than double the 9.4 percent of Maryland residents who live below the poverty line. The homeownership rate in Baltimore is 48.8 percent compared 68.1 percent in the state.

Baltimore City Background

Among the overall population, there are more women than men in Baltimore City, 52.9 percent versus 47.1 percent. Residents in the age range of 18 to 65 account for 59.8 percent of the population. In Baltimore City, African Americans constitute the largest population, accounting for 63.6 percent compared to 30 percent in Maryland; Whites as a group are the second largest population in Baltimore City with 28.2 percent versus 53.9 percent in the State of Maryland. In terms of education, 79.6 percent of the Baltimore population aged 25 years and above has high school diploma and 26.1 percent has bachelor's degree compared 88.5 percent and 36.3 percent, respectively at the state level. The median household income in Baltimore is $40,803, much lower than state's median of $72,999.

TABLE 1: Facts of Baltimore City

(2012)	Baltimore City	Maryland	United States
Population	621,342	5,884,868	313,873,685
Gender			
Male	47.1%	48.4%	49.2%
Female	52.9%	51.6%	50.8%
Age Group			
0-5	6.8%	6.2%	6.4%
6-17	21.5%	22.8%	23.5%
18-65	59.8%	58%	56.4%
65 or older	11.9%	13%	13.7%
Race/Ethnicity			
White	28.2%	53.9%	63%
Black	63.6%	30%	13.1%
Asian	2.5%	6%	5.1%
Hispanic	4.4%	8.7%	16.9%
Other	1.3%	1.4%	1.9%
Household Income	$40,803	$72,999	$53,046
Education (25+)			
High School degree	79.6%	88.5%	85.7%
Bachelor's degree	26.1%	36.3%	28.5%

Sources: *U.S. Census Bureau: State and County QuickFacts. Data derived from Population Estimates,*

American Community Survey, Census of Population and Housing, State and County Housing Unit Estimates, County Business Patterns, Non-employer Statistics, Economic Census, Survey of Business Owners, Building Permits Problem Statement.

When homeownership rates are examined at the city-wide level, the disparity seems favorable to African Americans. This should not be surprising in light of the high concentration African Americans in the city. As the chart on housing tenure in Baltimore by Race indicates, African American homeowners account for 53 percent versus 41.8 percent of Whites. On the other hand, African Americans are also more likely to be renters, 64.7 percent versus 26.2 percent for whites.

TABLE 2: Housing Tenure in Baltimore by Race

Estimate		White	Black	Asian	Latino	Others
Total:	240,630	83,346	144,699	5,903	6,620	6682
Owner occupied	117,500	49,131	62,250	1,452	1,817	2,850
%		41.8%	53%	1.2%	1.6%	2.4%
Renter occupied	123,130	32,241	79,677	3,951	4,131	3,130
%		26.2%	64.7%	3.2%	3.4%	2.5%

Source: *U.S. Census Bureau, 2008-2012 American Community Survey 5-Year Estimates.*

The Production of Neighborhood Distress

A collective set of theories on community benefits that result from homeownership were reviewed to develop a framework for comparing a traditional redlined community to a non-redlined community in Baltimore City. Contemporary literature on the effects of homeownership offers positive support for promoting it for both individual and community-level development. With increased homeownership it is expected that neighborhoods would improve along social and economic dimensions (e.g., increased stability, increased citizen participation, and more civility among youth and adults). It is commonly believed that the connection between homeownership and social stability is such that homeowners are more likely than renters to stay and invest in their homes. In turn, local property values tend to rise (Rohe and Stewart, 1996). More broadly, some theories describe the social and economic impact of homeownership as including positive effects on social engagement and political participation, improved school performance, reductions in teenage parenthood, lower illegal substance use, and more adherences to positive community norms.

This paper aims to explore using a case study analysis of the association between homeownership and neighborhood quality, as defined by socially and civically desirable be-haviors, in a manner that highlights the differences between a historically redlined and a historically non-redlined neighborhood in Baltimore City. The first level of analysis compares theoretically derived social indicators of the Baltimore neighborhood with the highest rate of homeownership (Cross Country/Cheswolde) to the neighborhood with the lowest rate of homeownership (Madison/East End), using the city-wide averages as a base for comparison. For the purpose of association, the Cross Country/Cheswolde neighborhood, which is located in Northwest Baltimore, appeared coded in the color blue on the 1930 Home Owner's Loan Corporation Residential Security Map for Baltimore, indicating a low-level of investment risk. On the other hand, the Madison/East End community, which is located is East Baltimore, appeared coded in the color red, indicating a high level of investment risk, and hence, has been redlined since the 1930s.

The Re-Production of Community Distress

Galster and Quercia (2000) provide a useful framework for comparing homeowner to renter communities. In a study of neighborhood threshold effects, Galster and Quecia (2000) found the homeownership serves as a trigger for neighborhood quality. Neigh-borhoods with low homeownership rates are associated with neighborhood distress, while those with high homeownership rates are associated with community benefits. Using fours social indicators—female headship rate, male labor force non-participa-tion rate, overall unemployment rate and poverty rate—they found that the rate of homeownership proved to be influential on the risk of neighborhood distress.

The Production of Neighborhood Advantage:
High Quality Neighborhood Indicators

This section seeks to compare the two neighborhoods at the extreme ends of home-ownership on community level characteristics that tend to accompany improvements in quality of life. It explores social indicators that have been linked to social, political and economic theory of group level behavior while presenting the comparison of two Baltimore neighborhoods with high and low rates of homeownership.

Neighborhoods with more residents are associated with higher quality of life because people are needed for social and economic markets to function productively. The more people in a community, the greater the capacity to produce goods and services, and the greater will be the ultimate demand for these outputs. When Table 5 is examined, it reveals that the population of residents in the non-redlined neighborhood is 1.7 times higher than that of the redlined neighborhood. It may be that the relationship between population and neighborhood quality of life is small; however, prior studies have revealed a favorable relationship.

Table 3 contains the comparison of socioeconomic characteristics. From this table we see that the median household income is 1.6 times higher in the non-redlined neigh-borhood compared to that of the redlined neighborhood. Neighborhoods with high levels of income are associated with higher levels of demand for goods and services, resulting in a higher quality of life for residents. Closely related to higher income effects are the following neighborhood indicators: percent of residents with a bachelor's degree or higher, fraction of residents between 25 and 64 years of age, and the unemployment rate. Using prior literature as a guide, the redlined and non-redlined neighborhoods were compared on these social indicators.

A striking difference exists between the non-redlined neighborhood and the redlined neighborhood on the adult education attainment indicator: the percent of residents with a Bachelor's degree or above. The non-redlined community has a rate that is 17.3 times higher than the redlined neighborhood. This is an important indicator of neighborhood quality of life because of its relationship to business growth. Autor (2001) reports a rising demand for a more highly educated workforce. Labor markets with higher concentrations of college-educated workers are attractive places for business to locate. Beyond serving as a source of highly skilled employees, neighborhoods with high percentages of college graduates exhibit a strong demand for the very goods and services produced by industry, thereby enhancing the attraction for business location. Another factor related to neighborhood quality is the possibility that college educated consumers may spend more on consumer goods than less educated consumers with similar incomes. Because this translates into a higher demand for goods and services, neighborhoods with more highly educated residents attract more business and industry, resulting in a relative higher quality of life for residents in such neighborhoods.

The relative age of the residents in a community generally serves as a draw for new business. In this case, the redlined community offers a more favorable age distribution. This finding does not support the notion that relatively young populations are more active consumers, resulting in a higher demand for goods and services. At the other end of the business attractiveness scale are the social indicators of unemployment and crime. These factors have a negative relationship with business growth, and as a result, could send neighborhoods into decline. The empirical studies of the influences of these variables on business are ambiguous. The causal relationships are difficult to establish. For example, it is unclear whether slow business growth causes higher unemployment or whether higher rates of joblessness results in slower business growth. On the matter of crime, the relationships are also challenging to model. While crime might deter business growth, increased economic activity also attracts crime. When the non-redlined community was compared to redlined community, the higher rates of unemployment and crime appeared in the latter.

TABLE 3: Economic Indicators

2011 Community Economic Indicators	Cross Country/ Cheswolde	Baltimore City	Madison/ East End
Percent of Properties that are Owner Occupied	83.4%	57.6%	24.%
Median Price of Homes Sold	$143,500	$100,000	$16,000
Percent of Homes Sold in Foreclosure (REO)	7.4%	33.1%	45.5%
Percent of Residential Property that Do Not Receive Mail	1.9%	7.5%	11.2%
Housing Affordability			
Affordability Index – Mortgage	48.1	40.5	35.6
Affordability Index - Rent	42.0	53.8	58.2
Housing Permits and Enforcement			
Percent of Properties with Rehab Permits (Over $5,000)	2.8%	2.4%	2.8%
Percent of Properties that are Vacant and Abandoned	0.2%	7.8%	22.7%
Percent of Vacant Properties Owned by Baltimore City	0.0%	19.7%	17.3%
Percent of Properties with Housing Violations	0.6%	4.7%	3.9%
Number of Demolition Permits per 1,000 Homes	0.7	1.6	7.6
Rate of Dirty Streets and Alley Reports per 1,000 Residents	8.8	61.1	267.7
Rate of Clogged Storm Drain Reports Per 1,000 Residents	2.2	6.4	13.0

Source: Baltimore Neighborhood Indicators Alliance (BNIA)

To compare a historically redlined community to a non-redlined community 50 years from 1963, the characteristics of the most advantaged community (in terms of homeownership) are compared to the least advantaged community. The importance of homeownership to neighborhood development is widely recognized. Research on the growth in homeownership offers links to economic benefits such as relative increases in property values. The relationship between homeownership and neighborhood development is theoretically ambiguous. This inquiry is further limited by the unobservable characteristics of both individuals and their neighborhoods that could potentially explain community benefits and the risks of community distress.

Table 4: Demographic Characteristics

2010 Age	Cross Country/Cheswolde	Baltimore City	Madison/East End
0-18	27.5%	21.5%	32.7%
19-24	9.8%	12.6%	13.2%
25-64	43.5%	54.2%	47.5%
65 & over	19.2%	11.7%	6.6%

Source: Baltimore Neighborhood Indicators Alliance (BNIA)

2011 Gender	Cross Country/Cheswolde	Baltimore City	Madison/East End
Total Population	13,034	620,961	7,781
Men	45.7%	47.0%	46.1%
Women	54.3%	52.9%	53.9%

Source: Baltimore Neighborhood Indicators Alliance (BNIA)

2011 Race/Ethnicity	Cross Country/ Cheswolde	Baltimore City	Madison/East End
Percent African American	20.4%	63.8%	90.3%
Percent White	72.1%	28.3%	3.1%
Percent Asian	3.7%	2.3%	0.8%
Percent of Persons of Two or More Races	1.2%	1.7%	1.2%
Percent of Person of all other Races	0.4%	0.5%	0.6%
Percent Hispanic	2.2%	4.2%	4.0%

Source: Baltimore Neighborhood Indicators Alliance (BNIA)

The demographic comparisons of the non-redlined versus the redlined neighborhoods are displayed in Table 4 along with the Baltimore City demographics. From this table we see that there is a homeownership gap of 59.4 percent between the non-redlined and redlined communities. The difference in the median sales price of homes in the two neighborhoods is $127,000, in favor of the non-redlined community. The redlined community has 4 percent more residents in the 25-64 age category. Communities with large populations of working age young people are more attractive to businesses willing to invest in new locations.

The percentage of African American residents in the redlined community is 69.9 percent higher than in the non-redlined community. On the socioeconomic level, large gaps appear between the redlined and non-redlined neighborhoods. The median household income in the non-redlined neighborhood is higher than the city-wide median, and is more favorable than that in the redlined neighborhood. The ratio of the median household income of the redlined neighborhood to that of the non-redlined neighborhood is 60.9 percent. A larger percentage of households in the redlined neighborhood earn less than $25,000 (42 percent versus 19.2 percent); while more households in the non-redlined community earn more than $75,000 (35.1 percent versus 10.7 percent).

The comparative analysis of the non-redlined to the redlined neighborhood show stark differences in quality of life and neighborhood distress factors. The homeownership rate in the redlined neighborhood is 59.4 percent lower than the non-redlined neighborhood, and is 33.6 percent lower than the city-wide percentage.

The Maintenance of Community Distress

Community distress (neighborhood stability) was measured with variables that have previously been associated with neighborhood decline (Galster and Quercia, 2000): female headship, labor force participation, unemployment and poverty rate. The female headship rate in the redlined community was over 70 percent in 2011, 15.1 percent higher than the city-wide rate, and 50.5 percent higher than the rate of the non-redlined neighborhood. The poverty rate in the redlined community was 2.5 times higher than the non-redlined community. The percent of residents without a high school diploma or GED was 5.2 times higher in the redlined community than in the non-redlined community. The percent of the population not in the labor force was 1.45 times higher in the redlined community when compared to the non-redlined community.

TABLE 5: Community Socioeconomic Profiles

2011 Socioeconomic Characteristics	Cross Country/ Cheswolde	Baltimore City	Madison/ East End
Income			
Median Household Income	$52,728	$40,100	$32,145
Percent of Households Earning Less than $25,000	19.2%	34.5%	42.0%
Percent of Households Earning $25,000 - $39.900	16.1%	17.0%	18.8%
Percent of Households Earning $40,000 - $59,900	20.6%	16.2%	18.8%

Percent of Households Earning $60,000 - $74.900	9.1%	9.2%	9.6%
Percent of Households Earning More than $75,000	35.1%	23.2%	10.7%
Percent of Female-Headed Households	19.5%	54.9%	70.0%
Percent of Household Living Below the Poverty Line	11.2%	17.7%	28.8%
Percent of Children Living Below the Poverty Line	16.0%	31.9%	45.2%

Program Participation

Percent of Families Receiving TANF	0.8%	9.4%	24.7%
Percent of Students Receiving Free or Reduced Meals	63.1%	82.8%	92.5%

Student Demographics

Percent of Students that are African American	75.2%	85.9%	95.6%
Percent of Students that are White (non-Hispanic)	8.4%	8.2%	1.0%
Percent of Students that are Hispanic	6.6%	4.1%	3.0%

Adult Educational Attainment (Population Aged 25+)			
Percent of Residents with Less than High School Diploma or GED	8.0%	21.5%	41.8%
Percent of Residents with High School Diploma/Some College/ Associates Degree	41.9%	52.7%	55.4%
Percent of Residents with a Bachelor's Degree or Above	50.1%	25.8%	2.9%
Community Assets and Engagement			
Percent of Population (18+) Who are Registered to Vote	83.1%	75.0%	78.3%
Percent of Population (18+) Who Voted in the General Election	54.5%	44.4%	30.6%

Source: Baltimore Neighborhood Indicators Alliance (BNIA)

Reproduction of Social and Political Participation

It is commonly believed that in order for democratic societies to function well, a commitment is required on the part of citizens to the values of voluntarism and political participation. Neighborhoods with higher rates of homeownership have been associated with higher levels of social capital, as defined by social and political participation. One argument offered in support of this assertion that there is a positive relationship between homeownership and social capital. Homeowners have a direct interest in protecting their real estate investments and view social and political participation as a means for doing so (Baum and Kingston 1984; Rohe and Stewart 1996). As a result, when compared to renters, homeowners are more likely to take action to protect their equity interest through involvement in social and political participation. It is further argued that such behavior results in community conditions that are often associated with a higher quality of life.

Cox (1982) offers another reason why we might expect more civic engagement among homeowners as compared to renters: the costs of moving are higher for homeowners than for renters. When renters move, their transaction costs do not typically involve selling a house and buying a new one. Neighborhood deterioration that may force homeowners to move could result in transactions costs of thousands of dollars. Homeowners are, as a result, provided with a greater incentive than renters to become more civically engaged in ways that may work to maintain or improve the physical and social conditions of their neighborhoods.

Baum and Kingston (1984, p. 163) suggest that the longer homeowners stay in their homes, the more they grow attached to them in ways that can measured along social and psychological dimensions. It is this greater level of attachment, they suggest, that serves as the motivation to participate in voluntary and political organizations more often than renters. When Table 5 is examined, it reveals a positive relationship between homeownership and political participation. Residents from the Baltimore neighborhood with the highest rate of homeownership were more likely to be registered to vote, and more likely to vote.

Homeownership Impacts on Youth Behaviors

Beyond neighborhood stability and social involvement, neighborhood quality is also affected by a third dimension: youth behavior. High quality neighborhoods are often characterized by more favorable school performance among youth, lower high school drop-out rates, lower rates of teenage parenthood, and less juvenile delinquency. Green and White (1997) suggest that homeowners pass on positive habits to their children, thereby resulting in a culture of homeownership that transfers skills and values to future generations. This assertion is supported by Boehm and Schlottman (1999) who demonstrate that children of homeowners are more likely to become homeowners. Haurin and colleagues (2002) posit that homeownership is related to the cognitive and emotional development of children. The logical link in this argument is that homeowners act as investors who recognize the negative impacts that anti-social behaviors of local children can have on their property values. As a result, homeowners are more apt to monitor the behavior of their children more closely.

A third line of reasoning in support of the positive effects of homeownership on youth behavior has its roots in the sociological theory of collective socialization. Sociologists such as Simmal (1971) and Weber (1978) developed theories of collective behavior that focus on the rate of social interaction in shaping individual attitudes, values and behavior. The general idea of this theory is that collective socialization offers the power to influence conformity to social norms, customs, and behaviors. Jencks and Mayer (1990) and Ellen and Turner (1997) applied the theory of collective socialization to the literature on the impact of homeownership with their assertion that the longer tenure status of homeowners produce a community culture that monitors and shapes the behavior of children. As a result, the aggregate level effect of community culture is thought to influence youth behavior in ways that extend beyond the influences of family and personal characteristics (Jencks and Mayer 1990; Ellen and Turner 1997).

Table 6 compares the school performance of children from the redlined neighborhood with those from the non-redlined neighborhood. The general patterns of the comparisons are consistent with the articulated theories on the impact of homeownership on youth behavior. Children from the non-redlined community were less like to be absent from school, more likely to perform better on state-level K-12 assessments, less likely to drop-out of school, and more likely to graduate high school. For example, 60.1 percent of students from the redlined community were chronically absent from high school, compared to 20.3 percent absentee rate among high school students from the non-redlined community. The school suspension rate for students from the non-redlined community was 3.1 times lower than the rate in the redlined community. The percentage of 8th grade student from the redlined community who passed the Maryland States Reading Assessment in 2011 was 45.1 percent, compared to the 76.5 percent among 8th grade students from the non-redlined community.

TABLE 6: Community Outcomes for Children

2011 Community Child Outcome Indicators	Cross Country/ Cheswolde	Baltimore City	Madison/ East End
Birth Outcomes			
Teen Birth Rate per 1,000 Females (aged 15-19)	15.5	46.6	86.1
Percent of Births Delivered at Term	95.9%	87.4%	85.6%
Percent of Babies Born with a Satisfactory Birth Weight	96.8%	88.4%	83.1%
Percent of Births Where the Mother Received Early Prenatal Care	68.3%	59.0%	53.8%
Lead Poisoning			
Number of Children (aged 0-6) Tested for Elevated Blood Lead Levels	351.0	19,036	353.0
Percent of Children (aged 0-6) with Elevated Blood Lead Levels	0.0%	1.4%	5.9%
Life Expectancy and Mortality			
Life Expectancy	88.0	73.5	66.8
Mortality by Age (Less than 1 year old)	9.2	11.7	14.0
Mortality by Age (1-14 years old)	0.7	2.8	1.0
Mortality by Age (15-24 years old)	2.2	13.5	23.1

Percent of 1st-5th Grade Students who are Chronically Absent	8.1%	16.6%	21.8%
Percent of 6th-8th Grade Students who are Chronically Absent	4.3%	16.7%	23.9%
Percent of 9th-12th Grade Students who are Chronically Absent	26.3%	42.1%	60.1%
Percent of Students Suspended/Expelled During School Year	3.2%	7.9%	9.9%
Student Performance (Elementary, Middle High)			
Kindergarten School Readiness at age 5	43.9	66.0	54.0
Percentage of 3rd Grade Students Passing MSA Math	83.0%	73.3%	64.8%
Percentage of 3rd Grade Students Passing MSA Reading	84.4%	69.4%	61.9%
Percentage of 8th Grade Students Passing MSA Math	54.3%	35.1%	23.9%
Percentage of 8th Grade Students Passing MSA Reading	76.5%	61.2%	45.1%
Percentage of Students Passing H.S.A. Algebra	40.0%	22.5%	18.2%
Percentage of Students Passing H.S.A. English	46.2%	36.2%	25.6%
Student Dropout and Completion			
High School Dropout/Withdrawal Rate	3.1%	4.2%	5.3%
High School Completion Rate	80.0%	80.3%	75.4%

Source: Baltimore Neighborhood Indicators Alliance (BNIA)

The high school drop-out rate in the Madison/East End Community (the redlined community) was nearly twice that of the Cross Country (non-redlined) Community. The high school completion rate from the non-redlined neighborhood was nearly 5 percentage points higher than of its comparison neighborhood. On the measure of teenage birthrates per 1,000 females, there were 70 more births per 1,000 females in the redlined neighborhood than there were in the non-redlined neighborhood. For each child born in the respective communities, the difference in the life expectancy was 21.2 years in 2011. In other words, a child born in the non-redlined neighborhood can expect to live, on average, 21.2 years longer than a child born on the same day at the same time in the redlined community.

When the rates of juvenile crime were examined across the low and high homeownership communities, a disturbing pattern was uncovered. The redlined community had a juvenile arrest rate per 1,000 juveniles that was 7.8 times higher than the rate in the non-redlined community. In addition, juveniles from the redlined neighborhood were 9.3 times more likely to be arrested for violent offenses, and extremely more likely to be arrested for drug related offenses.

Research and Policy Implications

The findings of this case study raise questions regarding the implementation of federal, state and local homeownership initiatives, and the role of employers in expanding opportunities for homeownership. Further research is needed to explore the contemporary variants of 21st century redlining to identify the organizational and structural impediments to low-income home-buying and reduced access to prime mortgages. In addition, future researchers should explore the circumstances under which homeownership results in positive versus negative outcomes as negative equity has become a real concern.

Increased enforcement of the regulatory environment could lead to an expansion in homeownership among low-income populations. Mortgage lenders are regulated by the federal government under the Community Reinvestment Act (CRA) where they "have a continuing and affirmative obligation to help meet the credit needs of the local communities in which they are chartered," and this includes low and moderate income neighborhoods (para. 802(a)(30, 12 USC 1901: Title VII of Public Law 95-128, 91 Stst. 1147, October 12, 1977). In Baltimore City, high unemployment rates are a challenge that could be met with the addition of minority employment as a new evaluation criteria during the CRA examinations. As is often the case, it is possible to negotiate diversity plans as a component in the agreements between community organizations and lenders.

Beyond the improvements to mortgage financing are the micro-level policies and programs needed to help low-income families save for down payments, build credit, and enhance the life skills needed to navigate the complex home buying and home-ownership management processes. Community Development Corporations can play an important role in such regard. They could work to expand the use of individual development accounts (Sherraden 1991) to help families save for down payments on a home, fund community-based organizations to provide financial counseling to improve program participant knowledge on the responsibilities of homeownership and the importance of investing in quality neighborhoods (Ratner 1996). Of particular need is assistance in navigating the financial complexities of a home purchase (Quercia and Wachter 1996) to avoid the pitfalls of predatory lending.

On the issue of race and housing, Baltimore is in need of policies that deal with its realities regarding the differences between its black and white residents. Too often, policy models rest on the assumption of equality of conditions that result in improved human capital through asset acquisition such as homeownership. Such assumptions offer little insight into the underlying causes of the persistent racial disparities in homeownership. In many respects, the differences are unobservable and more difficult to address through policy initiative than they are via model manipulation. The importance of multi-disciplinary perspectives in shaping well-designed policies to promote homeownership among the poor cannot be over-stated.

Summary and Conclusions

Using descriptive case study of social indicator data, quality of life, economic stability and neighborhood characteristics were compared between a redlined community and a non-redlined community in Baltimore City. This comparison revealed evidence consistent with the theory of positive social impacts of homeownership on neighborhoods. The weight of this case study descriptive analysis suggests that neighborhoods with high rates of homeownership are more stable; offer a higher quality of life, more social capital, and more socially acceptable youth behavior.

The strength of this case study lies in its ability to produce a way of knowing that overcomes the challenge with contemporary housing policy analysis which has strayed too far from the original aim of the field of policy sciences. This aim was fastened on a broader socioeconomic approach to multi-faceted problem solving (Lasswell, 1971). Instead, in the past 40 years we have witnessed the crowning of the rationality theorem as articulated in the discipline of economics.

Traditional policy analysis in housing is dominated by the proposition that we can resolve fair-housing controversies through traditional economic reasoning. Under classic welfare economics, it is argued that the systematic rationalization of market and housing-policy decision making is possible when housing and lending services are valued and weighed against the enhancement of market functioning so as to maximize society's collective welfare. This view has been intensively criticized and its efficacy has been challenged on the grounds of effectiveness and policy direction.

The traditional policy analysis approach with its emphasis on the welfare economics model and its positivist foundations is inadequate to improve policy decisions that address segregation and home ownership disparities. This framework lacks the tools to analyze this problem because of its complexity. The classic welfare economics framework is designed to identify efficient solutions at the expense of fairness and human dignity. Brown has argued that such models are incapable of incorporating the full complexity of people's thoughts about policy issues (Brown, 1980). For example, as a society we lack a consensus on how to value benefits and harms of homeownership. There are vast differences over what types of benefits and harms should be factored into a cost/benefit calculation. It remains unclear how such costs and benefits should be measured, and how society's competing demands for social welfare should be mediated (i.e., how do we balance the maximization of social welfare and provide the level of home ownership that individuals desire without regard to cost?). As a result, the model envisioned by classic welfare economics is beyond our cognitive and moral reach.

The traditional policy analysis approach is argued to be antiquated because it does not accurately reflect the contemporary practice of real estate and mortgage markets. We know little about the efficacy of most of mortgage products, and the complexity and variability of borrowers' ability to judge their creditworthiness make large advances in this knowledge unlikely in the foreseeable future. Traditional policy analysis approaches reflect a Newtonian/positivist worldview with a focus on empiricism (Hajer and Wagenaar, 2003). This view has been discredited by research in the fields of quantum mechanics, chaos theory, and cognitive science (Morcol, 2002). Fischer makes a similar argument and suggests that policy analysis in general needs to take into account the new realities of science (Fischer, 1995).

There is some promising research in the discipline of psychology, which helps to shed some light on the attempt to account for the reported racial disparities in homeownership. These studies have identified the influences of the internal psychological factors of the attitudes of real estate agents and mortgage professionals.

In an attempt to account for the shift in the practice and patterns of racial cognitive bias in recent years, researchers have increasingly focused their attention on individual-centered psychological variables. The question of whether (and to what extent has) the attitudes and beliefs of professionals influenced professional decision-making is the focus of this work.

Since the Civil Rights Movement of the 1960s, it has become socially unacceptable to express overt racial prejudice. As a result, there has been a marked decrease in reporting overt prejudice against racial and ethnic groups among white Americans (Devine et al., 2001). In fact, when asked in the form of a survey, white Americans are more likely to endorse social equity goals in schools, housing, employment, and politics (Dividio et al., 2001). Nevertheless, contemporary theorists of psychology have failed to dismiss the notion that prejudice is a thing of the past. Instead, they have developed new models of prejudice to uncover the new form in which racial prejudice now appears.

In light of the fact that current law and custom has eliminated many of the overt forms of prejudice, contemporary prejudice models have distinguished explicit, overt forms of prejudice from subtle, implicit forms. As a result of this new research focus, there have been substantial empirical findings indicating that implicit prejudice remains widespread even in individuals who, on an explicit level, are genuinely unprejudiced (Dividio et al., 2001). According to Devine, implicit prejudice can be found principally within two main cognitive domains: attitudes and stereotypes (Divine et al., 2001).

Greenwald and Banaji define attitudes as positive or negative dispositions toward objects in one's social environment. While pre-civil rights movement researchers have traditionally focused on attitudes that are consciously accessible, more recently there is a growing recognition that attitudes can be implicit as well as explicit. Implicit attitudes can be thought of as "introspectively unidentified (or inaccurately identified) traces of past experience that mediate favorable or unfavorable feeling, thought, or action toward social objects." (Greenwald and Banaji, 1995, 8). Thus, implicit attitudes, by explanation, are unconscious. Moreover, they are activated habitually by the mere presence of the attitude object.

Implicit stereotypes, though related to implicit attitudes, are theoretically, a distinct subset of implicit bias (Divine et al., 2001). As reflected above, attitudes are dispositions toward social objects; stereotypes, on the hand, are beliefs about particular groups (Divine et al., 2001). Greenwald and Banaji define implicit stereotypes as "the introspectively unidentified (or inaccurately identified) traces of past experience that mediate attributions of qualities of a social category." (Greenwald and Banaji, 1995, 15). Kunda (1999) describes implicit stereotypes as subconscious mental representations of social categories-representations which involve knowledge, beliefs, and expectations about social groups. In housing markets such beliefs may take the following form: "African American residents drive down the value of home in neighborhood where their percentage make-up exceeds certain thresholds."

When one considers the substantial amount of professional discretion available to real estate agents and mortgage bankers in their respective practices in conjunction with the prevalence of implicit cognitive bias, it seems more likely than not that racial disparity in home ownership will endure. To start, discretion plays a significant role as a source of disparities in homeownership. This is evident in the types of communities that real estate agents steer their black versus white clients. African Americans are more likely to be shown homes in predominately black communities. It is also clear that African American home buyers were more likely to be steered into sub-prime (high interest) home loans, even when they would have qualified for more favorable loans. A third form of unfavorable treatment emanates from the common practices of insurance companies who extend less desirable insurance coverage with higher prices to racial minorities. The dearth of research support for most real estate sales and mortgage lending decisions results in such wide variability in professional practice so as to render the notion of reaching evidenced-based conclusions about the appropriateness of practice variations beyond our current human capacity. The results are housing markets that are more idiosyncratic because of the heavy reliance on professional discretion. In other words, in far too many cases, the practice of real estate sales and mortgage lending relies on the kind of art like qualities of intuition and insight, which leaves these professionals unable to rationally justify their decisions. If the practice of real estate and banking industries, as we know it, does not proceed solely from om rationalistic assumptions, should our public policies, designed to regulate this activity, emanate from these assumptions?

Redlining in the 21st century must be represented and named before it can be combatted with policy and action. It has become a commonsense practice that is less overt and invidious and more subtle and in the shadows. The systematic practice of implicit redlining will continue to produce, reproduce and maintain social and economic racial disparities in Baltimore's communities until such practices are addressed.

References

Autor, D. H. (2001). Wiring the labor market. *Journal of Economic Perspectives*, 25-40.

Baum, T. and P. Kingston. 1984. Homeownership and Social Attachment. *Sociological Perspectives* 27(2): 159-80.

Boehm, T. P. and A. Schlottmann. 1999. Does Homeownership by Parents Have an Economic Impact on Their Children? Paper presented at the American Real Estate and Urban Economics Association Mid Year Meeting, New York, NY.

Brown, Steven (1980). *Political Subjectivity: Applications of Q-Methodology in Political Science*: New Haven, CT: Yale University Press.

Connolly, Sheelah, Dermot O'Reilly, and Michael Rosato. 2010. House Value as an Indicator of Cumulative Wealth is Strongly Related to Morbidity and Mortality Risk in Older People: A Census-Based Cross- Sectional and Longitudinal Study. *International Journal of Epidemiology* 39: 383-391.

Cox, K. 1982. Housing Tenure and Neighborhood Activism. *Urban Affairs Quarterly* 18(1): 107-29.

Devine, Patricia G., Ashby E. Plant, and Irene V. Blair (2001). "Classic and Contemporary Analysis of Racial Prejudice." In *Blackwell Handbook of Social Psychology Intergroup Processes, vol. 4*, edited by Rupert J. Brown and Samuel L. Gaertner, Oxford: Blackwell Publishers: 198.

Dietz, R. D., & Haurin, D. R. (2003). The social and private micro-level consequences of homeownership. *Journal of Urban Economics*, 54(3), 401-450.

Dovidio, John F., Kerry Kawakami, and K. Beach (2001). "Implicit and Explicit Attitudes: Examination of the Relationship between Measures of Intergroup Processes." In *Blackwell Handbook of Social Psychology: Intergroup Processes*, edited by Rupert J. Brown and Samuel L. Gaertner: Oxford: Blackwell Publishers:176-177.

Ellen, I. G. and M.A. Turner. 1997. Does Neighborhood Matter? Assessing Recent Evidence. *Housing Policy Debate* 8(4): 833-866.

Galster, G. C., Quercia, R. G., & Cortes, A. (2000). Identifying neighborhood thresholds: An empirical exploration. *Housing Policy Debate*, 11(3), 701-732.

Green, R. and M. White. 1997. Measuring the Benefits of Homeowning: Effect on Children. *Journal of Urban Economics* 41: 441-61.

Greenwald, Anthony G. and Mahzin R. Banaji (1995). Implicit Social Cognition: Attitudes, Self-Esteem, and Stereotypes, *Psychology Review* 102, no. 1 (January).

Hajer, Maarten and Hendrick Wagenaar, *Deliberative Policy Analysis: Understanding Governance in a Network Society.* (Cambridge: Cambridge University Press, 2003).

Haurin, D. R., Parcel, T. L., & Haurin, R. J. (2002). Does homeownership affect child outcomes?. *Real Estate Economics, 30*(4), 635-666.

Haurin, D. R., Dietz, R. D., & Weinberg, B. A. (2002). The impact of neighborhood homeownership rates: A review of the theoretical and empirical literature. *Journal of Housing Research, 13*(2), 119-152.

Jencks, C. and S. Mayer. 1990. The Social Consequences of Growing Up in a Poor Neighborhood. In Inner-City Poverty in the United States. Edited by L. Lynn and M. McGeary. Washington, DC: National Academy Press.

Kunda, Ziva (1999). *Social Cognition: Making Sense of People* (Boston: MIT Press).

Lasswell, Harold (1971). *A Preview of the Policy Sciences.* (New York: American Elsevier, 1971).

Manturuk, K. R. (2012). Urban Homeownership and Mental Health: Mediating Effect of Perceived Sense of Control. *City & Community, 11*(4), 409-430.

Manturuk, K., Lindblad, M., & Quercia, R. G. (2009). Homeownership and local voting in disadvantaged urban neighborhoods. *Cityscape*, 213-230.

Morcol, Goktu (2002). *A New Mind for Policy Analysis: Toward a Post-Newtonian and Postpositivist Epistemology and Methodology:* Westport: Praeger.

Page-Adams, Deborah and Nancy Vosler. 1997. Homeownership and Well-Being Among Blue-Collar Workers. Working Paper No. 97-5. St. Louis, MO: Washington University George Warren Brown School of Social Work Center for Social Development.

Quercia, Roberto G., and George C. Galster. 1997. "Threshold Effects and the Expected Benefits of Attracting Middle-Income Households to the Central City." *Housing Policy Debate* 8(2): 409-36.

Ratner, Mitchell S. 1996. "Many Routes to Home Ownership: A Four-Site Ethnographic Study of Minority and Immigrant Experiences." *Housing Policy Debate* 7(1): 103-45.

Retsinas, N. P., & Belsky, E. S. (Eds.). (2002). *Low-income homeownership: Examining the unexamined goal.* Brookings Institution Press.

Rohe, W. M., Van Zandt, S., & McCarthy, G. (2002). Home ownership and access to opportunity. *Housing Studies, 17*(1), 51-61.

Rohe, W. M., & Stegman, M. A. (1994). The effects of homeownership: on the self-esteem, perceived control and life satisfaction of low-income people. *Journal of the American Planning Association, 60*(2), 173-184.

Rohe, W. M., & Stegman, M. A. (1994). The impact of home ownership on the social and political involvement of low-income people. *Urban Affairs Review,30*(1), 152-172.

Rohe, W. M., & Stewart, L. S. (1996). Homeownership and neighborhood stability. *Housing Policy Debate, 7*(1), 37-81.

Sherraden, Michael W. 1991. *Assets and the Poor: A New American Welfare Policy.* Armonk, N.Y.: M. E. Sharpe.

Shlay, A. B. (2006). Low-income homeownership: American dream or delusion?. *Urban Studies, 43*(3), 511-531.

Simmel, George. 1971. *George Simmel on Individuality and Social Forms.* Chicago: University of Chicago Press.

Spilerman, S. (2000). Wealth and stratification processes. *Annual Review of Sociology, 26*(1), 497-524.

Weber, Max. 1978. Economy and Society. 2 volumes. Berkeley, CA: University of California Press.

Neighborhood Revitalization in Baltimore

Donn C. Worgs

Beginning in the 1950s, Baltimore was beset by the processes of deindustrialization and suburbanization that would ravage cities throughout the rust belt. As these processes accelerated in the 1960s and 70s, many of Baltimore's neighborhoods experienced a steady slide into distress. City leaders attempted to navigate the transition to a post-industrial economy by prioritizing investments in downtown and the redevelopment of the Inner Harbor into a tourist magnet through the development of Harborplace and other attractions (Levine 1987). There was little attention given to the neighborhoods. Since the 1980s, a few communities (like Federal Hill) that had been in decline have been transformed by gentrification, but there remain a number of neighborhoods that exist in a state of physical decay and social disarray as their thousands of residents, the vast majority of whom are Black, are disconnected from the mainstream economy. Although these conditions haves existed for decades, the city has yet to mount an extensive and focused effort aimed at revitalizing and transforming the hardest hit communities – for the residents.

In 2010, at the beginning of her tenure, Mayor Stephanie Rawlings-Blake's transition team produced a report assessing the city's agencies and the general performance of the city government. In their assessment of the city government's activities in the realm of community development and neighborhoods, the transition team concluded that the city was in need of a guiding "vision for neighborhood and community development" (Bell-McKoy et al. 2010, p.30).

The transition team acknowledged what myself and two colleagues had also come to understand about neighborhood revitalization in Baltimore. As that transition report was produced, my colleagues and I were in the process of examining neighborhood revitalization policies and politics in Baltimore as part of a comparative study of different cities by teams of scholars around the country. As we conducted our study, through interviews with dozens of officials, activists, and advocates, and reviews of various reports, studies, data etc., a picture of the contemporary politics and policies in this realm became clear.[1] Baltimore does not have a coordinated strategy to revitalize neighborhoods. But this is no surprise because most cities do not have such a strategy.

In this chapter, I will share some of our key observations relative to neighborhood revitalization policies and politics in Baltimore, and suggest what I think is the most likely path to significant progress in this realm. Rather than a coherent strategy, what one does find in Baltimore are various ad hoc arrangements brought together in search of/or in response to scarce resources. As of late, these efforts have been shaped (or

---

1   For a detailed description of our findings see In a New Era, Stone et al. forthcoming in University of Chicago Press.

confined) by desires to tap the forces of the market. We see the growing centrality of anchor institutions (like hospitals and universities) in the thinking of folks working in this arena, and a corresponding greater activity among these institutions. Much of the efforts in Baltimore are carried out by quasi-public corporations that are set up as private nonprofit corporations, but have access to government powers and resources. This arrangement intentionally distances them from the reach of traditional politics, and therefore have some important implications in terms of further disconnecting residents from the decisions that impact their lives. Ultimately, the most likely path for significant change for these distressed communities is the organization and mobilization of the residents. They will have to mobilize themselves and assert their own vision for their communities, otherwise their neighborhoods will either continue to be ignored or be the target of revitalization plans crafted by others. Regardless of how well-meaning these others might be, the needs of the residents will likely be left on the margins.

Neighborhoods in Distress
While there are some stable and vibrant communities in the city, some of which (like Northwood or Loch Raven) are predominantly African American, our focus here is on those communities that are distressed. The vast majority of the residents in these neighborhoods are African Americans. These areas are faced with high numbers of vacancies, low housing values (a key factor in lower levels of household wealth), low incomes and low levels of labor market participation, along with other social and economic challenges – all of which illustrate a disconnection from the mainstream.

The Baltimore Neighborhood Indicators Alliance has compiled census and other social and economic data for the city, and assigned the data to fifty-five community statistical areas (CSA). This data provide a snapshot of neighborhood distress. Consider the state of the housing markets. In 2011 the median price for homes sold in the Baltimore metropolitan area was $230,000. The median for the city was $100,000. Of the 55 CSA's there were six that had median prices of $230,000 or higher, while there were 32 areas that had median prices below $100,000, and 13 that had median home sales prices below $40,000. Southern Park Heights, Midway Coldstream, Southwest Baltimore, Clifton-Berea, and Madison/East End each had median sales prices below $19,000 (BNIA- JFI).

One of the most visible signs of disinvestment and decline are the vacant and abandoned houses. These vacancies of course are not distributed evenly across the city, though they are a problem for many neighborhoods. In 2011, there were 14 areas that had more than ten percent of houses vacant or abandoned, and five of which had more than 25 percent vacant or abandoned. The highest proportion was found in the Oldtown/ Middle East communities which had a rate of 40% (BNIA-JFI).

When we look at neighborhoods we also see the varying levels of poverty and its concentration in certain areas. The city of course has neighborhoods that are consistent with, or surpass the region's median household income of $68,000. But most are much lower. At the extreme are two areas with a combined population of over

20,000 people – Upton/Druid Heights and Old Town/Middle East—where the median income was below $14,000. That means that half the households in these areas have incomes below that mark. These areas are also among the seven CSAs (with a combined population of over 66,000 people) with over one-third of households living below the poverty line. The highest level was found in Upton/ Druid Heights with over 50 percent of households living below the poverty line. Unemployment and labor force participation further reflect the disconnection from the mainstream economy. In 2011, twelve CSAs had an unemployment rate over 19%. The picture is even more extreme when one considers that in eleven of the twelve areas, fewer than half of all residents age 16 to 64 were employed. At the bottom of the list again was Upton/Druid heights and Old Town/Middle East where barely a third of residents 16 to 64 were employed (BNIA-JFI).

Neighborhood Revitalization Politics in Historical Context

Neighborhood decline occurred in the wake of deindustrialization and suburbanization. As these trends began to be visible in the 1950s and 60s, city leaders responded by reinvesting in downtown and the city center (including highway development), and ignored the impact of these developments on the neighborhoods. Communities mobilized in opposition to those policies, and for a time there was a vibrant neighborhood movement in the 1970s (Crenson 1983; Stone et al). Yet, during the mayoralty of William Donald Schaeffer (1971-1986), there was still little focus on neighborhood revitalization. Schaeffer is regarded by many as supportive of neighborhoods, yet rather than a focus on neighborhood revitalization, his approach to neighborhoods was more consistent with the city's tradition of patronage politics; e.g., providing quick responses to specific constituent concerns and small grants for neighborhood projects. Schaeffer's priority and focus was on economic development – the center of which was the Inner Harbor redevelopment. As he earned accolades for the "Baltimore Renaissance", neighborhoods continued to decline – apparently untouched by the burgeoning tourist economy (Stone et al.). After Schaeffer left office, (and following the brief mayoralty of Clarence "Du" Burns), revitalizing distressed neighborhoods became more of a priority during Kurt Schmoke's mayoralty.

Schmoke took office at a time when the city, already experiencing the loss of industry, and a steady out migration, was hit by the increasing wave of crime and violence that came with the arrival of crack. Meanwhile, the Reagan administration had set about making massive funding cuts to the cities. At a time when cities across the country had become more dependent on federal aid, federal programs were cut severely (Eisinger 1998).

Within this changed context, Schmoke and other city leaders recognized neighborhood decline as more of a priority, and the mayor set about attempting to address it in a few targeted communities. The most significant attempt came in the form of an attempt at comprehensive community building in Sandtown-Winchester. The project was the product of a collaboration with noted builder Jim Rouse and his Enterprise Foundation and Baltimoreans United in Leadership Development (BUILD). BUILD is the Baltimore affiliate of the Industrial Areas Foundation (IAF), a national network of community organizations founded by Saul Alinsky and noted for its organizing philosophy and willingness to use confrontational strategies to leverage concessions from powerful actors (Brown et al., 2001; Orr 1999; McDougall 1993). BUILD's membership consists primarily of churches and other faith-based organizations.

The vision for the project was "comprehensive" in the sense that it was based on the notion that neighborhood transformation requires a broad effort that would address various community needs – including housing and various social services. The vision was that this effort would not only stave off decline but also spark the transformation of the community (McDougall; Brown et al.). During the 1990s the project gained national acclaim as a model of comprehensive community building (Brown et al.). But in Baltimore, the project led to disappointment in many circles. Although the project had successfully provided services to many in the community, produced hundreds of housing units that are still stable and have risen in value, and produced other neighborhood amenities that were a net gain for the community, it did not have the transformative impact that was hoped for or that many felt was necessary to justify the levels of financial and political investment. This led many local observers to shift their thinking about the possibilities of, and the keys to neighborhood revitalization.

While the Sandtown project was underway, Baltimore was designated for one of the Federal government's Empowerment Zones. This program, the marquee program under the Clinton Administration, provided an array of tax incentives for economic activities that take place within the zone, and awarded a $100 million Social Service Block Grant, to be invested in a manner directed by the local plan for reviving distressed areas. In Baltimore, the empowerment zone program had some marked positive outcomes, yet it too failed to have a transformative impact (Rich and Stoker).

Lessons from Sandtown - The Market Orientation
In our many conversations with policy makers and activists, it was striking how many made reference to the Sandtown project. For many, the lessons learned were clear, and thus came to shape the city's strategies in this area since. It was widely held that Sandtown failed because it had not tapped the forces or resources of the market. The project was not connected to any kind of economic anchor. Many concluded that the resources of the city government and the foundation sector are insufficient to transform communities in significant distress – private investment was also necessary.

Hence, future projects would have to be able to attract private investment in addition to the contributions of government and the foundation sector. To do so, these projects would have to somehow be connected to or create some kind of market advantage and also be of sufficient scale (major redevelopment) in order for the market dynamics to be unleashed. Thus, only major large-scale projects could be feasible. Small scale, piecemeal projects would likely be ineffective.

The approach coming out of the late 1990s was two-fold. First, revitalization efforts would have to tap market forces and be of a scale to leverage these market forces. Secondly, city leaders began to focus on deconcentrating poverty. During the Schmoke administration and continuing after, there was a sense that concentrated poverty (like what could be found in the public housing projects) could and should be addressed. New resources were made available for these efforts by the federal government. Thus, the city was one of the earliest and most thorough users of the Federal governments HOPE VI program, which provided local authorities funds for the demolition of public housing which would in turn be replaced by mixed-income developments.[2] Baltimore demolished its high-rise public housing and is still in the process of demolishing many of its remaining public housing units.

By the end of the 1990s, aside from the demolition of public housing, the general approach to neighborhoods amounted to a triage strategy: those neighborhoods that were stable would be left to thrive on their own. For the neighborhoods "in the middle" – those thought to be teetering on the brink of decline—some modest investments would be made to improve the local housing market (this was manifest through the Healthy Neighborhoods Initiative, for example). Lastly, for neighborhoods that were severely distressed, the strategy would essentially be large scale "redevelopment" (PlanBaltimore 1997). This was laid out in a four-part typology of neighborhoods presented in the city's comprehensive plan produced in 1997 (PlanBaltimore). Of course large-scale redevelopment could only be carried out when sufficient resources could be brought together, and would only make sense if there were some feasible way to tap into the market. This meant that the only neighborhoods that would even potentially be targeted would be those with some form of market advantage. Thus, most neighborhoods that were deemed severely distressed were left unaddressed.

As the Schmoke era ended and Martin O'Malley came in to office, this market orientation was consolidated – and accepted by not only city officials, but also many in the foundation sector and some at the community level. Neighborhood revitalization efforts in Baltimore for the past decade or so have been shaped (or confined) by these understandings. The project that most exemplifies the approach and this market orientation is the effort to redevelop the Middle East neighborhood.

Redevelopment in East Baltimore

The most high profile and extensive revitalization effort in the city over the last decade has been the redevelopment of an 88 acre area in the Middle East neighborhood just north of Johns Hopkins University's medical campus. The project reveals many of the key characteristics of the current landscape of neighborhood revitalization politics. It calls for the demolition of hundreds of houses and the relocation of hundreds of people to make room for new mixed income housing, a new school and other amenities, all anchored by a new biopark which the project's designers believed would house new biotech companies and provide jobs and an economic boost to the neighborhood and the city as a whole. A total of $1.8 billion in public and private investment is expected by the time the project is completed (EBDI 2006). Since the plans for the project were made public in 2001, it has been the subject of high aspirations, controversy,

---

2   Researchers have found that residents relocated through HOPE VI, have moved on to better housing, but still continue to have low incomes, and an assortment of health and other challenges (Popkin 2004).

protest, and quite a bit of frustration.

The target area was one of the most distressed in the city – with a vacancy rate between 60 and 70 percent. This stood in stark contrast to the prosperity of the Johns Hopkins campus. City leaders targeted the area for modest revitalization efforts for at least a decade before the current project was unveiled, yet the area continued to decline. Mayor O'Malley is credited with calling for a more extensive project.[3] The new project would entail a partnership comprised of the city government, Hopkins, and others. Eventually, the Annie E. Casey Foundation (AECF) was brought on board as a key partner. AECF is credited with shifting the vision for the project – somewhat; from being an old fashioned urban renewal project aiming to replace the existing community (through displacement of the residents and demolition of existing structures), and paying little attention to the well being of the current residents. AECF pushed for more concern regarding the residents – including more extensive relocation services, job training, and case management. Regardless, the linchpin would still be the biopark. It would attract investment, bring jobs, and serve as the magnet which would bring higher income residents to the new community.

To implement the project, the partners created East Baltimore Development Incorporated (EBDI), as an independent nonprofit entity. Its board consisted of some of the most influential business and foundation leaders in the city. Importantly, EBDI operates as a private corporation – but has access to (or can guide the use of) public powers and resources.

The ultimate plan that went forth from the partners was a plan that had been crafted without the community's input. The planners had essentially concluded that the solution to the community's problems was complete demolition and displacement. When they learned of the plan, many residents were outraged. Where the designers only saw distress, the residents saw a community of homes, relationships, traditions and connections that would be ripped apart. To make matters worse, the relocation packages were so limited that homeowners would not be able to purchase a comparable home in the metropolitan area. As a result, residents organized and formed the Save Middle East Action Committee (SMEAC) to try to resist the project and advocate on behalf of the residents.

SMEAC would have some significant successes. They garnered much more extensive relocation benefits, a new unprecedented demolition protocol (aimed at reducing the inconvenience and environmental hazards associated with demolishing structures which contained an array of harmful substances), and promises of a "House for a House" program which guarantee residents targeted for displacement a new (or renovated) home in the community if they desired to stay. After years of activism, SMEAC disbanded as most (though not all) of the residents they had organized to advocate for had been relocated. However, residents of the target area continued to protest and

---

3   We found some disagreement as to who initiated the project O'Malley or Johns Hopkins. While many believe the project was pushed at the behest of Hopkins, some insiders claim it was pushed by the mayor, and Hopkins was reluctant to participate.

contest the implementation of the project (Simmons 2011C).[4]

Three key observations related to this project stand out for the purposes of this discussion. First is the need for partners and contributors outside of government. The project may have been pushed by city hall, but city hall lacked the resources to make it happen. In fact, Hopkins and city hall together, still needed to tap an array of other public resources (from the state and Federal governments), and bring on other key partners, most importantly, AECF. This highlights a second key observation. The vehicle for implementing the project was a newly created corporation – EBDI. The use of such quasi-public corporations for major development projects has a long history in Baltimore, dating back to the days of the Schaeffer administration. This is related to the need to cobble together resources as potential contributors insist on such mechanisms for two reasons. First, there is a lack of faith in the capacity of city agencies to carry out such complicated projects. Secondly, there is a desire for some kind of insulation from "politics."

The latter is in part a response to the city's legacies of patronage politics. It is an attempt to avoid the challenges that ensue when local politicians distribute the benefits of a particular project. This process of distribution is distasteful and wasteful for these potential partners. Some officials believe that key partners would not participate without such a shield from "politics." The practical impact is an organizational form which shields the project from the levels of public scrutiny and accountability that would come with local government action. Even elected officials (other than the mayor) are left on the margins. This was evident when a number of elected officials claimed to not be fully aware of how EBDI used or accessed public funds. Although one might argue that this is at least as much of a criticism of these officials as it is of EBDI, the reality is that this reflects an insulation that may not be good for local democracy (Jacobson and Simmons 2011).

The third observation is perhaps the most ironic. The "market" did not deliver as promised. This was a project promoted on the basis of the power of the market potential of a biopark next to the Hopkins campus. The market was the justification and the linchpin. It is what makes this project different. But the market did not respond as the architects of the project expected. As the country experienced the greatest economic downturn in decades, the real estate market collapsed and the biotech companies failed to come in the numbers predicted. To date the project is behind schedule. So much so that the expected increase in property values has not been manifest.[5]

At the present, almost 600 families have been relocated and over $200 hundred million in public money has been invested. Though the project has made progress, it is behind schedule, and EBDI has made some significant adjustments. For example,

---

4   Interview with resident activist

5   Property tax revenues have been insufficient to cover the Tax Increment Financing (TIF) bond payments due in 2011 (Simmons, 2011B). TIF bonds are issued, with the expectation that they will be repaid with the increment in property tax revenue generated by the project for which the bonds were issued.

one of the proposed biotech buildings, is now slated to be a state Department of Health and Mental Hygiene's Public Health Laboratory, and the project leaders intend to construct smaller biotech buildings than they initially planned (Jacobson and Simmons 2011; EBDI 2011).

The changed context has driven the project's leaders to rework their plans and shift their emphasis as illustrated by the formulation of a new comprehensive plan (FC-NEBP 2011). There has been more emphasis on the array of amenities that will be required by the new community: a hotel, supermarket, and other consumer businesses have garnered more priority. Interestingly, it seems the discussion of "the market" shifted from the market potential of a biopark, to the untapped consumer market of the thousands of Hopkins employees (Simmons, 2011C).[6] Furthermore, the school, which is being run by Johns Hopkins and Morgan State University, has become the linchpin of the project. In a speech before a group of business leaders, Hopkins president Ron Daniels, stated that the school would "rise to the top of the list" of priorities in the East Baltimore project. He claimed, they "expect that the school will become the anchor of the East Baltimore development" (Simmons, 2011A).

Two recent controversies illustrate how the project – which started out with a grand vision of transformation garnering national attention—has in a sense been reduced to fights over the distribution of benefits. First, there was controversy and protests surrounding the lack of employment for Black East Baltimore residents during construction (Simmons, 2012). More recently, there was outrage over parents in the neighborhood not getting access to the school (Green, 2013). Both of these illustrate just what the partners hoped to avoid – being dragged into disputes over the distribution of benefits. Their vision was one of community and economic development, not distribution of construction jobs and seats in the school. But the reality is that the city is still struggling, people need work and parents are desperate for education opportunities. When residents see the public investment in EBDI and hear promises of transformation and improvement, they make the "mistake" of expecting their lives to be impacted as well. In actuality, one school will not be enough. And relying on the "market" means relying on market actors (like construction companies) who make decisions that continue to leave East Baltimore residents on the margins.

Building from Market Strength in Oliver

Just up the road from the EBDI target area is the site of a much smaller scale effort in the Oliver neighborhood that nevertheless offers a different set of lessons about neighborhood revitalization in the current context. The Oliver project, which focuses on building and renovating housing – with a plan to build or renovate as many as 800 units, is being led by BUILD in partnership with The Reinvestment Fund (TRF). This project displays the potential effectiveness of an organized community effort.

Much like Middle East, Oliver has suffered from disinvestment and a wide array of social challenges. Churches in the community have long been trying to push for change and alter the trajectory of the community. Yet it was in the aftermath of the Dawson

---

6   This is based on interviews with participants in the project

family tragedy that they began to get more support from the city government. When the seven members of the Dawson family were murdered in an arson in retaliation for their opposition to neighborhood drug dealers, the city could not continue to ignore the community (DeGregorio 2005; Kiehl 2007).

Churches in Oliver (which organized as part of BUILD) had been purchasing properties in the neighborhood in an attempt to stave off decline but initially did not have a clear vision of how to do it. Ultimately, through BUILD they began to craft a collective vision for the transformation of the neighborhood. Importantly, BUILD organizers had the experience of Sandtown-Winchester, and they too had drawn conclusions from the project. First, they reiterated the importance of community organizing as the backbone of any neighborhood effort, but also – much like many of the other policymakers, they concluded that foundations and the city government lacked sufficient resources for neighborhood transformation. They too concluded that market forces were needed. In their search for a market approach, they came to partner with TRF, an organization based in Philadelphia which has developed a market strategy for revitalizing distressed communities.

The TRF approach rests on the logic of rebuilding from market strength. Where Sandtown had implicitly aimed to rebuild from the "worst" spot in the worst neighborhood, TRF's strategy would be to rebuild from the "best spot" in the worst neighborhood. This might take the form of building on the edge of a distressed neighborhood that might be in proximity to a more stable area. The stable neighborhood would serve as a market strength. They would then work inward into the distressed area. In a twist, this meant that BUILD/TRF would begin their revitalization efforts – focused on housing – in the portion of the neighborhood closest to the EBDI target area. They banked on the market strength of EBDI to serve as leverage for their efforts in Oliver.

Ultimately, BUILD activists were able to pull together resources to implement the vision developed by TRF. How they did this is worth noting. Their fundraising began with the churches themselves raising $1 million. Beyond that, they tapped relationships with civic elites like Anthony Deering (former CEO of The Rouse Company, head of The Rouse Company Foundation, and an EBDI board member), who led the effort to raise funds for the project from foundations and other companies and individuals. They also used their political leverage to connect their project to EBDI, getting some slices of funds intended for EBDI and getting the city to commit to giving BUILD 155 vacant units it owned (Kiehl 2007).

One of the best examples of their efforts to garner resources for their work was the role BUILD played in the establishment of the city's affordable housing fund. When city officials announced plans to build a convention center hotel (what is now the Hilton), community groups, led by BUILD, protested. They argued that the city needed to invest in the neighborhoods, not just the Inner Harbor. This opposition was able to successfully negotiate the formation of a $59 million Affordable Housing Trust Fund. Subsequently, BUILD was able to get money from this fund for their work in Oliver (Donovan, 2005).

To date, the project has continued to progress, although they too were slowed down by the housing market collapse. Yet they have built and renovated dozens of houses, and have also built a multi-unit apartment building for artists on the west side of the neighborhood, intended to connect to the growing market presented by the Station North Arts District. Importantly, they have also developed a relationship with EBDI. The two organizations have collaborated on projects including the renovation of houses along a stretch of North Broadway, which connects the two communities.

There are a variety of lessons from these projects in East Baltimore, but the most important is that these are efforts being carried out by entities outside of government. Although they each make use of government resources and partner with government (and EBDI may have been initiated by government officials), they are being implemented by nongovernmental actors. Neighborhood revitalization in Baltimore is not driven by local government. It is driven by nongovernmental actors who cobble together resources from government, private sector and foundations to implement projects shaped outside of government.

The Future of Neighborhood Revitalization in Baltimore

Neighborhood revitalization in Baltimore will evolve in a landscape that is defined by some key characteristics. First, neighborhood revitalization is not a priority for the city government. After all, there is no city agency that has community development or neighborhood revitalization as its primary focus. As the Mayor's transition report noted, the city's department of Housing and Community Development had even taken out the term "Community Development" from its title. The city's Neighborhood Office is purely about constituent services not transforming neighborhoods. Thus, as evident from East Baltimore examples (and others)[7], these efforts are driven by actors outside of government.

A second key characteristic of the current landscape is the lack of resources. The city government has limited resources and there is very little flowing from the state and federal levels. This in turn enhances the importance of two other characteristics of the current context – the need to assemble resources for projects by attracting an array of partners, and the perceived need to leverage market forces.

The effort to pool resources and attract partners is a major factor in the use of quasi-public corporations like EBDI. These entities are viewed as more efficient than city government, and are ideal for pooling resources. Importantly, they allow the business and civic elites which lead these organizations to avoid politics – which they associate with patronage and the scramble to distribute benefits. Moreover, it reflects a level of unease with the broader populace. Ultimately, because of the "private" status of these corporations, community residents have a limited voice in the design and implementation of these projects. This has some major democratic implications for residents, as their elected representatives (council members) are left on the margins and the obstacles they pose for residents who wish to influence a project may serve

---

7   The Patterson Park neighborhood provides another example of revitalization driven by actors outside of government, but tapping government resources (Rutkowski and Pollack 1998).

to demobilize communities. Furthermore, a racial divide – predominantly Black residents, versus mostly white civic and business leaders cannot be ignored.

As noted, many actors, in varied positions, have concluded that revitalization efforts have to tap the forces of the market in order to have the kind of transformative impact desired. This ultimately means relying on market dynamics by strategically designing projects to: capitalize on existing or emerging market strengths; appeal to private investors; and to be nudges to unleash latent market potential. One major manifestation of this has been the emphasis on anchor institutions like the educational and medical institutions (eds and meds). This is not just a Baltimore phenomenon. The focus on anchor institutions has become a national trend (Taylor and Luter 2013). Driving this trend is the recognition that these institutions bring a significant amount of economic activity to a community and they are attached to their locations ("spatial immobility") in a way that most businesses are not. These institutions have been found to have a positive impact on their communities, as they themselves receive benefits from investments and expansion of their activities (Taylor and Luter 2013; Bates et al. 2011; Bartik and Erickcek 2008).

In Baltimore, we see the emphasis on anchors, not only in EBDI, but in a number of smaller projects as well (Sharper 2013). In recent years the Baltimore Neighborhood Collaborative (BNC) promoted eds and meds becoming more active in neighborhood revitalization efforts around the city. The BNC is also one of a number of partners in the Baltimore Integration Partnership – an initiative funded by the Living Cities Foundation—which aims to connect low income individuals to the mainstream economy – through economic development practices that rely heavily on anchor institutions (Baltimore Integration Partnership).

A last key characteristic of this current landscape is the level of community engagement around these policies and projects. Community engagement related to revitalization efforts is quite limited, and what does occur is largely reactive. Communities may have opportunities to express concerns in hearings or public forums, but this is not the kind of engagement that shapes a policy. These activities can modify a plan or its implementation, but are insufficient for re-framing the basic idea. This is what we saw with Middle East. SMEAC won some key victories, but for the most part the fundamental vision of the project was sustained.

The current landscape suggests that without some kind of drastic change, the future outlook is likely to be - more of the same. Given the limited resources and low level of prioritization, we can expect only limited government initiated efforts at neighborhood revitalization in Baltimore. We are, however, likely to see continued efforts in areas with some market advantage, particularly areas in proximity to anchor institutions. These efforts will likely be driven by actors outside of government, though likely will have some support from the city government. What does this mean for the residents? For those in neighborhoods that lack an anchor or "market advantage," – nothing will likely change. For those in distressed communities that have such advantages, past experience suggests that most residents will be left on the margins as other actors (many of them well meaning) determine their fate. The manner in which these projects are put together and implemented leaves very little opportunity for residents to express their interests and contribute to the guiding vision. They are left out of the planning and shaping stage, and their interests only get expressed as the residents of these communities react to proposals.

A Strategy for the Future

While the above may seem a bit dismal, there are some characteristics of the present context that make change possible; difficult but possible. To begin with, there are some advantages of the current context. There is limited political opposition to neighborhood revitalization. To the extent that there is resistance it is based on competition over resources, not on disagreement with the goal. Furthermore, there may be opportunities to connect neighborhood revitalization and community development to other policies such as transportation, economic development, and public safety. To the extent that these other policy priorities are pursued, neighborhood advocates may be able to attach neighborhood benefits to new projects or strategies. The planned Red Line for example has entailed a detailed "Neighborhood Benefits Agreement." While the ultimate impact remains to be seen, it does suggest an opportunity for accruing some benefits to neighborhoods. Another key advantage of the current context is a set of supportive philanthropic organizations. There are a number of foundations that are supportive of revitalization efforts (e.g. AECF, The Rouse Company Foundation, Enterprise, etc.). Importantly, however, any efforts at linking neighborhood revitalization to other policies, or partnerships with foundations would have to be driven by actors with neighborhoods as their priority.

The key determinant of the possibility of changed outcomes will ultimately come down to the residents. The outcomes will be dependent on the capacity of these communities to organize and mobilize. The examples described above demonstrate that mobilized community groups can have an impact. The challenge is to shift from "reactive" engagement to "proactive" engagement—much like BUILD was able to accomplish in Oliver. They crafted a vision with their partners, and were able to push and prod government officials to support their vision. Importantly, their effectiveness came from their capacity to organize.

This may sound deceptively simple, but Baltimore's own experiences suggest that it can be effective. We know that without a voice, community interests will be left on the margins; as has been and continues to be the case. The only way to alter that is for residents to insert themselves into the process. This would entail community organizing efforts that yield an organized collective which could in turn shape a vision of what the residents want, and then use their collective power to persuade, pressure and partner with other actors (including local government) to implement projects that come out of that vision.

Individual neighborhoods need to be organized, but there also needs to be a collective voice that speaks for neighborhoods, which can put forth a clear, coherent vision of how to address neighborhood decline – from the perspective of the neighborhoods and the residents. This collective voice is also crucial because the reactive, opportunistic way in which neighborhoods have mobilized can create competition between neighborhoods. Consider Oliver and EBDI. BUILD for example, could have supported EBDI as it offered some perceived advantages for revitalization efforts in Oliver, while SMEAC would of course not support it. Thus, there was the potential of putting two community groups, with comparable general goals (thriving East Baltimore communities) at odds over strategy.

The heavy lifting will ultimately have to come from the neighborhoods themselves but, there is room for potential partners. Foundations and other entities with sincere interests in the well-being of these communities need to be willing to partner with the residents and their representatives on an equal basis, and need to promote and contribute to neighborhood capacity building. When SMEAC was formed, they were funded by AECF. While this no doubt, made for some uncomfortable moments, if one is serious about empowering and transforming neighborhoods, one has to acknowledge that an organized and mobilized community is a necessity. This was acknowledged by Douglas Nelson, chair of the EBDI Board, and former president of AECF, when he testified before the City Council amidst controversy surrounding EBDI's funding and accountability highlighted by the series of critical articles in the *Daily Record* (Simmons and Jacobson 2011). Nelson acknowledged that they needed to:

> ... do a better job of engaging / involving / and being guided by community residents – both those who have relocated and those who live in and around the EBDI footprint. We need to find ways of supporting community organizations that can give clear voice to community interests...
> (Nelson 2011)

He also acknowledged the need to find ways to not only keep residents informed about the project, but to find ways to put residents in "a better position to shape its implementation" (Nelson). Foundations have done these things in the past, but need to return to these activities if they hope to increase trust, legitimacy and the effectiveness of their community efforts.

There is a need for more resources. There is a need for neighborhoods to be a higher priority for the city government. There is a need for civic actors to be more conscious of, receptive to and responsive to the needs and interests of communities. But none of that is likely to occur unless driven by organized, mobilized voices from the communities themselves. Once they are organized and have a clear vision of what they want, they can mobilize to persuade, pressure and partner with local government, developers and civic actors who can help implement that vision.

References

Baltimore Integration Partnership, "Baltimore Integration Partnership" website http://www.abagrantmakers.org/page/BaltimorePartnership/ Downloaded – November 1, 2013.

Baltimore Neighborhood Indicators Alliance – Jacob France Institute (BNIA) *Vital Signs* Data http://www.bniajfi.org/index (Downloaded: November 1, 2013).

Bartik, Timothy George Erickcek, (2008) "The Local Impact of 'Eds & Meds': How Policies to Expand Universities and Hospitals Affect Metropolitan Economies" Washington, C: The Brookings Institute.

Bates, Mary Ann, Justina Cross, Ilana Goli, and Elizabeth Redman, (2011) "Giving Back and Getting Back: An Analysis of the Return on Community Investments by Public Universities" Annie E. Casey Foundation

Bell-McKoy, Diane, Nicholas Ramos and Seema Iyer, (2010) "Mayor Stephanie Rawlings-Blake Transition Team – Community Development and Neighborhoods Final Report"

Brown, Prudence, B. Butler, and R. Hamilton. (2001). *The Sandtown-Winchester* Neighborhood Transformation Initiative: Lessons Learned about Community *Building and Implementation*. Baltimore: Annie E. Casey Foundation.

Crenson, Matthew (1983) *Neighborhood Politics.* Cambridge: Harvard University Press

DeGregorio, Jen (2005) "Baltimoreans United in Leadership Development demands meeting with City Council president." *The Daily Record* (May 26, 2005).

Donovan, Doug. (2005) "Deals secure council votes for city hotel ; O'Malley administration offers funding for projects; 9-6 vote is likely Monday; Hilton to cost $305 million, $72 million for community". *The Baltimore Sun* (August 12, 2005).

East Baltimore Development Inc. (EBDI) (2006) *Annual Report. -* (2011) "EBDI's response to the Daily Record".

Eisinger, Peter, (1998) "City Politics in an Era of Federal Devolution" *Journal of Urban Affairs* Vol. 33 No. 3.

Forrest City New East Baltimore Partnership (FCNEBP), (2012) "2011 Summary Recommendations".

Green, Erica L. (2013) "A community school divides the community; East-side families feel shut out from Henderson-Hopkins." *The Baltimore Sun* (June 22, 2013).

Jacobson, Joan and Melody Simmons. (2011) "Maryland elected officials short on financial details". *The Daily Record* (January 31, 2011).

Kiehl, Stephen. (2007) "Renewal Planned for Area: $10 Million Raised for Rehab in E. Baltimore". *The Baltimore Sun* (December 9, 2007) (January 13, 2013).

Levine, Marc V. 1987. "Downtown Redevelopment as an Urban Growth Strategy: A Critical Appraisal of the Baltimore Renaissance." *Journal of Urban Affairs* 9, 2: 103-123.

Nelson, Douglas (2011) Testimony Before Baltimore City Council, March 30, 2011.

Popkin, Susan J., Bruce Katz, Mary K. Cunningham, Karen D. Brown, Jeremy Gustafson, and Margery A. Turner (2004) "A DECADE OF HOPE VI: Research Findings and Policy Challenges".

Rich, Michael and Robert Stoker (Forthcoming) *Governance for Urban Revitalization.* Cornell University Press.

Rutkowski, Ed and Marcus Pollack, (1998) *The Urban Transition Zone: A Place Worth A* Fight: A Strategy for Urban Stabilization and Revitalization.

Scharper, Julie. (20013) "Down from ivory towers, into the neighborhoods: With universities seen as cities' 'anchor institutions,' those in Baltimore push to improve their communities". *The Baltimore Sun.*

Simmons, Melody (2012) "Second protest for local hiring held at East Baltimore Development Inc." *The Daily Record* (March 1, 2012). - (2011A) "Hopkins president lays out plans for East Baltimore Community School". *The Daily Record* (September 20, 2011).

— (2011B) "Baltimore finds funds for EBDI TIF" *The Daily Record.* (September 18, 2011).

— (2011C) "Middle East residents form new grassroots organization to advocate for increased representation on East Baltimore Development Inc. Board". *The Daily Record* (August 9, 2011).

Stone, Clarence, et. al (Forthcoming) *In a New Era.* Chicago: University of Chicago Press.

Taylor, Henry Louis and Gavin Luter (2013) "Anchor Institutions: An Interpretive Review Essay" Anchor Institutions Task Force.

Down to the Wire: Displacement and Disinvestment in Baltimore City

Lawrence Brown

"Look, the pawns, man, in the game, they get capped quick."
—D'Angelo Barksdale in *The Wire*

"Demolition. Dust. People. Children. Residents.
Where are they gonna go?"
—Sallie Gorham
Former Middle East resident and activist

In order to understand the state of black Baltimore today, we must always strive to understand the impact of the past. In the 50 years since the March on Washington for Jobs and Freedom, we have come, as the black laureate James Weldon Johnson reminded us, over a way that with tears have been watered. We have come over a way that has been and still is shaped and structured by racism. Racism, according to the People's Institute for Survival and Beyond, is defined as: race prejudice *plus* the misuse of power of systems and institutions, that is, both factors must be present. We must understand racism if we are to neutralize and destroy it.

We live in a moment where the destructive politics and seductive narrative of personal responsibility and "blame-the-victim" discourse dominate. Thus, this essay will explain the historical dynamics affecting black Baltimore in the Jim Crow era preceding the 1963 March on Washington before delving into the historical dynamics that shape where stand today. Only by accounting for these dynamics will we be able to take stock of what happened and where we need to go.

Racial Segregation and Health

As chronicled in *Not in My Neighborhood: How Bigotry Shaped a Great American City* (Pietila, 2010), white Baltimore city officials, bankers, and real estate agents engaged in racist practices and policies such as segregation, restrictive covenants, redlining, and disinvestment over a period stretching from the 1910 to the present. The cumulative impact of Jim Crow policies has been devastating to people of African descent, but particularly for low-income African American communities. As Massey and Denton (1993) articulated:

> Residential segregation is not a neutral fact; it systematically undermines
> the social and economic well-being of blacks in the United States. Because
> of racial segregation, a significant share of black America is condemned to
> experience a social environment where poverty and joblessness are the norm,
> where a majority of children are born out of wedlock, where most families are
> on welfare, where educational failure prevails, and where social and physical

deterioration abound. Through prolonged exposure to such an environment, black chances for social and economic success are drastically reduced.

Not only is there an economic impact, but there is also a health impact. As LaVeist and colleagues (2011) noted: "Racial segregation creates different exposures to economic opportunity and to other community resources that enhance health. Likewise, segregation produces differential exposure to health risks."

In other words, racial segregation—along with subsequent disinvestment—increases risk to health-negating factors and decreases access to health-enhancing factors. Marisela Gomez (2013) described the impact of more recent disinvestment on black communities:

> The unequal and discriminatory laws and policies resulted in disinvestment and marginalization of communities in which majority African Americans lived leading to unhealthy physical environments of unsanitary, abandoned, and run-down streets, schools, parks, health clinics, recreation centers, stores, and houses, and high crime. The consequences of living in such disinvested neighborhoods help to determine exposure to different levels of stress faced daily by individuals living, playing, working, and learning in these communities as well the internal and external resources to address these stressors in a healthy way.

During the Jim Crow era and beyond, black folks living in communities such as Sandtown-Winchester, Park Heights, Cherry Hill, or Middle East were living in environments that did not receive the same level of city investment as the dollars allocated to downtown, the Inner Harbor, or Harbor East. These investment decisions continue to reverberate and affect the health profile and economic well-being of black people living in disinvested communities.

Disinvestment, Uneven Development, and Neighborhood Health
Between 1970 and the early 2000s over $2 billion in public tax money was spent by city officials on developing the area in and around the Inner Harbor and downtown while many schools and city infrastructure crumbled, particularly in disinvested black neighborhoods (Levine, 2000). This unfair development—characterized by billions of tax money for wealthy developers while recreation centers and fire stations were shuttered—continues unabated and unrestrained into 2014.

City officials often use a mechanism known as a tax increment financing (TIF) to accomplish redevelopment aims. As described by Melody Simmons and Joan Jacobson in *The Daily Record* (2011a): "When City Hall approves a TIF to help finance a new development, bonds are sold to investors. The bonds are to be repaid not with city general funds but with future property taxes from the new development." But TIFs affect city finances (and therefore taxpayers) in three ways according to Simmons and Jacobson (2011a):

- TIFs impact the city's bond rating and a bad bond rating could impact the city's ability to take out bonds for other things like schools;

- Taxes are diverted from coming in for years with TIFs, thereby reducing the amount of tax revenues the city could be receiving to pay for things such as fire stations and recreation centers;

- If the holder of the TIF were to default, then ownership of the land would revert back to the city. This could mean that the city could have partially or fully developed structures that will need to be managed, sold to another owner, or perhaps demolished—costing taxpayers more money in the process and not realizing the promised tax revenues.

In spite of these risks, city officials have been handing out TIFs like sweets to children in a candy shop. In 2012, the city approved up to $35 million in TIF bonds for Under Armour (Scharper, 2012). Last year, the Baltimore City Council approved up to $125 million in TIFs for the Harbor Point development (Simmons, 2013a) although it could cost the city up to $283 million when all the costs are considered (Simmons, 2013b).

This critical context—first racial segregation and redlining, then disinvestment and unfair development—helps explain the data presented in the table below in the following table. Data were obtained from the Neighborhood Health Profiles generated by the Baltimore City Health Department (2011).

TABLE 1: Baltimore Neighborhood Health and Economic Comparisons

Community Area	% Black	Life Expectancy	MAHI*	% FIP*	% Unemployed
Upton/Druid Heights	94.3	62.9 years	$13,388	48.8	17.5
Southern Park Heights	96.1	66.7 years	$27,635	25.9	17.5
Cherry Hill	95.7	67.8 years	$19,183	45.1	28.2
Perkins/Middle East	87.1	68.2 years	$18,522	28.4	17.5
Morrell Park/ Violetville	18.8	70.7 years	$39,931	11.4	5.8
Highlandtown	9.2	74.0 years	$49,680	7.6	9.8
Baltimore City Average	63.6	71.8 years	$37,395	15.2	11.1

MAHI = median annual household income, FIP = Families in Poverty

Therefore, the state of black Baltimore is one where black folks living in disinvested neighborhoods are confronted with shorter lives, lower economic opportunities, disparities in health outcomes, and uneven economic investments across city neighborhoods. These outcomes are rooted in the inter-generational impacts of and exposure to structural racism embedded in policies practiced by city officials, bankers, developers, and real estate agents.

The Baltimore Displacement Equation

In addition to the dynamics of racial containment and marginalization via segregation, Baltimore City officials have more recently implemented the strategy of displacement and dispersal, clearing the poor out of the city and into the surrounding counties. The shifting and removal of black folks living in disinvested neighborhoods into less desirable spaces and less valuable land has been a core feature and function of Baltimore City policies under recent mayoral administrations, regardless of race. From the 1940s through the 1960s, Baltimore City leaders utilized comparable policies – starting with slum clearance and morphing into urban renewal – as exemplified by the Johns Hopkins Broadway Project, in order to obtain the land occupied by black residents near the Hopkins campus (Gomez, 2013). The Hopkins Broadway Project displaced over 800 black families (Gomez, 2013).

As a part of an aborted highway expansion project I-70, the city displaced 960 black families from the infamous "Highway to Nowhere" in West Baltimore on what is now known as U.S. 40 (Power, 2000; Lankford, 2010). Other families were displaced south of downtown when a 1.5 mile stretch of I-395 was completed in 1982. Since

1990, black Baltimoreans living in disinvested neighborhoods have experienced displacement in four main ways: eminent domain, gentrification, foreclosures, and the dismantling of public housing.

The late Lucille Gorham, long-time activist and president of Citizens for Fair Housing in East Baltimore starting in 1967, recalled in an interview with the author in 2011:

> The city has always been taking property for what they call 'urban renewal.' And they have been taking it for years and years and years… After all [that] urban renewal stuff, people had a right to come back to those neighborhoods. But what chopped that up is people's incomes—they didn't have the money. After these new houses were built, prices go up, up, up and up.

It is important to call forth into recognition that in the midst of Jim Crow and urban renewal forces, black folks living in segregated and disinvested communities were not sitting back as mere victims. They would organize in various ways and fight back—by participating in the 1963 March on Washington for Jobs and Freedom, engaging in the Holy Week Uprising in 1968 in the aftermath of the assassination of Dr. Martin Luther King Jr. (Yockel, 2007), and forming the Baltimore chapter of the Black Panther Party in 1968 (Royster-Hemby, 2006).

More recently, residents of public housing fought back against the decrepit conditions in their developments and HUD's racial segregation of public housing residents into disinvested communities (Williams, 2004). Residents facing eminent domain and city eviction protested and won concessions even as they were being displaced in the Middle East by the quasi-governmental, Hopkins-directed East Baltimore Development Incorporated or EBDI (Gomez, 2013).

The resilience and resistance of black people living in disinvested communities is characterized in *The Politics of Public Housing: Black Women's Struggle Against Urban Inequality* by Rhonda Williams. After Williams recounted the brave efforts of low-income black women in public housing to improve the quality of lives in their communities, she found that although black women living in public housing are marginalized and demonized, their efforts spoke to "their commitment to a humanistic agenda of social rights, progressive change, and fairness."

Although the mechanisms have changed, much of what has happened since the late 1970s was predicted by the late Morgan State economist and Goon Squad activist Dr. Homer Favor. In the October 3, 1978 edition of *The Baltimore Afro-American*, Dr. Favor prophesied:

> My concern is that presently the city is being prepared for the return of the genteel to its confines. …it seems to me that the city has indicated that it will attempt to solve the city's problems by bringing in middle class and upper middle class privileged—basically whites and dislocating blacks who are here and then viewing this transformation as a major accomplishment… I am concerned because I don't see the evidence of grappling with the very

difficult problem of what happens to people who are displaced, who are not involved, who are not counted into this particular equation (pages 8-9).

The rest of this chapter will outline how the displacement of black folks living in disinvested areas has (or will be) taking place via four primary mechanisms of urban redevelopment: eminent domain, gentrification, foreclosures, and the dismantling of public housing.

Eminent Domain

Marisela Gomez has written a historical narrative entitled *Race, Class, Power, and Organizing in East Baltimore* that discusses how black East Baltimoreans were displaced by Johns Hopkins' medical campus on multiple occasions during their campus and hospital expansions. From 2000 to 2010, the EBDI-Hopkins-Baltimore City triumvirate partnered with the Annie Casey Foundation and others to carry out forced relocation using eminent domain (Gomez, 2013). In the process, the aforementioned institutions and organizations forced over 700 African American families to uproot and leave their homes and community (Simmons and Jacobson, 2011b). This included many elders who organized and fought back as a part of the Save Middle East Action Committee (SMEAC). Many elders have since died after relocation, including Lucille Gorham, and others are facing foreclosure and uncertainty after taking out loans to help cover living expenses and/or fix the shoddy homes into which they were placed (Simmons, 2013c).

In 2013, city officials announced a new round of eminent domain that will force residents to relocate from the heart of the Upton/Druid Heights neighborhood near the 1700 block of Division Street. Several black homeowners and residents will be affected by this displacement. A recent story in the Baltimore Sun also raises several salient points:

> Norma Green, who lives in the West Baltimore neighborhood of Upton, where the city plans to tear down at least several blocks of vacant homes, spoke at a community meeting Tuesday evening in Druid Heights.
>
> "There's always been a great push to bring people back to the city, but the people who live here are always overlooked," she said. "How are you going to give someone fair market value for a house surrounded by vacants?"
>
> Some residents are suspicious of the process that will take their homes. Others can't wait to rid their neighborhood of blight, perhaps Baltimore's most visible problem (Wells, 2013).

Gentrification

In his book *Driven from New Orleans: How Nonprofits Betray Public Housing and Promote Privatization*, John Arena defines gentrification as "flows of capital into an urban core that create spaces for the affluent while displacing the existing low-income residents of the area." In Baltimore, gentrification has largely and negatively impacted the black community. In their 2012 report, the Joint Center for Political and Economic Studies in conjunction with the Baltimore Place Matters team (known as Equity Matters), has shown that formerly segregated and redlined neighborhoods such as Midtown, Inner Harbor, Downtown, Highlandtown, and Upper Fells Point have become gentrified over time.

The Poppleton community has experienced gentrification originating from the University of Maryland when the university crossed over Martin Luther King Blvd to build its BioPark. The threat and reality of gentrification is captured by real estate agent Debbie Kuper in a news article in *The Daily Record*:

> "Housing is going to be an issue once biotech really gets moving," she said. "People are feeling better about the neighborhood, thinking that there will be *better people* over there. [Emphasis mine]… Everyone's still a little nervous with the market, but the word 'biotech' is helping turn things around. A lot of people who come to me say they're looking for a 10-year investment, and that's smart" (Whelan, 2008).

The article goes on to state the following:

> Last year, four houses in a row on the 1000 block of West Fayette Street, less than two blocks from the BioPark, sold for an average of $371,000 apiece, helping to account for a 588 percent rise in the median home sale price in the neighborhood. In 2004, the median price of a home sold in Poppleton was $59,500.

> Audrey Robinson, president of the Poppleton Co-Op, which is subsidized by the U.S. Department of Housing and Urban Development, said local residents are already reaping the benefits of University of Maryland's investment in the neighborhood.

> "We're feeling so far so good, as long as we don't become displaced," she said.

The CDC has issued a brief outlining the following health effects of gentrification: stress levels, injuries, violence, crime, and mental health (CDC, 2009). For people who are facing the threat of displacement, affordable housing becomes an issue as the cost of living rises and tax bills increase.

Foreclosures

Data from the Baltimore Neighborhood Indicators Alliance—Jacob Francis Institute (BNIA-JFI) indicates that between 2000-2010, there were more than 45,000 foreclosures filings in Baltimore City (Kachura, 2012). Since the inception of the Great Recession, there have been over 22,000 foreclosures in Baltimore between 2008-2013 (Baltimore Neighborhood Indicators Alliance, 2013). Many of these foreclosures were the result of subprime mortgages or what is also known as predatory lending. As

Washington Post business writer Binyamin Applebaum noted:

> Between 2004 and 2007, bank affiliates made more than 1.1 million subprime loans, around 13 percent of the national total, federal data show. Thousands ended in foreclosure, helping to spark the crisis and leaving borrowers and investors to deal with the consequences.

In her affidavit in the case against Wells Fargo, Beth Jacobson charged that loan officers targeted the black community in Baltimore and Prince George's counties with subprime mortgages by partnering with black churches and community groups (Mui, 2012). This charge caused the Baltimore city officials to file a lawsuit against Wells Fargo and announced a settlement of $7.5 million to the city in 2012 (Broadwater, 2012). Targeting the black community for subprime lending is called reverse redlining.

How did this happen? How does the "Subprime Game" work so that black Baltimore can be aware of the inner workings of such devastating and predatory behavior? William Poole (2013) explains:

> As the decade proceeded, underwriting standards for subprime mortgages deteriorated. Mortgage brokers, who originated the subprime mortgages, lent to households without adequate income or assets to service the mortgages. Income and asset documentation was weak or nonexistent. Some of the mortgage borrowers were investors anticipating quick resale of the properties they purchased—the "flippers." Nevertheless, the market was so hungry for yield that investment banks found that they could easily package subprime mortgages…and peddle them to investors.

Yet another tool that can induce foreclosure is a financing tool known as a reverse mortgage. Although residents are able to obtain money for some needed expenses, particularly medical bills, reverse mortgages can leave survivors and descendants at risk for losing their home when the person holding the reverse mortgage dies (Simms, 2014).

The Dismantling of Public Housing in Baltimore City

Both Edward Goetz (2013) and Rhonda Williams (2004) have described the way in which public housing has filled a critical need for people without means around the country. Many public housing authorities have long waiting lists attesting to the demand for subsidized housing. Williams found that in 1994 "the Baltimore housing authority had a waiting list of 23,000 people." In 2007, the number had grown to 29,477 (Jacobson, 2007). Due to the neglect and mismanagement of the Housing Authority of Baltimore City (HABC) along with declining funding from HUD, many public housing buildings have fallen into disrepair.

In his book *New Deal Ruins: Race, Economic Justice, and Public Housing Policy*, Goetz gives extensive documentation that shows how housing authorities around the nation used a strategy of neglect to allow units to remain vacant and allow buildings to become decrepit—in a process he calls ***de facto demolition***—so that they could demolish public housing developments and sell the land to private corporate developers. In the process, several forces combine to promote and hype what Goetz calls "a discourse of disaster," promoting the idea that *all public housing is so bad* the only way to help public housing residents is to demolish public housing and displace them. In this way, the dismantling of public housing is a part of the broad strategy of pushing out black people for the profit of rich developers (Keene and Geronimus, 2011).

The HABC has increasingly dismantled public housing in the city by utilizing demolition and land disposition (selling the land to private developers) over the past 20 years. Rhonda Williams (2004) has noted the implosion of several Baltimore public housing developments starting in 1995:

- Lafayette Courts (1995)
- Lexington Terrace (1996)
- Murphy Homes (1999)
- Flag House Courts (2001)

Public housing has also been lost in the following Baltimore neighborhoods in the past 15 years: Oldtown, Westport, O'Donnell Heights, Cherry Hill, Belair-Edison, Armistead Gardens, Rosedale, and Washington Hill (Jacobson, 2007). Many of the public housing units were demolished and former residents were subsequently dispersed with the assistance of Section 8 vouchers. Many residents are now living in Baltimore County.

In Baltimore, the dismantling of public housing has occurred with a particular twist and irony. In 1995, residents fought back against the segregation practices of the city, HABC, and HUD (Williams, 2004). The U.S. District Court of Maryland ruled in favor of residents in a final consent decree that set up a housing mobility program where residents would be dispersed throughout the region. The initial partial consent decree involved demolition, relocation, and rebuilding public housing in neighborhoods that were not poor (Williams, 2004). It seems that somewhere along the way, the idea of rebuilding public housing in Baltimore City was set on the wayside. Thus, although residents won a significant victory against modern segregation as practiced by HUD and HABC, the HABC has actually been working to dismantle public housing in Baltimore City in a manner consistent with other housing authorities around the nation. The final consent decree features the housing mobility component without any rebuilding component which accomplishes the objective of dispersing black residents out of the city.

Beyond this, the HABC continues to use the classic methods of demolition and displacement to dismantle public housing in Baltimore. The Pedestal Gardens housing development in the Druid Heights neighborhood is scheduled to be demolished soon by The Community Builders out of Boston (Kay, 2011). In the Upton neighborhood, the residents of McCulloh Homes housing development may be threatened by forced relocation when the $1.5 billion State Center project begins construction (Mithun, 2013).

In February 2014, reporter Melody Simmons broke the news of HABC's heavy participation in HUD's Rental Assistance Demonstration or RAD program (Simmons, 2014a). Ten of the remaining senior high rise towers will be turned over to private developers and residents will have the option of moving out with Section 8 vouchers in two years (Simmons, 2014b). There are questions concerning whether or not RAD will lead to yet more dismantling of public housing around the city. As of now, the jury is still out. But groups such as the Right to Housing Alliance are raising critical questions about Baltimore's RAD implementation that HABC has not yet answered (Lewis, 2014).

Current Urban Redevelopment, High Unemployment, and Health Impacts

After displacement and dispersal takes place, new issues emerge for the displaced and those who remain nearby: employment in the redevelopment process. For instance, in the Middle East neighborhood, the triumvirate of EBDI, Johns Hopkins Medical Institutions, and the City of Baltimore (under then mayor Martin O'Malley) promised in 2001 to create 8,000 jobs and build affordable housing. As of late 2011, EBDI had only created 759 permanent jobs. Out of that amount, only 183 people were East Baltimore residents (Haber, 2011).

Black folks living in Baltimore's disinvested neighborhoods are systematically locked out of employment opportunities during the redevelopment process. But again, in spite of the callousness of developers and subcontractors, many black men and women living in disinvested neighborhoods have fought back in the effort to feed their families and create a higher quality of life. During 2011 and 2012, Community Churches United (CCU) for Baltimore Jobs fought to gain employment for unemployed African Americans it had organized under the leadership of lead organizer Richie Armstrong (Hare, 2011; Simmons, 2012). CCU engaged in street protests at EBDI headquarters and the Baltimore Development Corporation. CCU members flooded city hall during hearings concerning the tax money being allocated to Under Armour and Superblock developers. Their goal has been to enforce a community workforce agreement with the mandate of employing over 50% of the construction workers from among Baltimore city residents.

Yet, they often faced pushback from black political officials. Rhonda Williams explained why low-income black folks could not count on its predominantly black city leaders for assistance in their struggle to work: "In some cases, black elected officials' urban reform agendas did not benefit low-income residents, but focused on maintaining and luring businesses and professionals to declining cities through tax breaks and incentives."

John Arena (2012) attested to this dynamic when he observed:

> This type of regime, which governed New Orleans from the late 1970s until the late 2000s, is on that emerged in many majority black cities in the post-civil rights era. These political formations are characterized by a "governing coalition" composed of a primarily black public wing that holds

a majority of the leading positions in local government and their allied, primarily black cadre of professionals, contractors, and ministers. Assembled on the other side of the power structure is a mainly white corporate private wing that controls the most important economic institutions. These elites are, for the most part, committed to a neoliberal urban entrepreneurial development model, with their collaboration often taking the form of "public-private" partnerships. The governing elite favors constructing policy through these private and sometimes quasi-public entities, since they are buffered from extensive citizen participation and pressure.... These corporate or entrepreneurial regimes facilitate and subsidize corporate-led economic development, while redistribution and welfare are jettisoned.

This arrangement where public goods are subsidized to satisfy private corporate objectives is facilitated by a class of black elites that partner with wealth white developers. This arrangement of black elites and wealthy whites leaves black folks living in disinvested neighborhoods locked out and disproportionately unemployed. Gomez (2013) has noted the impact of unemployment on residents:

The effect of having a low-paying job or no job, being African American or part of a racial minority, and education below high school level independently and together affects the health of an individual. These socioeconomic factors or social determinants increase the likelihood of an individual having a variety of physical and mental illnesses and a shorter lifespan.

This argument is further laid out in a recent article in the *American Journal of Public Health*. McLoed and colleagues (2012) find a higher risk of dying for unemployed Americans, but not Germans, suggesting that being unemployed in America is dangerous for one's health, both mentally and physically.

The War on Drugs and the Prevalence of Violence

The sustained impact of racial segregation, economic disinvestment, and serial forced displacement has created conditions contributing to high crime and anti-social behavior (Gomez, 2013). Without gainful employment, unemployed people turn to illegal ways to gain money for survival. Persons involved in the illegal drug trafficking are exposed to higher levels of violence both from other dealers and police fighting the War on Drugs (Kostroff-Noble, Simon, Pelacanos, Burns, et al, 2008). This is most vividly and heart-wrenchingly illustrated in the television drama called *The Wire*. In the Baltimore-based, ethnography-inspired drama, violence is intimately connected with the drug economy.

In a social environment that does not provide sustainable employment and opportunities, men have historically turned to an illegal drug economy to earn income. During American Prohibition, recently arrived Italian immigrants turned to organizing gangs (i.e. the American Mafia) and started "bootlegging" to make ends meet (unknown, 2013). In Central and South America, some Latinos are engaged in "large scale drug gangs and cartels" in places such as Mexico, Colombia, and Brazil (Becker and Murphy, 2013). Locally, a number of African American men in Baltimore are no different from their counterparts and are also operating drug organizations or "hustling" to make ends meet.

Whether hustling or bootlegging, such activity is inimical to the health and well-being of vulnerable populations when drug dealers and gangsters often murder each other and innocents, increase the levels of stress already experienced by disinvested communities, and lure young boys and male teenagers away from formal education and schooling into a life on the corner (*The Wire*, especially season 4). Again, such activity can flourish in an environment where racial segregation "reduces exposure to economic opportunities" (LaVeist et al, 2011). The same is true in disinvested communities under constant threat of displacement and dispersal vis-à-vis eminent domain, gentrification, foreclosure, and the dismantling of public housing.

Organizing and Policy Solutions

When we analyze "the way that with tears have been watered" in Baltimore and bear witness to the state of black Baltimore, it is clear that we have not yet overcome nor achieved the realization of some post-racial nirvana. In fact, we might call the combination of segregation, disinvestment, and serial forced displacement along with their subsequent impacts by another name: Jim Crow Jr. If strong organizing and powerful policies were needed to defeat Jim Crow, then the same if not more will be needed to defeat Jim Crow Jr. and the neoliberal urban redevelopment model that proliferates the displacement, disinvestment, unemployment, and poor health.

It is clear that we are a community divided—the black elites are separated from black folks living in disinvested communities. Given the trauma of racism and what the People's Institute for Survival and Beyond calls *internalized racial oppression*, there are many internal community dynamics we must address if we are to heal and unify around an agenda to uplift the entire community. The internal Du Boisian "double consciousness" has now manifested itself into our social fabric, manifesting as an external reality as we move into the next chapter of our American saga.

In concert with this occurrence is the reality of a class of black political elites who are not accountable to the issues affecting the people living in disinvested black communities. Finding a way to heal what Eugene Robinson calls "the splintering of black America" and hold black political elites accountable to the disinvested and displaced is the preeminent organizing challenge of our time. We are down to the wire and must develop strategies to make black politicians more responsible to the needs of the displaced and disinvested. Our challenge is to push, pass, and implement policies to address the damage caused by the Frankenstein we now know as Jim Crow Jr. Given the harm done and damage inflicted on disinvested black communities, we need to think along the lines of community-level solutions.

First, we need anti-displacement legislation to prevent city officials, corporate developers, and members of the nonprofit industrial complex from engaging in practices and processes that lead to what Mindy Fullilove (2001) has called "root shock." This means devising policies that protect homeowners from being pushed out and making it illegal to engage in displacing vulnerable populations for private profit or an institution's gain.

Second, we must strengthen the capacity of residents to draft and require developers sign on to progressive community benefits agreements (CBAs). Progressive CBAs will allow communities to share in the wealth of redevelopment and obtain employment and job experience in the process. Unlike the regressive CBA promoted by a cadre of black elite city officials and ministers that doubled down on the exploitation of the people of Perkins Homes during the Harbor Point TIF debate in 2013 (Reutter, 2013; Litten, 2013), a progressive CBA would ensure both community control by historical residents and benefits accrue to black residents who actually live in disinvested neighborhoods. If people living in disinvested black communities agree to partner with a developer, shared wealth components (e.g. stock options, land ownership, profit sharing) should be built into the progressive CBA.

This strategy should be implemented in the Druid Heights community where private development (The Community Builders) threatens to displace the residents of Pedestal Gardens. Pedestal Gardens residents and the surrounding community should have a legally binding CBA that guarantees one-for-one housing replacement in the new development, resident employment and job training before and during construction, and a substantial incorporation into the decision-making apparatus of the project. Without these protections, the residents of Pedestal Gardens will become the next in a long line of residents impacted by the dismantling of public housing.

Third, another community-level solution is the establishment of resident-led community benefits districts (CBDs) in disinvested neighborhoods such as Upton, Sandtown-Winchester, or Middle East. Richer communities such as Midtown have their own community benefits district which provides cleaning, maintenance, and safety services on top of city services (Midtown Development Corporation, 2013). In the Middle East neighborhood, EBDI has endeavored to set up a CBD and would allow only business owner and homeowner control (BRACE, 2012). This is not the model we need. We need an anti-racist model that provides unfettered funding designed for community residents to come together in a participatory and democratic way to voice the types of programs they would like to see. Some examples of services provided could be paid community organizers, anti-racism training workshops, and community health workers going door-to-door to provide health resources information and navigation similar to the work being done by the Men and Families Center and Charm City Clinic in East Baltimore (Charm City Clinic, 2013). Using this strategy, people can organize to address conditions that affect health and well-being while working to improve and directly address health outcomes.

Fourth, the local hiring mandate passed by the Baltimore City Council is wholly insufficient as it only applies to new hires that a contractor might bring on board in a project where they are receiving a certain amount of public funding. Passing a full-throated local hiring mandate is an imperative to ensure that black folks living in disinvested communities will have access to jobs where public money is being used to subsidize corporate developers. We know that job employment will not be enough alone. We should therefore also look at micro-lending and entrepreneurial strategies to boost self-employment.

Fifth, black Baltimoreans living in disinvested neighborhoods need policies that will effectively end the War on Drugs, especially with respect to marijuana. The criminalization of marijuana possession, combined with the disproportionate arrests and convictions of black people, leads to the development of a criminal record that negatively affects the life trajectory of thousands of black youth in the city (Duncan, 2013). We can put an end to much of this with legislation legalizing marijuana.

Sixth, we need policies authorizing restorative justice for those who have been harmed by Jim Crow Jr. This means an infusion of subsidized wraparound social services and health insurance. People cannot improve their wealth until they address their health. We know from the research that the impacts of Jim Crow and Jim Crow Jr. have harmed the physical and mental health states of black Baltimoreans.

Finally, all of the organizing and policies that is discussed here and will emerge in other arenas need to take place with an anti-racist framework in mind. The People's Institute for Survival and Beyond conducts undoing racism workshops that should be mandatory for all people interested in doing this work. Or, some other anti-racist models—National Coalition Building Institute, Teaching Tolerance, or Everyday Democracy (formerly the Study Circles Institute), The Public Conversations project, or the Public Narrative Approach. If we do not address the threat of internalized racial oppression in our communities, we will merely spin our wheels in the mud and essentially create multicultural racism. Only a fully and authentically anti-racist framework will equip us with the insights and tools we need to create life-giving, life-affirming, and life-sustaining equity and social justice for all people in all communities. Unemployed marcher James Johnson captured the task before us succinctly in his interview with *The Daily Record* during the protest for jobs at EBDI in March 2012:

> It's about time that our city officials and leaders that's supposed to be looking out for our well-being start doing so…. What's going on is ridiculous. It's about time we stand for ourselves and our politicians to do what we hired them to do which is stand up for the people in this city.

Citations

The Afro-American. (1978). Urbanologist scores Baltimore: Excerpts from an AFRO interview with Dr. Homer Favor. *Baltimore Afro-American*, pp. 6-9. Retrieved from: http://news.google.com/newspapers?nid=2205&dat=19781003&id=rYIlAAAAIBAJ&sjid=I_UFAAAAIBAJ&pg=2030,1860211

Ames, A., Evans, M., Fox, L., Milam, A. J., Petteway, R. J., & Rutledge, R. (2011). Baltimore City Neighborhood Health Profiles. Retrieved from http://www.baltimorehealth.org/neighborhoodmap.html

Applebaum, B. (2009). Fed held back as evidence mounted on subprime loan abuses. *The Washington Post: Business*. Retrieved from: http://www.washingtonpost.com/wp-dyn/content/article/2009/09/26/AR2009092602706.html

Arena, J. (2012). *Driven from New Orleans: How nonprofits betray public housing and promote privatization.* Minneapolis: U of Minnesota Press.

Baltimore Neighborhood Indicator Alliance—Jacob Francis Institute. (2013). Baltimore City Foreclosure Data. Retrieved from: http://foreclosures.bniajfi.org/filings-ratified-sales.php

The Baltimore Redevelopment Coalition for Empowerment. (2013). BRACE website. Retrieved from: http:// bracebaltimore.blogspot.com/

Becker, G. S., & Murphy, K. (2013). Have we lost the War on Drugs? After more than four decades of a failed experiment, the human cost has become too high. *The Wall Street Journal*. Retrieved from: http://online.wsj.com/news/articles/SB10001424127887324374004578217682305605070

Broadwater, L. (2012). Wells Fargo agrees to pay $175M settlement in pricing discrimination suit: Settlement calls for payments of $7.5 million to city of Baltimore, $2.5 million directly to 1,000 area residents. *The Baltimore Sun*. Retrieved from: http://articles.baltimoresun.com/2012-07-12/news/bs-md-ci-wells-fargo-20120712_1_mike-heid-wells-fargo-home-mortgage-subprime-mortgages

The Centers for Disease Control and Prevention. (2009). Health Effects of Gentrification. Retrieved from: http:// www.cdc.gov/healthyplaces/healthtopics/gentrification.htm

Charm City Clinic. (2013). Community Need. Retrieved from http:// charmcityclinic.wordpress.com/who-we- are/about-us/our-vision/

Duncan, I. (2013). Racial disparity in marijuana arrests has grown, ACLU finds: Blacks arrested at increasingly disproportional rates. *The Baltimore Sun*. Retrieved from: http://articles.baltimoresun.com/ 2013-11-13/news/bs-md-sun-investigates-marijuana-arrests-20131113_1_marijuana-arrests-racial- disparity-drug-laws

Franz, M. (2012). Protest at EBDI leads to arrests Baltimore: The Dolan Company.

Fullilove, M. T. (2001). Root shock: the consequences of African American dispossession. *J Urban Health*, 78(1), 72-80.

Fullilove, M. T., & Wallace, R. (2011). Serial forced displacement in American cities, 1916-2010. *J Urban Health*, 88(3), 381-389.

Fullilove, M.T., Hernadez-Cordero L., Fullilove R. "The Ghetto Game: Apartheid and the Developer's Imperative in Postindustrial Cities." In Hartman, C. W., & Squires, G. D. (2010). *The integration debate: Competing futures for American cities.* New York: Routledge.

Garcy, A. M., & Vagero, D. (2009). The ghetto game: apartheid and the developer's imperative in postindustrial American cities. In *The integration debate: Competing futures for American cities*. Routledge.

Goetz, E. G. (2013). New Deal ruins: Race, economic justice, and public housing policy. Ithaca: Cornell University Press.

Gomez, M. B. (2013). *Race, class, power, and organizing in East Baltimore: Rebuilding abandoned communities in America.* Lanham: Lexington Books.

Gorham, L., & Brown, L. (2011). Ms. Lucille Gorham on Baltimore's Urban Renewal. Retrieved from: http://www.youtube.com/watch?v=hPJLCMav2u8

Haber, G. (2011). EBDI not creating jobs residents say. *Baltimore Business Journal*. Retrieved from: http://www.bizjournals.com/baltimore/blog/real-estate/2011/11/ebdi-biopark-project-not-creating.html? page=all

Hare, M. G. (2011). E. Baltimore residents rally for jobs at EBDI development. *The Baltimore Sun*. Retrieved from: http://articles.baltimoresun.com/2011-12-20/news/bs-md-ebdi-protest-20111220_1_ebdi- construction-jobs-residents-rally

Jacobson, J. (2007). The dismantling of Baltimore's public housing: Housing authority cutting 2,400 homes from its depleted inventory. Abell Foundation.

Kachura, M. (2012). Children and foreclosures in Baltimore City: The foreclosure crisis and student mobility. *The Baltimore Neighborhood Indicators Alliance—Jacob Francis Institute*.

Kay, L. F. (2011). HUD grant to fund redevelopment planning in West Baltimore: Pedestal Garden complex is focus of effort to reconnect Bolton Hill to neighboring communities. *The Baltimore Sun*. Retrieved from: http://articles.baltimoresun.com/2011-03-18/news/bs-md-hud-funding-west- baltimore-20110318_1_hud-grant-mount-royal-improvement-association-bolton-hill-shopping-center

Keene, D. E., & Geronimus, A. T. (2011). "Weathering" HOPE VI: The importance of evaluating the population health impact of public housing demolition and displacement. *Journal of Urban Health*, 88, 417-435.

Kostroff-Noble, N., Simon, D., Pelecanos, G. P., Burns, E., Johnson, C., West, D., Doman, J., ... (2008). *The Wire: The Complete Series*. New York, N.Y.: HBO Video.

Lankford, E. (2010). Rooted/Unrouted: West Baltimore and the Highway to Nowhere. PRX. Retrieved from: http://www.prx.org/pieces/51755-rooted-unrouted-west-baltimore-and-the-highway-to

Laveist, T., Pollack, K., Thorpe, R. J., Fesahazion, R., & Gaskin, D. (2011). Place, not race: disparities dissipate in southwest Baltimore when blacks and whites live under similar conditions. *Health Affairs (project Hope), 30*(10), 1880-1887.

Levine, M. V. (2000). A third-world city in the first world: Social exclusion, racial inequality, and sustainable development in Baltimore. In M. Polese & R. Stren (Eds.), *The Social Sustainability of Cities: Diversity and the Management of Change* (pp. 123-156). Toronto: University of Toronto Press.

Lewis, J. (2014). HABC refuses to answer these essential questions about RAD. Right to Housing Alliance website. Retrieved from: http://rthabaltimore. org/2014/08/habc-refuses-to-answer-these-questions-about-rad/

Litten, K. (2013). Clergy would support Harbor Point if developer gives community $25M: $1 billion project sits between Harbor East and Fells Point. *Baltimore Business Journal*. Retrieved from: http:// www.bizjournals.com/baltimore/blog/real-estate/2013/08/clergy-would-support-harbor-point-if.html? page=all

Massey, D. S., & Denton, N. A. (1993). *American apartheid: Segregation and the making of the underclass*. Cambridge, Mass: Harvard University Press.

McLeod, C. B., Lavis, J. N., MacNab, Y. C., & Hertzman, C. (2012). Unemployment and mortality: a comparative study of Germany and the United States. *Am J Public Health*, 102(8), 1542-1550.

Midtown Development Corporation. (2011). What we do. Retrieved from: http:// midtownbaltimore.org/benefits-district/ what-we-do/

Mithun. (2013). State Center. Retrieved from: http://mithun.com/projects/ project_detail/state_center/

Mui, Y. Q. (2012). Ex-loan officer claims Wells Fargo targeted black communities for shoddy loans. *The Washington Post*. Retrieved from: http://www.washingtonpost. com/business/economy/former-wells-fargo-loan-officer-testifies-in-baltimore-mortgage-lawsuit/2012/06/12/gJQA6EGtXV_story.html

Pietila, A. (2010). *Not in My Neighborhood: How Bigotry Shaped a Great American City*. Chicago: Ivan R. Dee.

Reutter, M. (2013). Clergymen seek $25 million from Harbor Point developer for "community benefits". *Baltimore Brew*. Retrieved from: http://www.baltimorebrew.com/2013/08/05/clergymen-request-25-million-from-harbor- point-developer-for-community-benefits/

Royster-Hemby, C. (2006). Fighting the power: The Black Panther Party in Baltimore. *Baltimore City Paper*. Retrieved from http://www2.citypaper.com/story.asp?id=11419

Scharper, J. (2012). Council approves benefit for Under Armour campus: City to fund infrastructure improvements as company expands. *The Baltimore Sun*. Retrieved from http:// articles.baltimoresun.com/2012-09-24/news/bs-md-ci-under-armour-tif-20120924_1_improvements- issue-bonds-council-members

Simmons, M., & Jacobson, J. (2011a). Daily Record investigation: TIFs increasingly fuel city projects. *The Daily Record*. Retrieved from http://thedailyrecord.com/2011/01/31/daily-record-investigation-tifs- increasingly-fuel-city-projects/

Simmons, M., & Jacobson, J. (2011b). Too big to fail? Betting a billion on East Baltimore. The Daily Record. Retrieved from http://thedailyrecord.com/too-big-to-fail-betting-a-billion-on-east-baltimore/

Simmons, M. (2012). Four arrested in protest at EBDI. The Daily Record. Retrieved from: http:// thedailyrecord.com/2012/03/29/four-arrested-in-protest-at-ebdi/

Simmons, M. (2013a). Full City Council advances Harbor Point TIF. *The Daily Record*. Retrieved from http://thedailyrecord.com/2013/08/12/full-city-council-advances-harbor-point-tif/

Simmons, M. (2013b). Harbor Point TIF could cost $283 million: Repaying tax beak more than double initial $107 million request. *The Daily Record*. Retrieved from http://thedailyrecord.com/2013/07/15/ harbor-point-tif-could-cost-283-million/

Simmons, M. (2013c). Activist's children fear foreclosure of her home. *The Daily Record*. Retrieved from: http://thedailyrecord.com/2013/04/29/activists-children-fear-foreclosure-of-her-home/

Simmons, M. (2014). City selling Baltimore's high-rise public housing to private entities: Participation in new federal program will mean housing subsidies for developers – and uncertainty for tenants. The Baltimore Brew. Retrieved from: https://www.baltimorebrew.com/2014/02/27/city-selling-baltimores-high-rise-public-housing-to-private-entities/

Simms, B. (2014). Reverse mortgage stipulations could leave some homeless: Md. couples say younger spouse taken off deed to get loan approved. *WBALTV: Channel 11*. Retrieved from: http://www.wbaltv.com/news/maryland/i-team/reverse-mortgage-stipulations-could-leave-some-homeless/24696028#ixzz2xO6NJOT6

Unknown. (2013). America in the 20th Century: Immigration and Prohibition. *Google Sites*. Retrieved from https:// sites.google.com/site/americainthe20thcentury/ italian-american-mafia/immigration-prohibition

Wells, C. (2013). Baltimore residents in largely vacant blocks to be uprooted: City's plans meet mixed reaction. *The Baltimore Sun*. Retrieved from: http://articles. baltimoresun.com/2013-05-21/news/bs-md- ci-eminent-domain-20130521_1_ baltimore-residents-west-baltimore-vacant-blocks

Williams, R. Y. (2004). *The Politics of Public Housing: Black Women's Struggles against Urban Inequality*. New York: Oxford University Press New York.

Whelan, R. (2008). BioPark drawing home buyers west. *The Daily Record*. Retrieved from: http://www.umbiopark.com/ News/BioPark-drawing-home-buyers-west/134

Yockel, M. (2007). 100 Years: The Riots of 1968. *Baltimore*. Retrieved from: http:// www.baltimoremagazine.net/features/2007/05/100-years-the-riots-of-1968

HBCUs, Future at Stake in Fight Against Segregation in Maryland Higher Education

J. Wyndal Gordon

February 1, 2012

Thank you Doc Cheatham of the National Action Network (NAN) for being an ardent court observer of the HBCU litigation in downtown Baltimore, Courtroom 7D, Garmatz Building, U.S. District Court of Maryland on Lombard Street. Cheatham was invited by me to speak with the Monumental City Bar Association's ("MCBA") General Body on January 26, 2012, to give members details on the case and to explain the import of supporting and participating in this most crucial litigation of our time. Our mere presence in the courtroom as conscientious observers was all that he had asked in exchange for the information shared.

On January 31, 2012, I accepted Cheatham's request, walked down to the Federal Court and spent the entire day observing; and I was glad I did. The case was truly a clash of the Titans. It was so intriguing that I couldn't leave until the day was almost done. I urge anyone who believes in justice to do the same. The HBCU litigation is serious. It is the *Brown v. Board of Education* of our day and is being watched all over the country by everyone except, perhaps, by those it should matter to the most—Us. The Plaintiffs, Coalition for Equity and Excellence in Maryland Higher Education ("Coalition") consists of Maryland's four HBCUs: *Morgan State University, Coppin State University, Bowie State University, and the University of Maryland Eastern Shore.* They are represented and lead by none other than the esteemed nationally renowned civil rights attorney, John C. Brittain, Micheal D. Jones, et al. The Defendant, State of Maryland ("State"), is being represented and lead by Craig A. Thompson, Kenneth L. Thompson, et al. The identified cast are well respected attorneys on a local and national scale, joined at center court for a battle royale—and they happen to be African Americans pitted against one another in a fight for equality that would make Armageddon seem like a schoolyard tussle. Yesterday, I do not believe a single spectator in the entire courtroom was disappointed by the performances on either side of the trial table. Not to mention Craig A. Thompson and Kenneth L. Thompson are erstwhile members of MCBA, although I firmly believe they are on the wrong side of this issue.

> Be that as it may, perhaps the most obvious and strange irony of the day was remembering when Craig A. Thompson hosted the radio show "The Front Page" on Morgan State University Radio WEAA, 88.9 FM. I used to listen to the show and it was actually pretty good. Interestingly, he's now fighting to maintain vestiges of segregation at the very institution that was at least partially responsible for his professional development. This is not to single out and slight my good friend Craig; I have a great deal of respect for him, his body of work, and stellar accomplishments—but it is a fact that is undeniably newsworthy

and worth mentioning. Arguably, it either shows him to be the consummate professional who believes that everyone is entitled to competent legal representation, no matter how unpopular the cause—including the State of Maryland, or that he has come back to dine off of the hand that once nourished him. However, it has absolutely nothing to do with the fact that I just happen to be Morgan State University alum, *tongue in cheek* :o). Craig requested that I invite him to speak with MCBA about the State's position in the litigation. I graciously accepted and we are humbled by his courage, as we are too, humbled by the courage of those lawyers who challenged the State on this issue. We will invite them as well.

The fact is many of us have benefitted from HBCUs whether we attended them or not. They offer opportunities that are not readily available in other venues. To me, the Coalition's case is about extending those same opportunities to all manner of people. It is about forcing the State to expand its HBCUs mission(s), programs, and funding, as required by law, and to honor its 2000 Partnership Agreement with the US Office of Civil Rights. It is about ensuring that HBCUs become more competitive in their quest to increase enrollment and educate more students around the world. In other words, HBCUs want the capacity to do the things well-funded traditionally white Maryland institutions have been doing with our State and federal tax dollars for years —educate more people. Now, who can legitimately argue with that?

The Coalition sued the State of Maryland for violating the 14th Amendment of the Constitution as interpreted by *US v. Fordice*, 505 U.S. 717 (1992). They argue that Maryland has "fail[ed] to eradicate policies and practices regarding its institutional mission, programmatic duplication and inequality, and operational and capital funding that are traceable to the prior system of *de jure* segregation." The HBCU litigation is about diversity and inclusion. In these modern times of multi-cultural and diverse student backgrounds, Maryland's HBCUs seek to encourage *all* races, nationalities, and social statuses to consider HBCUs for a quality education –*not solely* African Americans and the disadvantaged. Although HBCUs are proud of their heritage and remain committed to their historic mission, unless the State: (1) expands its HBCUs' limited mission that segregates African Americans and the disadvantaged from others, (2) provides for lawful operational and capital funding to attract a more diverse student body, and (3) stop permitting the unlawful duplication and inequality of unique HBCU flagship programs by traditionally white institutions in close geographical proximity, HBCUs will become less attractive, and less able to compete in the ever changing global market. As a result, the educational experience offered by Maryland's HBCUs will become less enticing and their very existence less relevant.

As agreed by the members assembled at our meeting on January 26, 2012, MCBA stands firmly against segregation and other forms of discrimination. We vehemently support with fervor the Coalition's quest to force the State of Maryland to comply with the Equal Protection Clause of the US Constitution, and to honor its contractual agreement to eradicate *de jure* segretation in education. I am asking all of our lawyers to please join us in supporting the HBCU litigation by "making" time to sit in the courtroom and observe this most important litigation of our day. I encourage our members to stand among our passionate and committed comrades in academia, and to truly take note of what is at stake—the future of our children and our beloved HBCUs.

Higher Education
Readiness, Access, and Completion

Associated Black Charities

Education, and specifically college readiness, access and completion were priorities in the 1960s and remain so today. The following is an excerpt of key findings from a full-length, comprehensive, by the same title, African American Higher Education Readiness, Access, and Completion, which can be accessed in full via the wesiite (http://www.abc-md.org) of Associated Black Charities.

FOREWARD

The More in the Middle Initiative is a strategic intervention of Associated Black Charities (ABC) and its Collaborative Partners, targeted at creating an economically healthier Baltimore City and region. The initiative is focused on human capital development, specifically, creating and growing greater economic assets among Baltimore City's largest and the region's statistically significant population group—African Americans. The wealth of this population profoundly affects the prosperity of the region now and in the future. More in the Middle's five strategies address:

- Homeownership and foreclosure prevention

- Workforce development/career training and advancement

- Higher education: college readiness, access, and completion
  Business and economic development

- Asset--building and financial literacy

The economic case for including higher education is clear. Baltimore's 21st century economy is powered by brains, not brawn. The economic opportunity case is equally clear. The key to widely--shared prosperity among its citizens is education beyond high school. "Higher levels of education lead to elevated wages, a more equitable distribution of income and substantial gains in productivity. For every additional average year of schooling U.S. citizens complete, the GDP increases by about 0.37 percentage points – or by 10% – over time."[1]

And yet, a tragic leakage of potential economic health for the City and its residents is taking place every time a student is not able to complete high school, every time a high school graduate does not apply to college, or applies and is accepted and yet fails to matriculate, or matriculates but never earns a degree. The rates of these leakages are greater for African American students, who make up 88 percent of Baltimore City Public Schools' population, than for white students. If the 7,481 BCPS 9th graders in 2009 are able to earn Associate's (AA) or Bachelor's (BA) degrees, economists at College Board estimate that the median earnings they and their families and the Baltimore economy will enjoy will be 26 percent (AA) to 60 percent (BA) higher than if they have only a high school diploma, and 68 percent (AA) to 107 percent (BA) higher than if they drop out before finishing high school.[2] The contributions to the tax bases of local, state, and federal governments will be similarly enlarged at the same time that these citizens will need fewer tax--funded services. It is estimated that if high school dropouts in 2008--09 had graduated with their class, the Maryland economy would enjoy $5.5 billion more in resident earnings over their lifetimes.[3]

Associated Black Charities' More in the Middle higher education work began with research funded by the Bill and Melinda Gates Foundation. During the academic year 2007--2008, and later in spring/summer 2009, a consultant team assessed African American students', parents', and school personnel's awareness of and perceptions about higher education preparation, access, and associated benefits. The two phases of the project focused first on schools that did not have defined college readiness pro-grams and subsequently on high schools with established college readiness programs or foci.[4]

In November, 2009, ABC convened 200 preK--20 educational leaders, foundation program managers, researchers, and community--based educational access service providers for a day--long African American College Completion Summit. Plenary sessions and break--out groups addressed opportunities, barriers, and policy issues in three areas: college--going culture and attitude, college readiness and access, and college completion. Later in the spring, summit participants were reconvened to report the results of the break--out groups. Three focus groups of local experts were then held to refine and supplement the work of the summit participants and identify relevant research.[5]

This policy discussion paper6 summarizes the findings and conclusions of these meetings along with additional research and cited promising practices. It is intended to provide a shared base of information and policy issues for discussion and action by all of us who have a vested interest in enhancing the region's economic health by removing barriers to postsecondary readiness, access, and completion by African American students.

We are deeply indebted to Citi Foundation for funding this work and grateful to participants in the

African American College Completion Summit and focus groups, who shared their wisdom and knowledge about research and practice in this important field.

Diane Bell McKoy
CEO
Associated Black Charities

SUMMARY OF FINDINGS AND CONCLUSIONS

The Annenberg Institute's study of schools that are "beating the odds" for students who begin ninth grade not on a college--going track concludes that the exemplary schools used the following key strategies: academic rigor, a network of timely supports for students and parents, school culture focused on preparation for life after high school, and effective use of data.[7]

Aspirations, Exposure, and College--going Culture Findings

- Students learn in families, communities, and schools. However, more than 80 percent of African American parents of all income levels expressed the opinion in a 2007 Public Agenda survey that the "vast majority of qualified students do not have the opportunity to attend college."

- Early outreach initiatives seek to build student interest, motivation, and preparation for college, starting as early as middle school.

- Whether planning to enter college or workforce training programs or a job after graduation, all high school students need to be educated to a comparable level of readiness in reading and mathematics.

- Studies show that teachers and principals often do not believe that all students can succeed. The assessment by parents, teachers, principals, and counselors of students' ability and potential profoundly affects their aspirations and academic performance.

- Fostering a college--going culture for all students in a school requires college preparatory tools for students and parents; embracing social, cultural, and learning style differences in the environment, activities, and assessments at the school; involving leaders at all levels in establishing policies, programs, and practices; adequate financial and human resources; assessing policy, programs, and practices regularly to test their effectiveness; taking preventive rather than reactive steps; and assuring that positive youth development is understood and fostered by caring adults.

- Schools in which the focus is on college--going, not just high school graduation, are better able to retain and motivate students.

- Most Baltimore City public school students aspire to college educations. Over three--quarters of Baltimore City students took SATs in 2009, exceeding both state and national participation averages.

CONCLUSIONS

- We cannot afford to channel and teach students in separate "college" or career" tracks. Continuing to "untrack" high school education in Baltimore City will enable all students to aspire to and achieve a place in college or a career with advancement potential.

- Teachers and principals must believe that all students can succeed.

- Community partners – higher education institutions, faith communities, college alumni and others – can be mobilized to increase BCPS students' exposure to college and college graduates throughout their school years.

- The task for the adults in students' lives – parents, teachers, school administrators, community mentors – is to support their college--going ambitions with affirmation, opportunities, and practical help in planning a path, overcoming obstacles, and perseverance. Many students and parents – and too many teachers and counselors – do not know what is required for college admission and success. This is a community, systemwide, and school--by--school challenge. Many college access supports are in use in Baltimore City public schools but reach only a fraction of students.

- Within the context of school--based governance, a comprehensive effort is needed to 1) assess needs and attitudes of students, parents, and school personnel, 2) use the results to repurpose each school as a college--going environment, and 3) marshall all available resources to achieve system--wide goals of college enrollment and success.

High School Preparation, College Expectations and Access Findings

- Secondary school preparation and college expectations are not now aligned.

- The new states--led effort to define common college--and--career readiness standards and common core K--12 standards will propel the State into a new era of academic achievement.

- The most important factors in college admission and success are the rigor of the high school curriculum, students' course--taking, and student effort.

- Advanced math is key to college and careers, and frequently screens out minority and lower income students.

- Students need a network of supports in order to successfully meet requirements for rigor. These include emotional, instrumental, informational, appraisal, and structural support.

- Students expect to go to college but they and their families lack accurate information and guidance on what they will need to do to get there and succeed.

- Continuing professional development for teachers and counselors enables them to be effective in reaching college-going and persistence goals.

- Data can be better used to improve goal-setting, instruction, and preparation.

- Financial aid for students and institutions is vital. A "downpayment" on the President's ambitious proposals for bolstering access and completion, particularly for low income students, was included in the health care reform bill signed in March.

- Nationally, African American undergraduates are awarded five percent more financial aid per student on average than whites, the majority from federal sources, while the median income of African American families in the U.S. is only 62 percent of the white median and the typical African American family holds only one-tenth the wealth of the average white family.

- Approximately 12 percent of African American college students nationally attend Historically Black Colleges and Universities (HBCUs). If Baltimore City Community College were considered an HBCU, the overwhelming majority of Baltimore City public high school graduates matriculate at HBCUs. HBCUs have historical missions to provide access to higher education for African American students; 90 percent of their students nationally receive financial aid. Their tuition rates tend to be 50 percent lower than predominantly white institutions (PWI). Students typically use the benefits of lower tuition, Pell Grants – received by 46 percent of African American undergraduates – and other support and institutional aid in order to attend.

- Only four HBCUs have endowments greater than $100 million. Endowments in all American colleges and universities returned 19 percent less in 2009 than in 2008. African American students are looking for aid from the federal government and help in identifying and accessing other non-institutional sources of financial assistance. Like their institutions, the financial pressures on students have become intense.

CONCLUSIONS

Maryland has recently adopted the K-12 common core state standards and has begun implementation. This should address the major concern of summit attendees – the lack of alignment between high school achievement and college expectations. Particular emphasis on production of high-quality curriculum and teacher support materials will be needed, as well as textbook selection.

Federal funding can help Maryland and Baltimore's curriculum upgrades and student achievement. President Obama's education budget includes a five year $3.5 billion College Access and Completion Fund; $1.2 billion over three years for Graduation Promise Grants for high schools; and $65 million for Statewide Data Systems, an increase of $6.8 million to help States improve the availability and use of data on student learning, teacher performance, and college- and career-readiness. There is no assurance that these funds will be accepted by the new Congress in 2011.

The pending reauthorization of the federal Elementary and Secondary Education Act (ESEA) would support high expectations and accountability for all student groups and the closing of achievement gaps to ensure that all students, including poor and minority students, graduate from high school college-- and career--ready. The reauthorization, scheduled to take place in 2009, may be considered by Congress in 2011.

Advanced math is the key. Because advanced math is so critical to the college prospects of African American students, the importance of an integrated course of mathematics study for all BCPS K--12 students that prepares them to successfully complete high school advanced math courses is magnified. The Common State Standards for math represent a departure point for this effort.

Weekly advisories or other cohort--based strategies can be used to build peer support and connections with caring adults throughout high school. Many summit participants recommended requiring an individual postsecondary plan of all graduates, built over the four years of high school.

Step--by--step information is needed by all parents and students to enable them to navigate timelines, and learn how to investigate colleges, college application procedures, financial aid, college selection, college matriculation, college placement tests, and college course selection. Maximizing the use of on-- line resources will reserve counselor time for one--on--one customized college/career advising, which should be available in all high schools. Principals who are being held responsible for the college--going and persistence of their graduates will need to allocate a healthier share of their budgets – for both dedicated staff and external providers – to this function.

The availability of financial aid for college--going students needs a dramatic boost, making sure that as many Baltimore families benefit from recent federal increases as possible. Students and families also need help with financial planning that allows students to fulfill or find substitutes for family obligations for income production or child care and to continue to make efficient use of funds available. Maryland community college and public four--year institution students with the largest amounts of unmet financial need had the lowest retention rates. This was particularly evident among students in the lower income categories."

Education and continuing professional development centered on college advising will be increasingly important for teachers and school counselors, whose ranks need augmentation as the pace of college readiness efforts picks up.

Making college entry, need for remediation, and college completion key components of public school metrics is a critical component of infusing a "college--going culture" throughout the BCPS Sytem. The common state assessment systems are under development and Maryland has pledged to use them. Data should allow students and their parents to know exactly where they are on the college--readiness path at every point in their high school careers. Teachers and administrators need the same information in real time so that they can take appropriate steps to ensure mastery. Data on schools and districts should also be available to policymakers and the public. Data, including attendance, on students throughout the K--12 system should be used for early identification of students who are at risk of failure in ninth grade and dropping out.

Student and school assessments should focus on incentives and assistance for improvement rather than sanctions whenever possible.

College Completion Findings

In Baltimore City:

- 43 percent of African American public high school graduates enrolled in college

- Half of the BCPS college--going graduates enrolled in two--year institutions and half in four--year institutions

- Of the graduates of Baltimore's selective college--preparatory high schools, 37 percent required math remediation upon college enrollment, as did 69 percent of graduates from "non--core" (the remainder) schools. Ten percent and 36 percent, respectively, needed English remediation; and 16 and 40 percent, respectively, needed reading remediation.

- Of all BCPS graduates, 8.7 percent earned a two--year degree and 1.7 percent earned a four--year degree.

- Of BCPS graduates who ever enrolled in a postsecondary institution, 15 percent earned two--year degrees, and three percent earned four year degrees.

Predictors of college success are those identified in the college readiness and access discussion, most notably academic achievement. Race and gender also had influence on college performance in a Maryland Higher Education Commission (MHEC) analysis.

First generation college students say that their challenges are academic, financial, and social/emotional.

Many college academic, financial, and social/personal problems stem directly from inadequate academic preparation and college counseling – including financial planning – in high school.

Effective practices for helping students succeed in college include the same set of emotional, informational, instrumental, appraisal, and structural supports that they need to prepare for college. Examples include SuccessBoston College Completion Initiative, On Point for College (Syracuse, NY), Gates Millennial Scholarship Program, Meyerhoff Scholars Program (UMBC), and University of Washington's Dream Project. They highlight key requirements for keeping students in college: academic success, engagement with advisors, faculty, fellow students, others in the school community; and financial stability. Once again, the critical role played by staff and faculty has been highlighted.

High impact educational practices are known and can be adopted by institutions of higher education that want to improve African American student retention. They are: first year seminars and experiences; common intellectual experiences, learning communities, writing--intensive courses, collaborative assignments and projects, undergraduate research, diversity/global learning, service learning/community--based learning, internships, and capstone courses and projects.

Promising examples in Baltimore include: longtime intentional retention efforts at University of Maryland Baltimore County and more recent initiatives at Towson State University, Johns Hopkins' Baltimore Scholars, University of Baltimore's new undergraduate program, the recent announcement of a $2.5 million fund to support degree completion by University System of Maryland students, and CollegeBound's college retention program.

"Swirling" has become more common as students "consume" higher education. The proportion of undergraduate students attending more than one institution during their academic careers has grown from 40 percent in the 1970s to over 60 percent today. Students swirl among colleges and universities to maximize time in lower cost institutions and to accommodate scheduling preferences. Students from lower socioeconomic backgrounds were more likely than economically advantaged students to swirl with breaks in schooling. Engaging in this type of swirling is negatively associated with timely bachelor's degree completion.

Developmental (remedial) education at both the high school and college levels can benefit from research--based improvement. The Getting Past Go initiative of the Education Commission of the States is compiling a comprehensive set of policy research and data, and convening advisory team meetings, online dialogues among a community of practice, and case studies that can be tapped as they are produced.

The largest share by far of Baltimore City public school graduates enroll at Baltimore City Community College. It is clear, however, that they are not succeeding there – after four years, only one percent of African American students had graduated with a two--year degree, and seven percent had transferred to four--year institutions.

CONCLUSIONS

Administering the Accuplacer test in 10th grade along with PSATs would familiarize students with the tests and enable school personnel to target areas that need focused attention for each student before they graduate.

Formulas and budgets for higher education institutions need to be revisited to ensure that adequate resources are available and being dedicated to providing the student supports necessary for successful retention of students and advancement toward a degree.

Well--designed, research--proven high--impact college retention practices that have had their most positive impact on minority students are available from higher education peers for Maryland higher education institutions that want to make a concerted effort.

Swirling needs direct attention. Sara Rab (2004) and other education researchers recommend that policymakers improve the portability of credits and articulation agreements among institutions to increase completion rates of swirling students, and focus on creating a more integrated system of higher education that retains students of all backgrounds to full degree completion.

Developmental instruction quality improvements in both public schools and colleges will help Baltimore City students who have lagged to catch up and achieve success in college.

Public school, higher education, business, philanthropic, government, and community resources could be usefully focused on helping Baltimore City Community College realize its promise as a high quality first resort for Baltimore City Public School graduates and to become a valuable partner for BCPS as it ramps up its college readiness efforts.

More in the Middle

Closing the Wealth Gap – Expanding the Economics for the Baltimore Region

African American Higher Education

Readiness, Access, and Completion

CALL TO ACTION FINDINGS

- Policymakers, parents, and students agree that higher education for African American students is the key to both Baltimore's economic prospects and economic opportunity for its citizens.

- The situation today is dire. For every 100 students entering high school in 9th grade:

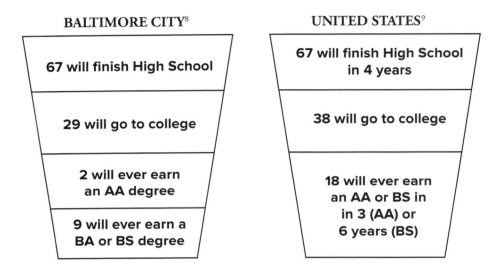

BALTIMORE CITY[8]

67 will finish High School

29 will go to college

2 will ever earn an AA degree

9 will ever earn a BA or BS degree

UNITED STATES[9]

67 will finish High School in 4 years

38 will go to college

18 will ever earn an AA or BS in in 3 (AA) or 6 years (BS)

This track record represents a tragic leakage of potential economic health for the City and its residents.

WORK TO BE DONE IN 2011 AND BEYOND

- Forcefully defend existing budgets and advocate the President's proposals for expansion of federal funding for African American higher education preparation, access (including financial aid), and completion. All of these monies are at risk in the new Congress.

- Invest in a cadre of professionals who support student and parent aspirations for higher education, and mobilize community resources to extend their reach o Share the belief that all students can realize their aspirations

- Expose students to higher education

- Mentor/counsel students and parents about all aspects of preparation for and completion of college: academic, financial, and emotional

- Actively support Baltimore City Public Schools efforts to meet college and employer expectations of all their graduates as now required by the common core state standards adopted by Maryland. A BCPS diploma should be a powerful signal that Baltimore students are ready and reduce the need for "developmental education" post high school.

- Support the leadership of Baltimore City Community College in transforming the school into a high quality first resort for BCPS graduates. Improve the portability of credits.

- Support the leadership of Morgan State University, Coppin State University, and Baltimore County Community Colleges – among the top four educational institutions chosen by Baltimore City students) in their efforts to decrease college dropout rates and increase college completion.

- Advocate the adoption of proven retention practices by all higher education institutions that receive public funding.

Notes

[1] Achieve (2010), "What is College and Career Ready?"

[2] College Board (2008). "Education Pays 2007: The Benefits of Higher Education for Individuals and Society."

[3] Alliance for Excellent Education (2009). "High Cost of High School Dropouts."

[4] Local education agencies in Maryland call these "non-core" and "core" schools.

[5] See list of planning committee members, summit speakers and panelist, focus group members, and advisors at the end of this report.

[6] Prepared by Marsha R. B. Schachtel, Senior Fellow, Johns Hopkins Institute for Policy Studies.

[7] Ascher, Carol and Cindy Maguire (2007). "Beating the Odds: How Thirteen NYC Schools Bring Low- Performing Ninth Graders to Timely Graduation and College Enrollment," Annenberg Institute for School Reform at Brown University.

[8] Feldman, Benjamin (2009). "Local Data on College Enrollment and Completion 2001-2008, prepared for ABC More in the Middle's African American College Completion Summit, Nov. 3.

[9] College Board (2006). "CollegeEd Creating a College-Going Culture Guide."

Part One
Resources for Education and Change

In addition to the strategies and resources in the chapter in Part One, some resources that give more information about the chapters in this section include:

Baltimore City Public Schools
www.baltimorecityschools.org

Census Quick Facts for Baltimore
http://quickfacts.census.gov/qfd/states/24/24510.html

Unemployment Rates for Baltimore
http://www.bls.gov/eag/eag.md_baltimore_msa.htm

http://www.ctdatahaven.org/
Data Haven for Community Action

Health Equity Alliance, Measuring and Reporting Health Equity: What Produces Impact?
http://www.communityindicators.net/system/medias/600/original/
Fri_2D_-_S._Thomas_-_Measuring_and_Reporting_Health_Equi-
ty_-_CIS12.pdf?1354803086

Kids Count Data Center, Annie E. Casey Foundation
http://datacenter.kidscount.org

Healthy People/Healthy Economy: A Coalition to Make Massachusetts the National Leader in Health and Wellness, Annual Report 2014
http://www.tbf.org/~/media/TBFOrg/Files/Reports/HPHE%204thRe-
port%20Card.pdf

Connecticut Economic Resource Center, Inc.
http://www.cerc.com/

Connecticut Commission on Families
http://www.cga.ct.gov/COC/index.htm

The Boston Foundation (nonprofits)
http://www.tbf.org/impact/objectives-and-strategies/education-to-career

Pietila, A. (2010). Not in My Neighborhood: How Bigotry Shaped a Great American City. Chicago: Ivan R. Dee

Part Two:
Public Health

Editor's Introduction

At the peak of the U.S. Civil Rights Movement, the health outcomes of Black Americans in many parts of the country were impacted by Jim Crow's blocked access to medical facilities. Over the last forty years, we have seen the legacy of decades of unequal access to adequate health care and economic resources reflected in an expansive body of literature on the issue of health disparities. The underlying causes of health disparities are generally characterized as socioeconomic risk factors, environmental risk factors, behavioral/lifestyle risk factors and medical bias.

Despite an increase in the awareness of health disparities and improved medical surveillance systems, public health reform that emerged in the 1980s and 1990s continues to see little progress in combatting some areas of racial health disparities across the life cycle from maternal health and infant mortality to preventable, chronic diseases such as hypertension, diabetes, end stage renal disease, cardiovascular disease, cerebrovascular disease, and some cancers which, contribute to elevated morbidity and mortality rates among African Americans. The authors in this section of the volume look more closely at the issues of race and clinical trials, diabetes, and sexually transmitted diseases as specific instances and indicators of the continuing struggle for health among Black Baltimoreans.

Black Baltimore and Blue Babies: Digging Deeper into the Social Determinants of Health & Transforming Clinical Trials

Nicolette Louissaint and Lawrence Brown

When the magnificent group of 250,000 people for justice and freedom marched on Washington DC in 1963, Baltimore was not yet a chocolate city. Black Baltimore was 38.3% of the population (Farber, 1963) as opposed to 63.6% of the population that it is now (US Census Bureau, 2014). When Baltimore marchers joined the 1963 March on Washington for Jobs and Freedom (and for racial equity), Dr. Robert Farber was serving as their Health Commissioner. In his introduction to the 1963 annual health report, Dr. Farber noted problems with syphilis and high rates of infant mortality among nonwhite infants.

Back in 1963, infant mortality in Black Baltimore was a staggering 38 per 1000 live births (Farber, 1963). Nearly 50 years later, the infant mortality rate is slightly less than half the rate at 18 per 1000 live births in Black Baltimore, which is *still* a staggering rate (Spencer et al, 2011). Nationally, the overall rate of infant mortalities is 6.15 per 1000 live births, for blacks the rate is 12.4 per 1000 live births (CDC and World Bank 2013 data). While the black infant mortality rate dropped 50.7% in roughly 50 years in Baltimore, white infant mortality dropped 83.7% during the same time. Thus, black babies are not only still dying at a higher rate in Baltimore, with few signs of improvement in the rate of decrease.

What was Dr. Farber's thinking regarding the tremendous health crisis during his time? Did he mention social determinants of health? In some ways, he did. In the 1963 report, he mentions the challenges of poverty and people living in "socially distressed conditions." But Dr. Farber's strongest remarks rest on the need for more personal responsibility and a lack of morality. He writes: "Logical efforts at control can only be based on efforts to encourage a change in moral climate among residents of the city living in socially distressed conditions." In other words, the moral problem was not that of the pervasive racist climate of the time or the active practitioners of Baltimore-style racism. For Dr. Farber, the moral problem and righteous responsibility did not rest with white Baltimoreans who helped pioneer restrictive covenants as a weapon of mass segregation and disinvestment. The burden of improving health was among those who were the victims of segregation and racism—Black Baltimore.

Fast forward nearly 50 years. The current Health Commissioner, Dr. Oxiris Barbot, is stepping down and headed back to New York City (Broadwater, 2014). What was Dr. Barbot's thinking regarding the health challenges she faced during her tenure? In her May, 2011 Op-Ed in the *Baltimore Sun* entitled "What's Killing Baltimore? Health Department on a Quest to Find Out," she highlights such health issues such as liquor outlet density, childhood obesity, and infant mortality. In her Op-Ed and in the *Healthy Baltimore 2015* report published under her watch, Dr. Barbot outlines her vision and discusses her plan to confront Baltimore's seemingly invisible and intrepid killers. In her quest to address the ills affecting Baltimoreans, Dr. Barbot writes: "I have met with all of the CEOs of the city's hospitals, as well as many of the leaders within the world-class academic institutions we are fortunate to have in this city."

Much like Dr. Farber, Dr. Barbot's strategy for improving health is decidedly one-sided: tilted strongly in favor of the powerful and wealthy. It seems she did not consider how "world-class" universities such as Johns Hopkins University and the University of Maryland practiced *de jure* segregation for decades, excluded black students from enrolling, and prevented black faculty members from teaching. Dr. Barbot did not demonstrate an understanding of the racial history and legacies, both good and bad, which exists in Baltimore. In order to understand the actual contributions of academic and medical institutions, we must be cognizant of their history, which includes recognition that both Johns Hopkins University and the University of Maryland were founded by white men (Charles Benedict Calvert and Johns Hopkins) whose personal or familial wealth had been obtained from slavery (Students of History 429, 2009; Johns Hopkins University, 2014).

Public Health and the Tenure of Dr. Oxiris Barbot

In Dr. Barbot's editorial and *Healthy Baltimore 2015*, no mention is made of the dynamics discussed in Malcolm Gladwell's bestselling book *The Tipping Point* (see excerpt below), where he makes the connection between retrenchment of public health spending, the displacement of public housing residents, and a syphilis outbreak in the mid-1990s. Gladwell's work illustrates how city decisions in the allocation public health resources and decisions regarding public housing can determine whether disease rates remain stable or erupt into epidemics.

Malcolm Gladwell's, The Tipping Point, Chapter One - The Three Rules of Epidemics

"In the space of a year, from 1995 to 1996, the number of children born with the disease increased by 500 percent. If you look at Baltimore's syphilis rates on a graph, the line runs straight for years and then, when it hits 1995, rises at almost a right angle. ... 'In 1990-91, we had thirty-six thousand patient visits at the city's sexually transmitted disease clinics,' Zenilman says. '*Then the city decided to gradually cut back because of budgetary problems.* The number of clinicians [medical personnel] went from seventeen to ten. The number of physicians went from three to essentially nobody. Patient visits dropped to twenty-one thousand. There was also a similar drop in the amount of field outreach staff. There was a lot of politics - things that used to happen, like computer upgrades, didn't happen. It was a worse-case scenario of city bureaucracy not functioning. They would run out of drugs.' When there were 36,000 patient visits a year in the STD Clinics in Baltimore's inner city, in other words, the disease was kept in equilibrium. At some point between 36,000 and 21,000 patient visits a year, according to

Zenilman, the disease erupted. ... There is a third theory, which belongs to John Potterat, ...His culprits are the physical changes in those years affecting East and West Baltimore, the heavily depressed neighborhoods on either side of Baltimore's downtown, where the syphilis problem was centered. *In the mid-1990s, he points out, the city of Baltimore embarked on a highly publicized policy of dynamiting the old 1960s-style public housing high-rises in East and West Baltimore"* (Gladwell, 2000).

As the reader can witness from the above excerpt, both public health cutbacks and the demolition of public housing were key factors in explaining how syphilis became an epidemic in the city. Therefore, city policies in public health and housing—two social determinants of health—help explain health outcomes in Baltimore. When the Health Commissioner of the city refuses to look in the mirror and ignores critical social determinants and policies that disproportionate burden the Black community, the health of Black Baltimore suffers. In a city filled with institutions such as the world-renowned Johns Hopkins Medical Institutions and the University of Maryland's Medical Centers, black Baltimoreans have neither been allowed to enjoy full equity in access to health care, nor benefit from health-generating policies that promote health and well-being.

Key Definitions

In order to understand the complexities of the health policy in Baltimore, we believe that it is imperative to provide the definitions with which we will operate. The WHO definition of health is comprehensive, defining it as: "Health is a state of complete physical, mental and social well-being and not merely the absence of disease or infirmity". The CDC defines both health disparities and health inequities (http://www.cdc.gov/healthyyouth/disparities/):

Health disparities are preventable differences in the burden of disease, injury, violence, or opportunities to achieve optimal health that are experienced by **socially disadvantaged populations.** Populations can be defined by factors such as race or ethnicity, gender, education or income, disability, geographic location, or sexual orientation. Health disparities are inequitable and are directly related to the historical and current unequal distribution of social, political, economic, and environmental resources.

Health disparities are called **health inequities** when they are the result of unfair and systematic social, political, economic, and environmental policies and practices.

Health inequities are thus those subset of health disparities that are unjust and avoidable. These inequities stem from the inequitable distribution of the social, economic, and political resources, power, and opportunities that promote and enhance health. (Source: CDC, adapted from Equity Matters, 2013)

According to the World Health Organization's Commission on Social Determinants of Health, both inequality and the social determinants of health can be described as follows:

> "Inequity in the conditions of daily living is shaped by deeper social structures and processes. The inequity is systematic, produced by social norms, policies, and practices that tolerate or actually promote unfair distribution of and access to power, wealth, and other necessary social resources. Every aspect of government and the economy has the potential to affect health and health equity – finance, education, housing, employment, transport, and health, just to name six. Coherent action across government, at all levels, is essential for improvement of health equity." (WHO Commission on Social Determinants of Health, 2011)

> "The *social determinants of health* are the conditions in which people are born, grow, live, work and age. These circumstances are shaped by the distribution of money, power and resources at global, national and local levels." (WHO Commission on Social Determinants of Health, 2011)

Health Equity, Health in All Policy, and Public Health at the Grassroots

While both Dr. Barbot and Dr. Farber cursorily address the social determinants of health in their writings, neither commissioner saw fit to describe how Baltimore's history of racism and racial exclusion functioned as a negatively impactful social determinant of health for Black Baltimoreans. These two commissioners skimmed the surface of what the social determinants of health are. Our next Health Commissioner must dig deeper and understand that racism and racial discrimination remain deeply embedded in Baltimore's history with respect to city policies, elite institutions, the local health care system, and allocation of resources. Not only does racism harm the immediate victims at the point of their experience with discrimination, **racism damages future patient-provider relationships by reducing the trust in both the provider and the health care system by members of the Black community. The same holds true for participant-researcher relationships.**

Figure 1 demonstrates a proposed framework to balance the traditional "medical model" with a socio-ecological model that demonstrates a wider array of influences, or causes, health outcomes. Given that many of the Health Commissioners of the past come from a traditional medical background, their view of the factors that cause disease are often limited to individual behavior (the "medical model"). Even many public health professionals do not take into account the socio-ecological factors at play, that is, factors relating to discriminatory policies, institutional power, neighborhood conditions, and residential segregation. But the socio-ecological model make it clear that all individual behavior occurs in a specific social and ecological context that must be taken into account. This explains why factors such as displacement and disinvestment, segregation and separation, and the power of institutions and policies of government agencies must all be taken into full account in order to address the health needs of Black Baltimore.

Figure 1. Health Equity Framework

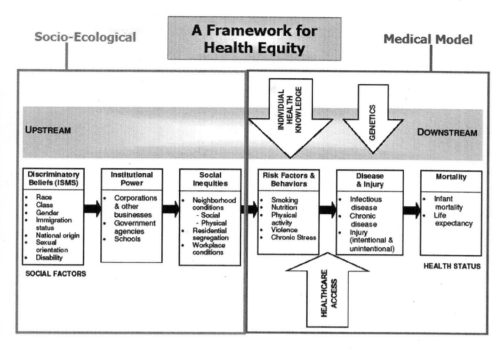

- Adapted by ACPHD from the Bay Area Regional Health Inequities Initiative, Summer 2008

As Antero Pietila documents in his book *Not in My Neighborhood: How Bigotry Shaped a Great American City,* black people living in Baltimore during formal segregation (from 1896 until the late-1960s) have experienced a long series of abuses at the hands of medical and academic institutions in Baltimore. Sometimes the abuse is softer, coming in the form of verbally blaming and shaming individuals for their behavior, while ignoring and neglecting social determinants and systems that impair health. This "blaming and shaming" is evidenced in Dr. Farber's 1963 report where he remarks: "Some of the health problems which face the community exist because adult individuals fail to take the initiative or exert the discipline which can gain for themselves and their children a better state of health or a longer lifetime" (Farber, 1963).

Apparently, it never occurred to Dr. Farber—a Johns Hopkins University graduate—that residential segregation might sap initiative or that racism manifested as disinvestment and discrimination might disrupt a person's attempt to impose discipline and order in their lives. This report and this type of one-sided statement was endorsed by a board of consultants which included four medical professionals from the School of Medicine at the University of Maryland, four medical professionals from the Johns Hopkins School of Medicine, and the dean of the School of Hygiene and Public Health at Johns Hopkins University. No one from this board came from Coppin State or Morgan State Colleges. This illustrates another form of discrimination—exclusion from the opportunities to shape knowledge and inform health policy. This happens when individuals from powerful institutions are the only ones invited to serve as decision-makers and consultants on matters that pertain to addressing health inequities affecting Black Baltimore.

The following list contains even more disturbing instances of abuse by Johns Hopkins Medical Institutions:

- Scientist Dr. George Gey (in a cancer treatment clinic owned by Dr. Howard Kelly) stole the immortal cells of East Baltimorean Henrietta Lacks during her clinical visit in 1951 (Washington, 2006);

- The Broadway Project in the 1950s during which Johns Hopkins University and the city forcibly removed over 800 African American families to create space for the expansion of Johns Hopkins University (Gomez, 2013);

- Johns Hopkins Hospital was segregated and had a colored ward from 1894-1960 (Cavagnaro, 1992);

- The lead study led by Johns Hopkins University and Kennedy Krieger Institute in the 1990s placed black children in homes with varying levels of lead exposure (Bullard and Wright, 2012);

- The East Baltimore Development Incorporated (EBDI) project which from 2001-2012 forcibly removed over 700 African American families to create space for a biotechnology park. EBDI facilitated the expansion of Johns Hopkins University into 88 acres of land in the Middle East community. EBDI-Hopkins promised 8,000 jobs and a community reinvestment fund. Black families were displaced and the promises were never fulfilled. EBDI was started by 3 Johns Hopkins University presidents (William Brody, Edward D. Miller, and Ronald R. Peterson) along with then mayor Martin O'Malley (Gomez, 2013).

We might also add to this list the neglected but brilliant contributions of Dr. Vivien Thomas whose story was chronicled in the powerful 2004 movie, *Something the Lord Made*. During segregation, Dr. Thomas developed a surgical technique to save babies from dying due to congenital heart defects that led to babies turning blue and dying from the lack of blood. Due to racism and the racial barriers of the time, Dr. Thomas was not allowed to perform surgeries on humans. Dr. Thomas did not receive the acclaim of Dr. William Blalock nor was he ever given the Doctor of Medicine degree or title of medical doctor (MD). He was only honored with an honorary Doctor of Laws 35 years after he began his groundbreaking, pioneering work (Rasmussen, 2007).

In combination with this critical history, the next Health Commissioner of Baltimore should understand the concept of health-in-all-policy. Although people usually speak of health-in-all-policy according to the usual breakdown of governmental functions (i.e. housing, criminal justice, transportation, economic development), the concept of health-in-all-policy should include all policies—past and present. Past social and institutional policies such as restrictive covenants, urban renewal, segregation at every level of education, and medical apartheid are a part of the reason why health inequities persist by race and disproportionately impact black Baltimoreans.

Although Dr. Barbot and Dr. Farber presented their reports as guiding documents for public health efforts, the critical attention to equity and history were missing in their analyses. Due of these missing elements, health providers, academic researchers, and public health practitioners have been unable to conduct a power analysis of the dynamics shaping public health in Baltimore. Public health efforts have usually consisted of top-down approaches as reflected in Dr. Barbot's attention to hospital CEOs and high-class academic institutions and Dr. Farber's exclusive group of medical professionals serving as consultants. Instead of focusing on empowering the people working at the grassroots level who are engaged in prevention and first-response efforts with few funds and little fanfare, the Baltimore City Health Department has instead given the lion's share of attention to the tertiary care sector. The prestigious and well-heeled hospital sector including both Johns Hopkins Medical Institutions and the University of Maryland Medical Center have wielded the majority of influence over decisions that predominantly affect the black community.

We know this to be even truer from a health-in-all policies perspective given the city's development policies with respect to these two academic medical institutions. Both institutions were empowered by the city to displace black residents for the construction of a biotechnology park. For Johns Hopkins University, it was a biotechnology park that was to be built by the East Baltimore Development Incorporated (Gomez, 2013). For the University of Maryland, it was their BioPark which has spurred rising home prices and set off a wave of gentrification in nearby neighborhoods (Kelly, 2013; Kaplan and Farooq, 2011; Wheelan, 2008). Again, given a health-in-all-policy lens, the new Health Commissioner would understand and act against development imperatives that threaten the health of the Black community and induce what Mindy Fullilove calls "root shock" (2004). According to Mindy Fullilove:

> Root shock, at the level of the individual, *is a profound emotional upheaval that destroys the working model of the world that had existed in the individual's head* [emphasis ours]. Root shock undermines trust, increases anxiety about letting loved ones out of one's sight, destabilizes relationships, destroys social, emotional, and financial resources, and increases the risk for every kind of stress-related disease, from depression to heart attack.

When the billions of total dollars in tax credits, tax increment financing, payments in lieu of taxes, and tax expenditures are accounted for, we can then comprehend that the city's priorities and investments in health are backwards (Levine, 2000). Somehow it is believed that the public health of Baltimoreans will magically improve when the city actually invests more money to cater to the interests of the tertiary care sector (i.e. hospitals, medical technology, and large academic medical institutions) as opposed to primary care, preventative care, and public health. Since primary care is also treatment-oriented, the real hope for improving health outcomes in Baltimore is investing deeply in public health and preventative care at the grassroots and in community-led, community-focused settings. At the same time, changing the public's health for the better also involves a participatory approach that seeks to undo racism, eliminate white privilege, stop the welfare for the wealthy (tax expenditures), and include equity as the central principle and driving force in all actions.

Public health at the grassroots means increased focus and funding must go to the city's HBCUs. Due to policies deriving from Jim Crow, institutions such as Sojourner-Douglass College, Coppin State University, and Morgan State University have lagged behind historically white universities in state and local funding support. A recent court case *(The Coalition for Equity and Excellence in Higher Education vs. the Maryland Higher Education Commission)* offers an opportunity to partially remedy this long-standing segregation in education (The Lawyers Committee, 2011).

The effort to ensure anti-racist scholarship and thinking is brought to the public health table to inform and shape programs and policies is even more vital when one considers how institutions such as the University of Maryland were founded by slaveholding individuals and engaged in segregative practices (Students of History 429, 2009). The unique role of HBCUs is appreciated even more when efforts to improve public health takes into account how deeply curricula and perspectives in higher education have been tainted by racist scholarship emerging from Ivy League and "little Ivies" (Wilder, 2013). If we hope to change the current system and approach to public health, we cannot rely solely on institutions that have benefitted so heavily from slavery, segregation, and the status quo.

Black Baltimore and Democratizing Clinical Trials

As this transformation towards complete equity takes place, Black Baltimore can begin to participate more fully in clinical trials that can be beneficial to the community. It is important to use the medical definitions that classify clinical research: "A clinical study involves research using human volunteers (also called participants) that is intended to add to medical knowledge. There are two main types of clinical studies: clinical trials and observational studies. ... In a *clinical trial* (also called an interventional study), participants receive specific interventions according to the research plan or protocol created by the investigators. ... In an *observational study*, investigators assess health outcomes in groups of participants according to a protocol or research plan" (ClinicalTrials.gov, accessed 2014). Clinical studies are a critical step in the research process, as findings from studies better inform researchers about potential interventions that can benefit human health. Clinical trials are the primary focus on clinical studies, as trials are the last step of the research process for potential drugs and medical products (including vaccines, devices, etc.). It is important to have complete representation of all types of people (races, gender, ethnicities, ages, etc.) in order to understand the effect of these medical products in all sorts of people. Diversity (beyond, but including, race) is critical to the development of safe and effective drugs.

When scientific research is conducted in a manner consistent with equity, transparency, shared benefits for all, accountability, and high ethical standards, then clinical trials can contribute to improved health for Black Baltimore. But the benefits of research involving black Baltimoreans should also be shared with the community. Unfortunately, the history of clinical research protection for study volunteers has created mistrust. Furthermore, the sullied history of clinical trials has opened up questions of the remuneration structure and protections for people, especially people of color.

This may mean creating a new community-based system or restorative justice compensation structure so that benefits (including financial incentives and healthcare) also flow to Black Baltimore. The wealth derived from Henrietta Lack's immortal HeLa cells should be (and should have been) shared equitably with her family. Henrietta Lacks was young Black woman who lived in East Baltimore who went to Johns Hopkins Hospital complaining of sharp, unusual, abdominal pain. It turns out she had cervical cancer. Scientists at Johns Hopkins confiscated some of her cells without her permission and those cells are still alive today (Skloot, 2010). Ms. Lacks died from cervical cancer at the age of 31. The cancerous cells, which were taken from her cervix, were the first cells which could be expanded and grown (known as cell culture) in the laboratory setting. This ability to "culture" the cells allowed for the cells to be "immortalized". That is, the cells could be grown and used for experiments across the world. The cells were termed "HeLa" cells, and have been grown and shared across the world for scientific experiments that have benefited millions of people, through research at universities and biotechnology companies.

HeLa cells have been credited with the discovery of several landmark discoveries, including: the polio vaccine, understanding cancer and various viruses, studying the effects of radiation (the atom bomb), in vitro fertilization, modern genetics, and much more. Alongside the countless research discoveries, and ubiquitous use of HeLa cells in laboratories across the globe, the Lacks family was left in the dark. The family was never fully informed of the use of her cells. Many of the scientific discoveries resulted in financial gain and prestige for many researchers (and research institutions) who have used HeLa cells in their work – in the form of research grants and funding, commercialized medical products, and other incentives. However, to this day, none of that wealth has been shared with her family, who still resides in the Baltimore area.

In 2010, Rebecca Skloot published the first full narrative of the story of Henrietta Lacks, entitled *The Immortal Life of Henrietta Lacks*. She captures the life and experience of Henrietta Lacks (often mistakenly called "Helen Lane") and the Lacks family. Below is Skloot's description of the treatment of Lacks following her death:

> There was no obituary for Henrietta Lacks, but word of her death reached the Gey lab quickly. As Henrietta's body cooled in the "colored" freezer, Gey asked her doctors if they'd do an autopsy. Tissue culturists around the world has been trying to create a library of immortal cells like Henrietta's, and Gey wanted samples from as many organs in her body as possible, to see if they'd grow like HeLa. But to get those samples after her death, someone would have to ask Henrietta's husband for permission.
>
> Though no law or code of ethics required doctors to ask permission before taking tissue from a living patient, the law made it very clear

that performing an autopsy or removing tissue from the dead without permission was illegal.

The way Day [Lacks' husband] remembers it, someone from Hopkins called to tell him Henrietta had died, and to ask permission for an autopsy, and Day said no. A few hours later, when Day went to Hopkins with a cousin to see Henrietta's body and sign some papers, the doctors asked again about the autopsy. They said they wanted to run tests that might help his children someday. Day's cousin said it wouldn't hurt, so eventually Day agreed and signed an autopsy permission form. (Skloot, 2010)

Other patent-generating research conducted with predominantly black participants who live in disinvested communities should also result in wealth shared with and controlled by disinvested Black communities. When science is conducted in a deeply democratic and equitable way, positive benefits can accrue to both the vulnerable and the powerful. Again, the tragic story of the treatment of the Lacks' family has echoed in the Black Baltimore community. The excerpt below highlights the sentiment that has to be overcome with a new approach:

Bobbette laughed. "My mother-in-law's Henrietta Lacks but I know you're not talking about her – she's been dead almost twenty-five years."

"Henrietta Lacks is your mother-in-law?" he asked, suddenly excited. "Did she die of cervical cancer?"

Bobbette stopped smiling and snapped, "How'd you know that?"
"Those cells in my lab have to be hers," he said. "They're from a black woman named Henrietta Lacks who died of cervical cancer at Hopkins in the fifties."

"What?!" Bobbette yelled, jumping up from her chair. "What you mean you got her cells in your lab?"

He held his hands up, like *Whoa, wait a minute.* "I ordered them from a supplier just like everybody else."

"What do you mean, 'everybody else'?!" Bobbette snapped. *"What* supplier? Who's got cells from my mother-in-law?"

It was like a nightmare. She'd read in the paper about the syphilis study at Tuskegee, which has just been stopped by the government after forty years, and now here was Gardenia's brother-in-law, saying Hopkins had part of Henrietta alive and scientists everywhere were doing research on her and the family had no idea. It was like all those terrifying stories she'd heard about Hopkins her whole life were suddenly true, and happening to her. *If they're doing research on Henrietta, she thought, it's only a matter of time before they come for Henrietta's children, and maybe her grandchildren.*

[...]"I wish I knew," he said. Like most researchers, he'd never thought about whether the woman behind HeLa cells had given them voluntarily.

Bobbette excused herself and ran home,... , yelling for Lawrence, "Part of your mother, it's alive!" (Skloot, 2010)

We can avoid such tragic pain and heartache if we conduct clinical trials and practice science in a fully democratic and equitable fashion. It was through teamwork and the painstaking process of trial and error that Dr. Vivien Thomas and Dr. William Blalock were able to pioneer the surgical techniques to correct the congenital heart defects that led to Blue Baby Syndrome. Through an arduous scientific process, Dr. Vivien Thomas discovered and developed the surgical method to save Blue Babies decades ago. If we democratize science, research, and clinical trials, then we can save Black babies and Black Baltimore now. If we find ways to make the scientific process increasingly anti-racist, then in the future, today's youth can develop the type of medicines, procedures, programs, and policies to improve the health outcomes of Black Baltimoreans living in Cherry Hill, Park Heights, and Upton.

We argue that the way research and clinical trials have been conducted in the past constitutes a threat to Black Baltimore's public health today and thus also needs to be transformed. Many black Baltimoreans avoid preventative care or primary care because of medical abuses that engendered medical mistrust and increased suspicion of all health related efforts due to abuses in medical experimentation. In other words, racist and racially exclusive actions in the past have damaged the willingness of black Baltimoreans to trust in public health today (Washington, 2008).

Transforming Clinical Trials in Baltimore

Therefore, the next Health Commissioner will have to acknowledge this dynamic, living history and work assiduously to regain the trust of many in the city. The challenge for Black Baltimore is to also acknowledge this history so that we can develop the type of structures to create more equity and shared benefits in clinical trials. We suggest the following steps to reform the clinical trials process:

1. *Confront the history of clinical trials, especially within Baltimore.*

   Clinical trials research has evolved over centuries, beginning as questionable experiments performed on prisoners of war, to a structured scientific endeavor designed to produce meaningful scientific data. Over this course, unethical practices have tainted trials. The evolution of clinical trials is a key to understanding the terror and mistrust that exists between lay people, especially within the Black community, and scientific researchers. Many historians have argued that the abuse of enslaved Africans and poor blacks during the infancy of the American research system has altered the manner in which blacks, especially black Americans, interact with medical institutions. As Harriet Washington explains in *Medical Apartheid* (2006):

Slavery created a medical partnership between physician and planter that eclipsed the patient-physician dyad, the traditional Western healing relationship. In the slaveholding United States, where the planter owned the slave and employed the physician, owners made their complaints or treatment wishes known to physicians and gave or withheld consent for procedures, from sterilization to amputation to autopsy. The planter, not the slave, had to be satisfied with the results. The planter, in every important sense of the word, was the patient.

2. *Build trust by engaging key community institutions as anchor institutions, to educate and engage researchers.*

Until now, most health and science interactions have been one-directional. That is, an individual/community member interacts with a medical institution by visiting a clinic or physician. Rarely do medical professionals continuously interact with the community. We propose that the creation of a bi-directional relationship between researchers and community members would build trust. Creating a structured relationship will require communities to form "anchored communities", using trusted institutions within the community to engage researchers and institutions.

3. *Build community structures which hold researchers accountable, including reporting the findings of research studies.*

Anchored institutions within communities can serve a vital role in upholding the relationship between medical researchers and community stakeholders. Anchored institutions have been defined as organizations that have a vested interest in a community, operating as a fixated presence in said community. We argue that there should be community-centered anchored institutions, organizations (preferably, non-profit organizations) that are community operated and have secured the trust of the community through continuous and equitable engagement. As a part of this structure, there should be a forum for scientists and researchers to communicate their research findings, and discuss scientific/medical progress.

An example of such a structure includes community institutional review boards (IRBs). The community IRB structure has been illustrated by the Albert Einstein College of Medicine, the Bronx Health Link, Community-Campus Partnerships for Health (2012) in a report. As the authors of the report state, community IRBs:

…routinely examine issues that institution-based IRBs typically do not, such as community risks and benefits of the research and the cultural competency of the research team and study design. Their primary benefits were giving communities a voice in determining which studies are conducted in their communities and ensuring that studies are relevant, feasible and build community capacity.

4. *Focus on cultural competency to equip research teams with skills to team with study volunteers.*

   Research teams should be trained to confront their own unconscious bias and to work to understand how this bias could affect their research. Tools such as the implicit association test (IAT) are valuable resources for study teams, who can use this test to understand their own bias. There are biases and prejudices that can affect the way that researchers interact with study volunteers, or worse, how researchers interpret the data that they collect. Recognizing that this bias exists is the first step to improving relationships between study teams and community members. The IAT and similar tools should equip researchers with new insights to relate to their study volunteers and conduct research in an anti-racist manner.

5. *Retain (and support) minority researchers and trainees to ensure that research teams benefit from a range of perspectives.*

   In addition to confronting existing unconscious bias, we should also work to support minority researchers and researchers in training. There are several studies, including a recent paper published by Kenneth Gibbs and Kimberly Griffin (CBE Life Science Education, 2013), which discuss the challenges that newly-minted scientific researchers face, especially researchers from underrepresented and underserved populations. Confronting the racial dynamics that exist in research require minorities to be present on both sides of the relationship. Black researchers can bring critical perspectives and insights to the research enterprise, and, as noted by Gibbs and Griffin, talented researchers are choosing to leave the "bench" for careers outside of research institutions. The lack of diversity in science affects the quality of research performed. More so, this lack of diversity affects the dynamics between the researchers and study volunteers. We (both communities and institutions) should work to support the retention of biomedical researchers, so ensure that diverse and broad perspectives are influencing medical research.

The list above is by no means exhaustive, but is intended to create an outline of the key components of a transformed clinical trials system. Confronting the sordid history of trials, and understanding the protections that resulted from these experiments, will enable researchers (and research institutions) to rebuild trust with the community. It is known that community participants are a critical component of the clinical trials system. Though there are medical protections in place for study volunteers, few researchers engage their volunteers as partners in the scientific process. This has created a transactional relationship, study participants never learn about the findings from the study (or studies) in which they have participated.

The model proposed above addresses the histories of clinical trials and institutions, which have been carried down in stories through generations. Most importantly, the model proposes a way forward, a new approach to engaging communities of potential study participants in the research process. The creation of a new process to engage community members in the trials process may appear cumbersome at first glance, but we should remember that communities are also filled with individuals who interact with the healthcare system in a host of ways. These community structures (#3) will also serve to increase medical education of the lay population, which is vital to encouraging healthy behaviors.

Conclusion

By acknowledging the devastating impact of racism and racial exclusion in public health and clinical trials, we gain the insight into the power dynamics that interplay and interfere with all efforts to eliminate health inequities and erase health disparities. Only by digging deeper into the policies and practices that constitute the social determinants of health are we able to forge a path towards improved public health efforts while simultaneously democratizing clinical trials. We shine a spotlight on how people from powerful institutions wield their power and privilege to exclude and marginalize people from less powerful institutions to perpetuate and maintain an unsustainable status quo.

We challenge the next Health Commissioner to work with and provide more support for public health at the grassroots. HBCUs are an untapped resource, with a wealth of expertise and analyses that can enrich and empower stale approaches that are ultimately ineffective and unethical. We know the current approaches to be ineffective because in the course of the past 50 years, although infant mortality rates have fallen, the magnitude of differences in infant mortality rates has actually increased from a difference of 1.6 times higher (38 per 1000 for black/23.6 per 1000 for white) to 4.75 times higher (18 per 1000 for black/3.85 times 1000 for white) when comparing black infant mortality rates to white infant mortality rates (Farber, 1963; Spencer et al, 2011). The higher rate of infant mortality for Black Baltimore is unacceptable. We cannot continue to pursue the same failed course of action rooted in shallow thinking.

Black Baltimore must also take action by aggressively challenging the social determinants of health that contribute to widening health inequities. The architects of the status quo are not invincible. As Dr. King reminds us: "No lie can live forever." Blues artist Queen Slyvia Embry reminds us that we as a people must develop a deep and abiding sense of divine dissatisfaction with abuse and oppression when she sings: "I'm so tired of always being pushed around." If we create the necessary and empowering social movements, we shall live and not die. Only by engaging in uncompromising social action to upend unethical power dynamics, practice public health from the grassroots, undo racism, demand health in all policy, and democratize clinical trials, will Black Baltimore live…and thrive!

References

Albert Einstein College of Medicine et al. (2012). Community IRBs and Research Review Boards: Shaping the Future of Community-Engaged Research. Albert Einstein College of Medicine, The Bronx Health Link and Community-Campus Partnerships for Health. Retrieved from:

Baltimore City Health Department. (n.d.). Retrieved March 21, 2014, from http://www.baltimorehealth.org/

Barbot, Oxiris. (2011). What's killing Baltimore? Health Department on a quest to find out. Retrieved from: http://www.baltimoresun.com/news/opinion/oped/bs-ed-city-health-20110509,0,1007204.story

Bay Area Regional Health Initiative. (2008). A framework for health equity. Bay Area Regional Health Initiative. Retrieved from: http://www.barhii.org

Boulware, L., Cooper, L. A., Ratner, L. E., Laveist, T. A., & Powe, N. R. (2003). Race and trust in the health care system. *Public Health Reports,* 118(4), 358-365. doi: 10.1016/S0033-3549(04)50262-5

Broadwater, Luke. (2014). City health commissioner to resign for N.Y. job. (n.d.). *The Baltimore Sun.* Retrieved from: http://www.baltimoresun.com/news/maryland/politics/blog/bal-city-health-commissioner-resigns-for-ny-job-20140312,0,4792324.story

Bullard, R. D., & Wright, B. (2012). The *Wrong Complexion for Protection: How The Government Response to Disaster Endangers African American Communities.* New York: New York University Press.

Cavagnaro, Louise. (1992). *A History Of Segregation and Desegregation at The Johns Hopkins Medical Institutions.* Baltimore: Johns Hopkins Medical Institutions.

"Learn About Clinical Studies". http://www.clinicaltrials.gov/ct2/about-studies/learn. (Accessed April 2014)

Farber, R. E. (1963). One hundred and forty-ninth annual report of the Baltimore City Health Department, 1963: Report of the health department. Baltimore City, Maryland. Retrieved from: http://www.baltimorehealth.org/dataresearch.html.

Fullilove, M. T. (2004). *Root Shock: How Tearing Up City Neighborhoods Hurts America, and What We Can Do About It.* New York: One World/Ballantine Books.

Gomez, M. B. (2013). *Race, Class, Power, and Organizing In East Baltimore: Rebuilding Abandoned Communities In America.* Lanham: Lexington Books.

Gibbs, K. D. and Griffin, K. A. (2013). What do I want to be with my PhD? The roles of personal values and structural dynamics in shaping the career interests of

Recent Biomedical Science PhD Graduates. *CBE Life Sci Educ.* 2013 Winter; 12(4): 711–723.

Johns Hopkins University. (2014). Johns Hopkins, his family and slavery: A first look back at the Civil War, from the Johns Hopkins perspective. Johns Hopkins University Government, Community, and Public Affairs. Retrieved from: http://perspectives.jhu.edu/2011/04/johns-hopkins-the-abolitionist/

Jones, H. W. (1997). Record of the first physician to see Henrietta Lacks at the Johns Hopkins Hospital: History of the beginning of the HeLa cell line. *American Journal of Obstetrics and Gynecology.* 176(6).

Kaplan, M., Farooq, U. (2011). Poppleton: A neighborhood in waiting. Indypendent Reader.

Kelly, Jacques. (2013). UM BioPark takes root in west Baltimore: Buildings surround venerable neighborhoods. *The Baltimore Sun.* Retrieved from: http://articles.baltimoresun.com/2013-11-08/news/bs-md-ci-kelly-column-biopark-20131108_1_baltimore-city-community-college-genome-sciences-west-baltimore-street

The Lawyers' Committee for Civil Rights Under Law. (2011). Maryland Historically Black Colleges and Universities Litigation. Retrieved from: http://www.lawyerscommittee.org/projects/education/page?id=0018

Levine, M. V. (2000). A third-world city in the first world: Social exclusion, racial inequality, and sustainable development in Baltimore. In M. Polese & R. Stren (Eds.), *The Social Sustainability of Cities: Diversity and the Management of Change* (pp. 123-156). Toronto: University of Toronto Press.

Rasmussen, F. N. (2010). Louise Pearl "Cavi" Cavagnaro dies: Longtime volunteer and former administrator helped lead the way in desegregating Hopkins Hospital. Retrieved from: http://articles.baltimoresun.com/2010-06-29/news/bs-md-ob-louise-cavagnaro-20100629_1_east-baltimore-hospital-nursing-patient-services

Rasmussen, F. N. (1997). Vivien Thomas: 'Technician' helped Dr. Alfred Blalock and Dr. Helen Taussig develop the 'blue baby' operation at Johns Hopkins. *The Baltimore Sun.* Retrieved from: http://www.baltimoresun.com/features/bal-blackhistory-thomas,0,833906.story?page=2

Spencer, M., Pettaway, R., Bacetti L., and Barbot O. (2011). Healthy Baltimore 2015: A city where all residents realize their full health potential. Baltimore City Health Department. Retrieved from: http://www.baltimorehealth.org/info/Healthy_Baltimore_2015/HealthyBaltimore2015_Final_Web.pdf

Skloot, R. (2010). *The Immortal Life of Henrietta Lacks.* New York: Crown Publishers.

Students of History 429. (2009). Knowing our history: African American slavery and the University of Maryland. University of Maryland. Retrieved from: http://cdm16064.contentdm.oclc.org/cdm/ref/collection/p266901coll7/id/2614

Washington, H. A. (2006). *Medical apartheid: The dark history of medical experimentation on Black Americans from colonial times to the present.* New York: Doubleday.

Wheelan, R. (2008). BioPark drawing home buyers west. The Daily Record. Retrieved from: http://www.umbiopark.com/News/BioPark-drawing-home-buyers-west/134

Wilder, C. S. (2013). *Ebony and Ivy: Race, Slavery, and The Troubled History Of America's Universities.* New York: Bloomsbury Press.

United States Census Bureau. (2014). State and County Quick Facts: Baltimore City, Maryland. Retrieved from: http://quickfacts.census.gov/qfd/states/24/24510.html.

Environmental Challenges Boosters Diabetes Epidemic
"Let My People Go"

Maurice Hunt

As a minority examining the current environmental health struggle, I cannot help but reflect on the Civil Rights Movement. "Outside agitators" was the language used to describe characters of the Civil Rights Movement. Civil Rights leaders often used the metaphor of the Children of Israel released from Egypt to describe their present day beckoning of the social justice issues of slavery and Jim Crow.

The rhetoric of that day highlighted human suffering that occurred during the Civil Rights Movement. Some onlookers describe the rhetoric as pulling the scab off a wound that is healing. Although this article seeks to shed light on environmental health challenges with the clarion call "Let My People Go", it's also meant to inspire, enlighten, and more importantly a call to action.

My name is Maurice Hunt and I am a current resident of Maryland. I am 28 years old and thought I was mentally able and physically fit but more importantly healthy. I thought I was the picture of health and worked out on a regular basis. I am a former coveted high school all conference basketball and football recruit before deciding to serve my beloved country by enlisting in the United States Navy.

During my enlisted career as a Hospital Corpsman, I worked my way up through the ranks to become a decorated veteran serving during the Iraq and Afghanistan conflicts which tested all my mental, physical, and emotional strength.

It was September 30, 2011 and I woke up feeling badly thinking I had a stomach virus. I was vomiting and could tell I was losing a little weight. My business partner suggested that he take me to the VA Hospital in Baltimore, Maryland if my conditions did not improve.

There was a hard knock on the door, but I did not hear it. Lo and behold, I passed out and nearly comatose. My business partner did not want to overreact but figured something was wrong. He walked next door and asked my neighbors to call 911. The Annapolis City Police arrived, looked through the window and saw me on the floor. The officer tapped on the window in an attempt to speak to me. The officer asked if I had the strength to crawl on the floor to open the door rather than break their way in to gain access.

The Emergency Medical Technicians rushed me to Anne Arundel Medical Center. My sugar level was over 1600mg/dL. I was facing death and or permanent brain damage because of diabetic ketoacidosis. My life as I had previously known it flashed before my very eyes.

At 28 years old, I have a diagnosis of type2 diabetes. As a result of this revelation and near death experience I have dedicated my life to educate others and myself about the chronic disease diabetes and its risk factors.

Diabetes is a growing epidemic, and it has become arguably one of the biggest health challenges of our time. Currently, more than 26 million Americans have diabetes, and Centers for Disease Control and Prevention estimate that in the last 15 years, the number of people in the United States with diabetes has more than doubled.

> "Fifty years ago, children did not avoid chronic diseases such as diabetes by making healthier choices but rather lived in a world with less pollutants."

Unfortunately, the impact and incomprehensible damage created by air pollution is unevenly distributed. Research has shown that disadvantaged minority populations are the recipients of higher exposure to pollutants and may endure the greatest effects of the remnants of pollution. Much of the research paints a clear picture of disparity of pollution equal to health disparity.

Air pollution is unequivocally one of the largest avoidable causes of the chronic disease diabetes on earth in particularly the United States. Changes in diet and regular exercise are often encouraged to tackle the ills of diabetes. Such remedies are effective however focusing on non-behavioral change remedies such as technology that deters pollutants could reap high rewards. Off-the-shelf technology can be retrofitted onto sources of pollution at minimum cost, with far reaching health benefits. The benefits are to include less premature deaths, lower risk of chronic diseases such as diabetes, and lower overall medical cost.

Over the last decade a massive amount of evidence has been gathered to suggest that exposure to air pollution has disadvantageous known health effects. 1,2 Long-term studies have exposed that individuals dwelling in polluted cities have lower life expectancy and more likely to expire earlier than those residing in less polluted areas. If we dig a little deeper, we will find that such mortality is mostly due to chronic diseases such as diabetes and strongly associated with an increase in air particulate matter (PM).

Ambient air contains a range of particles that vary in size over 5 orders of magnitude (from 0.001 to 100 μm). Larger particles (≥10 μm; PM_{10}) are derived from wind-blown soil or dust or volcanic activity and often consist of sea salts, pollen, mold, and spores. Human activities such as mining or agriculture also generate such particles. Fine particles (0.1 to 2.5 μm; $PM_{2.5}$) spawn from combustion emissions such as automobile exhaust or wood or coal burning and industrial emissions from smelters, paper and steel mills, or cement plants. Considered to be of greater health significance are fine and ultrafine (<2.5 μm) particles. These particles penetrate deeper in the lung and could potentially appear in our circulation. Several time-series analysis studies show a consistent association between $_{PM}10$ and $_{PM}2.5$ levels and daily mortality due to myocardial infarctions, arrhythmias, and heart failure.

Although the link is largely statistical, studies that demonstrate even a short-term decrease in air pollution linking a decrease in area deaths argue in favor of a causal relationship between PM exposure and mortality. The most striking examples are shown by studies from Utah, where a 13-month closure of a local steel mill led to a significant (3.2%) decrease in mortality. Further, studies from Dublin, illustrate that a decrease in PM due to a ban on coal was consistent with a 5.7% decrease in all-cause death rates.2 Such data is indicative that a large decrease in death after a reduction in air pollution within a few weeks to years provide a natural control for other variables. The aforementioned statement validates the hypothesis that long-term exposure to particulate air pollution has lasting health effects.

Pollutants other than air particulates have also been shown to exacerbate insulin resistance and diabetes. In a recent study, Navas-Acien and coworkers3 found that in a population exposed to low to moderate arsenic levels in the United States, there was a positive association between urine arsenic levels and the prevalence of type 2 diabetes mellitus. This study corroborates extensive data collected previously from exposed populations in Taiwan, Bangladesh, and Mexico confirm that chronic exposure to high levels of arsenic in drinking water is in accordance with a higher frequency of diabetes.4 In animal studies, the striking diabetogenic effect of arsenic, albeit at high concentrations is also affirmation of the correlation among the same. It is possible that both arsenic and PM engage similar mechanisms and that the increase in insulin resistance in arsenic-exposed populations is also a result of chronic low-grade inflammation.

The evidence supported by reputable research laid out in this article speaks for itself. As an advocate for health who survived a near death experience, I call for a paradigm shift.

A paradigm shift can be defined as an event that instantly and drastically alters the customary way of life and has worldwide transforming effects. If we are to live out our true creed as Americans and protect the yet unborn, a paradigm shift must take place.

Reducing pollution is the human rights issue of the day. The increase in population has been shadowed by increased air and water pollution that adversely affect our health. If we are to celebrate in this great achievement global unity will be essential. Reducing pollution means a clean and healthy environment but more importantly a healthy you and I.

Tackling the pollution problem will not be an easy task, because of many sources. In the spirit of Moses, I say to big industry Let My People Go! I say to fossil fuel generating automobiles Let My People Go! I say to unclean agriculture Let My People Go! We must, we will, we can Let My People Go!

Join the Diabetes Awareness Project and me in a statewide wide initiative t to educate the public on the dangers and symptoms and treatment of Diabetes: The Silent Killer! Diabetes Awareness Project will test 1 million residents of Maryland, DC and Virginia for diabetes. For more information, visit www.diabetesawarenessproject.org and Contact Maurice Hunt at mhunt@diabetesawarenessproject.

REFERENCES

Bhatnagar A. Environmental cardiology: studying mechanistic links between pollution and heart disease. *Circ Res.* 2006; 99: 692–705.

Pope CA 3rd, Dockery DW. Health effects of fine particulate air pollution: lines that connect. *J Air Waste Manag Assoc.* 2006; 56: 709–742.

Navas-Acien A, Silbergeld EK, Pastor-Barriuso R, Guallar E. Arsenic exposure and prevalence of type 2 diabetes in US adults. *JAMA.* 2008; 300: 814–822.

Navas-Acien A, Silbergeld EK, Streeter RA, Clark JM, Burke TA, Guallar E. Arsenic exposure and type 2 diabetes: a systematic review of the experimental and epidemiological evidence. *Environ Health Perspect.* 2006; 114: 641–648.

Diabetes and the Aging Population
Baltimore and Maryland

Roderick C. Willis (NewsULM)

As we analyze the progress of overall health of African Americans in 2014, it is necessary to place this analysis in the historical perspective of the total civil rights era. In the year 1960, the statistics for African Americans were frightening, with the average life expectancy of African Americans being seven years less than white Americans. African American children had only half the chance of entering and completing college and about one third the chance of entering a profession. In the early 1960s, African Americans earned half as much as white Americans and were twice as likely to be unemployed. In those days, the clear enemy was Jim Crow, institutional racism and the vestiges of poverty.

As we reflect on the tremendous progress made over the last six decades, African Americans in Baltimore and throughout the country, in many respects, have not closed the life expectancy gap. According to life expectancy figures released by the Baltimore City Health Department, the life expectancy of predominantly African American Upton and Druid Heights residents is an average of 62 years, while their white counterparts in Roland Park are expected to live to 82 years. The enemies that robbed African Americans of 20 years of their life may not be so clear in the year 2014. Much of Jim Crow is outlawed and not openly practiced, yet African American children born in Upton die 20 years younger than their white counterparts five miles away. Is the answer still poverty of the mind and ignorance? African Americans in 2014 have often traded hunger and malnutrition for obesity and diabetes in epidemic proportions. Why then, are residents of Upton and Druid Heights who live about five miles away from Roland Park expected to die 20 years earlier? Is it the food they eat, and the diet that's different, or the lifestyle they lead? Is it access to medical care? The one single disease that has reached epidemic proportions and contributes to a 20-year lower life expectancy is called "The Silent Killer"…diabetes. Diabetes contributes significantly to heart attack, stroke, blindness, amputation, kidney disease, Alzheimer's, and dementia.

The Greater Baltimore region has a serious diabetes epidemic and it is quietly eating away the health and financial resources of its senior citizens. As Baltimore and the rest of Maryland move well into the second decade of the 21st Century, the number of seniors living in Maryland is increasing. Of the 5.3 million people in Maryland in 2000, 15 % (801,036) were over the age of 60.

According to the Centers for Disease Control and Prevention (CDC) and National Institutes of Health (NIH), diabetes is an epidemic throughout the United States. The Centers for Disease Control's figures released in 2014 estimate that there are about 29.1 million people with diabetes or 9.3 percent of the population. These figures reveal that there are 21 million people diagnosed with diabetes with 8.1 million or 27.8 percent of those undiagnosed and not knowing they have the disease.

Diagnosed and undiagnosed diabetes in the United States, all ages, 2012

Total: 29.1 million people or 9.3% of the population have diabetes
Diagnosed: 21.0 million people
Undiagnosed: 8.1 million people (27.8% of people with diabetes are undiagnosed)

FIGURE 1:

According to National Institutes of Health and its National Diabetes Educational Program, it is estimated that another 79 million adults aged 20 and older have pre-diabetes. Pre-diabetes is a condition where blood glucose levels are higher than normal but not high enough to be called diabetes. Studies have shown that by losing weight and increasing physical activity people can prevent or delay pre-diabetes from progressing to diabetes.

According to the Centers for Disease Control and Prevention, by the year 2030, the percentage of senior citizens over the age of 60 is expected to increase to 25% of Maryland's projected population of 6.7 million or approximately 1.675 million. While the Greater Baltimore region's population showed a modest increase of about 4 percent from 2000 through 2007, the number of residents ages 55 to 64 and those 85 and older

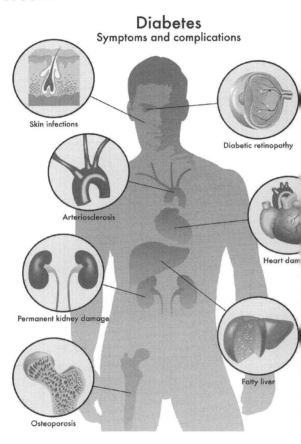

increased by about a third, according to an analysis of U.S. census released in 2008. According to statistics released by Maryland Department of the Aging, of the State's aged 60+ minority population in 2000, 32.3% lived in Baltimore City, with 15.7% in Montgomery County and 24.4% in Prince George's County. Of the population of older minority Marylanders who are 85+, 35% lived in Baltimore City in 2000.

What do these numbers mean to an ever-growing number of senior residents who will discover that they have diabetes? What will the cost of care be to those who suffer from diabetes? How will the budgets of the families and caretakers who must bare the burden of healthcare including supplies, medicine and hospital visits, be affected? What will the total bill for diabetes be and how will it impact public policy and the regional budgets?

The Epidemic of Type 2 Diabetes

According to Centers for Disease Control and Prevention, Type 2 diabetes, once called non-insulin-dependent diabetes is on the rise in epidemic proportions and accounts for 90%–95% of the 26 million Americans with diabetes. As many as 1 in 3 U.S. adults could have diabetes by 2050 if current trends continue, according to a new analysis from the Centers for Disease Control and Prevention. In 2010, the CDC released research that revealed that 1 in 10 U.S. adults has diabetes now. The prevalence is expected to rise sharply over the next 40 years due to an aging population more likely to develop type 2 diabetes, increases in minority groups that are at high risk for type 2 diabetes, and people with diabetes living longer, according to CDC projections published in the journal Population Health Metrics.

FIGURE 2:

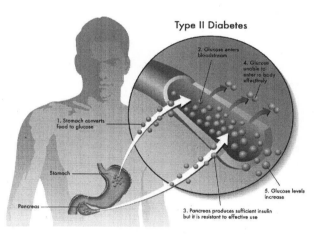

Type II Diabetes

1. Stomach converts food to glucose
2. Glucose enters bloodstream
3. Pancreas produces sufficient insulin but it is resistant to effective use
4. Glucose unable to enter to body effectively
5. Glucose levels increase

Stomach

Pancreas

Unlike people with type 1 diabetes where no insulin is produced by the pancreas, the bodies of people with type 2 diabetes actually produce insulin. But either their pancreas does not make enough insulin or the body cannot use the insulin well enough. When this condition occurs, this is called insulin resistance.

In the instances where there isn't enough insulin or the insulin is not used as it should be, glucose (sugar) can't get into the body's cells. When glucose builds up in the blood instead of going into cells, the body's cells are not able to function properly.

Because the study factored in aging, minority populations and lifespan, the projections are higher than previous estimates. The report predicts that the number of new diabetes cases each year will increase from 8 per 1,000 people in 2008, to 15 per 1,000 in 2050.

Seniors are at greater risk because Type 2 diabetes is usually associated with older age, obesity and physical inactivity, family history of type 2 diabetes, or a personal history of gestational diabetes. Diabetes rates vary by race and ethnicity, with American Indian, Alaska Native, African American, Hispanic/Latino, and Asian/Pacific Islander adults about twice as likely as white adults to have type 2 diabetes. Type 2 diabetes can be prevented through healthy food choices, physical activity, and weight loss. It can be controlled with these same activities, but insulin or oral medication also may be necessary.

Complications of Diabetes

Seniors with diabetes have an increased risk of developing a number of serious health problems. Over time, the high glucose levels in the blood can damage the nerves and small blood vessels of the eyes, kidneys, and heart and lead to atherosclerosis, or hardening of the arteries that can cause heart attack and stroke. Consistently high blood glucose levels can lead to serious diseases affecting the heart and blood vessels, eyes, kidneys, nerves and teeth. In addition, people with diabetes also have a higher risk of developing infections. In almost all high-income countries, diabetes is a leading cause of heart attack, stroke and other cardiovascular disease, blindness, kidney disease, kidney failure, and lower limb amputation.

Diabetic Eye Disease

Seniors are at greater risk of diabetes, and seniors are at greater risk of diabetic eye disease. Diabetic retinopathy is the most common diabetic eye disease and occurs when blood vessels in the retina change. **FIGURE 3:**

Sometimes these small blood vessels swell and leak fluid or even close off completely. In other instances, the formation of new abnormal blood vessels occurs and begins to grow on the surface of the retina. Diabetic eye disease has no warning signs. Early detection and treatment of diabetic eye disease, before it causes vision loss or blindness, is the best way to control diabetic eye disease. Seniors with diabetes should make sure they receive a dilated eye examination at least once a year.

Normal

Diabetic Retinopathy

Nonproliferative Retinopathy

Hemorrhage
Cotton wo
Macula
Microaneury

Proliferative Retinopathy

Abnorma
of blood

Diabetic retinopathy more often than not affects both eyes. People with diabetic retinopathy often don't notice changes in their vision in the disease's early stages. But as it progresses, diabetic retinopathy usually causes vision loss that in many cases cannot be reversed. Consistently high levels of blood glucose, together with high blood pressure and high cholesterol, are the main causes of retinopathy. It can be managed through regular eye checks and keeping glucose and lipid levels at or close to normal.

Seniors with diabetes are at greater risk of heart attack and stroke

Heart disease is the number one killer of people in the United States, and elderly people are at greater risk of dying from these diseases. But the number one cause and risk factor of heart attack is diabetes. Baltimore's and Maryland's senior citizens should pay particular attention to the symptoms of diabetes and take preventive measures to address the root causes of the rising diabetes epidemic.

Dr. Elijah Saunders is a world-renowned cardiologist who has practiced medicine in Baltimore for over 40 years. He has pioneered research of African Americans with hypertension, also known as high blood pressure, and is a founding member of the International Society of Blacks with Hypertension. Dr. Elijah Saunders, a board certified cardiologist and professor of medicine at University of Maryland was recently interviewed for a documentary film, Faces of Diabetes. In that interview he revealed there is a connection between diabetes and cardiovascular disease. He further revealed that 60% or more of people with diabetes would ultimately die from a heart attack or stroke. This means that we must heed his warnings and pay increased attention to our seniors with diabetes.

"Diabetes is called the silent killer because its symptoms often go unnoticed", continued Dr. Saunders. "Hypertension or high blood pressure is extremely prevalent in African American patients I have treated over the years and is often one of the conditions to look for with in people with diabetes." Dr. Saunders recommends exercise and a change in African Americans' diets from heavy meat diets to those with more fruits and vegetables.

Diabetes and the Baltimore Region's Veteran population

Diabetes Awareness Project has launched a statewide awareness, testing and anti-smoking program targeted at veterans, especially those who smoke, and for good reason. Approximately 1 in 4 of veterans in the Veterans Health Administration (VA) have been diagnosed with diabetes. Diabetes is clearly a leading cause of blindness, end stage renal disease, and amputation in the US and in the VA. The older age of veterans perhaps may be a contributing factor to the high rate of diabetes compared to the rest of the US population. About 11 million people in the USA 65 and older have diabetes or about 27 percent of seniors.

Many veterans, especially those of the Vietnam War era, are suffering from diabetes.

To get a clear picture of the severity of the impact of diabetes on veterans, one only has to look at the mortality rate of patients visiting the VA. The mortality rate associated with VA patients with diabetes averages approximately 5% per year, compared with an average of 2.6% among patients without diabetes, and the majority of deaths and hospitalizations related to diabetes, both inside and outside VA, are due to macrovascular complications such as heart attack and stroke. (http://www.ncbi.nlm.nih.gov/pmc/articles/PMC2219704/ US National Library of Medicine National Institutes of Health)

Veterans, and others with diabetes should get eye exams once each year to detect diabetic eye disease or diabetic retinopathy, and should also get their feet examined for cuts or sores on the feet. Because diabetics often have cuts that will not heal, toes and feet become infected and may have to be amputated. To avoid this fate, veterans and all seniors with diabetes should check their feet each day and visit the podiatrist if problems are detected.

For veterans with diabetes, the presence of specific risk factors such as inadequately regulated and controlled high blood pressure (also referred to medically as hypertension), higher levels of glucose in the blood stream, have been proven to increase the probability of devastating consequences. To the contrary, the appropriate management of these risk factors (both medical management and self-management), coupled with the early diagnoses and treatment of conditions such as foot ulcers, retinal disease, and renal impairment are known to be successful in reducing end organ complications and death.

Vietnam War Veterans should particularly be concerned about diabetes and the possibility that they were exposed to chemical agents and dangerous herbicides. Agent Orange was one such chemical agent widely used in the Vietnam conflict. Vietnam Veterans who were exposed to Agent Orange do not have to prove a cause/effect relationship between their type 2 diabetes and military service to be eligible for VA benefits.

TestaMillion Campaign key to testing Marylander's seniors for diabetes

Diabetes is known as "The Silent Killer" because many people who have the disease are unaware that they have it. Diabetes Awareness Project has launched a statewide outreach initiative and media to test one million Maryland residents for diabetes. With more than 800,000 Marylanders over the age of 60, this campaign is critical to help identify senior citizens and others who are unaware that they have the disease.

The TestaMillion Campaign provides free testing for seniors throughout Maryland and has formed strategic partnerships with churches, community associations, assisted living facilities and civil organizations. Maurice Hunt, a decorated US Navy Veteran of the Iraq War and Afghanistan War who experienced a near-death experience, launched the TestaMillion initiative. Six months after he was discharged from the Navy with a clean bill of health, he was found on the floor of his home half-unconscious with a 1600 sugar level. Annapolis Fire Department Emergency Medical Technicians rushed him to the emergency room of Anne Arundel Medical Center. According to his emergency room physician, Dr. Kanak Patel. "Had Maurice Hunt arrived here at the Anne Arundel Medical Center 20 minutes later, he would have died or suffered severe brain damage". Mr. Hunt suffered a condition called, diabetic ketoacidosis (DKA) or extreme blood sugar levels. DKA is considered a medical emergency that without treatment, leads to death.

First described in 1886 until the introduction of insulin in the 1920s, the condition was almost always fatal. Timely diagnosis and insulin therapy are the keys to survival from this deadly condition. DKA results from a shortage of insulin, and in response the body switches to burning fatty acids and producing ketone bodies that cause most of the symptoms and complications. The fact that an otherwise healthy 26-year-old US Navy veteran with no known history of diabetes could suffer an attack of ketoacidosis (elevated blood sugar levels with no warning) underscores the danger of diabetes to Maryland's senior citizen population. Inspired by his near-death encounter with DKA, Hunt founded Diabetes Awareness Project and the TestaMillion People for Diabetes Campaign to test one million people in Maryland for diabetes. TestaMillion targets veterans, especially those from the Vietnam War era and approximately 800,000 seniors in Maryland over the age of 62.

Diabetes : Is Alzheimer's Type III diabetes of the brain?

In 2005, a game-changing discovery was made that may trigger a whole new paradigm with respect to medical treatment and management of Alzheimer's disease. Researchers at Rhode Island Hospital and Brown Medical School have discovered that insulin and its related proteins are produced in the brain, and that reduced levels of both are linked to Alzheimer's disease. The findings are reported in the March issue of the Journal of Alzheimer's Disease (http://www.j-alz.com<http://www.j-alz.com/>), published by IOS Press. The discovery leans heavily to the conclusion that there is a link between diabetes and Alzheimer' disease and vascular dementia. "What we found is that insulin is not just produced in the pancreas, but also in the brain. And we discovered that insulin and its growth factors, which are necessary for the survival of brain cells, contribute to the progression of Alzheimer's," says senior author Suzanne M. de la Monte, MD, MPH, a neuropathologist at Rhode Island Hospital and a professor of pathology at Brown Medical School. "This raises the possibility of a Type 3 diabetes."

In an academic paper published in Current Alzheimer Research (2012), Dr. de la Monte reviews the growing body of evidence suggesting that Alzheimer's is fundamentally a metabolic disease in which the brain's ability to use glucose and produce energy is impaired. In one study, for example, de la Monte and her colleagues found that blocking insulin's path to the brain resulted in Alzheimer's-like neurodegeneration in rats.

Dr. de la Monte has also found that chemical preservatives we eat get past the blood brain barrier and cause neurodegeneration. She says the worst chemical is nitrosamines that are ingested or are made in our bodies that have the ability to enter the brain to cause the degeneration. Dr. de la Monte also says that the brain makes its own insulin and when the toxic chemicals enter the brain, it makes the brain become insulin resistant. Evidently the brain needs insulin to function and if it is not there the brain starts to atrophy allowing the amyloid plaque to form in the brain. (http://www.ncbi.nlm.nih.gov/pmc/articles/PMC3349985/)

Another expert is of the opinion that declining insulin levels might be an important feature of Alzheimer's disease, but may not be the entire story. "There is now increasing evidence primarily from observational studies that diabetes, its predecessor metabolic syndrome, and insulin resistance are implicated in increasing the risk for Alzheimer's disease," said Hugh C. Hendrie, M.D., professor of psychiatry and co-director of the Center for Alzheimer's Disease and Related Neuropsychiatric Disorders at Indiana

University Center for Aging Research in Indianapolis, Indiana.

Other researchers at Albany University in New York concur that there is a growing body of evidence that Alzheimer's is actually a late stage of another disease, type 2 diabetes. Research and experiments that involves feeding laboratory rats a diet designed to give them type 2 diabetes leaves their brains riddled with insoluble plaques of a protein called beta-amyloid – one of the indicators of Alzheimer's. It is a scientific fact that insulin plays a key role in memory. These two findings, coupled together give a strong indication that Alzheimer's might be caused by a type of brain diabetes. Research performed by Professor Ewan McNay, Ph. D. at Albany University in New York found that Alzheimer's, a neurodegenerative disorder may actually be a late stage of Type 2 diabetes. (http://timesofindia.indiatimes.com/topic/Alzheimer%27s-Disease, http://timesofindia.indiatimes.com/topic/neurodegenerative-disorder)

The findings also suggest that losing weight and exercising may ward off Alzheimer's, at least in the very early stages. His research indicates that the extra insulin produced by those with Type 2 diabetes also gets into the brain, disrupting its chemistry, which can lead to the formation of toxic clumps of amyloid proteins that poison brain cells. "The discovery could explain why people who develop Type II diabetes often show sharp declines in cognitive function, with an estimated 70 per cent developing Alzheimer's - far more than in the rest of the population," said Ewan McNay at Albany University in New York. "People who develop diabetes have to realize this is about more than controlling their weight or diet. It's also the first step on the road to cognitive decline," Dr. McNay said. McNay's research aimed at discovering the mechanism by which Type II diabetes might cause Alzheimer's. McNay fed rats on a high-fat diet to induce Type II diabetes and then carried out memory tests, showing that the animals' cognitive skills deteriorated rapidly as the disease progressed. An examination of animals' brains showed clumps of amyloid protein had formed, similar to the kind found in the brains of Alzheimer's patients. McNay suggests that, in people with Type 2 diabetes, the body becomes resistant to insulin, a hormone that controls blood-sugar levels - so the body produces more of it. He further suggests, however, that some of that insulin also makes its way into the brain, where its levels are meant to be controlled by the same enzyme that breaks down amyloid.

"High levels of insulin swamp this enzyme so that it stops breaking down amyloid. The latter then accumulates until it forms toxic clumps that poison brain cells. It's the same amyloid build-up to blame in both diseases - Type II diabetics really do have low-level Alzheimer's," McNay said. Should that be the case, the memory problems that are frequently associated with type 2 diabetes may in fact be early-stage Alzheimer's rather than mere cognitive decline. What does this potentially mean for Baltimore and Maryland seniors with Type II diabetes? It is estimated that approximately 35 million people have Alzheimer's disease. Statistics bare out that most patients have Alzheimer's long-term care that is very expensive.

It is estimated that by 2050 that number of people having Alzheimer's is expected to approach 105 million. We still don't really know what causes the disease or how it destroys the brain. With no known way to prevent Alzheimer's disease and the concurrent spike in the diabetes epidemic the cost of Alzheimer's could cost into the trillions

Other complications of seniors with diabetes

Managing diabetes or preventing diabetes also may help prevent Alzheimer's disease and other dementias. Preventing diabetes or managing it successfully may help people avoid other complications, such as:

- Heart disease
- Stroke
- Eye damage
- Kidney disease
- Damage to the nerves, which may cause pain in the feet or hands (diabetic neuropathy)
- Digestive problems
- Gum disease
- Carpal tunnel syndrome

Several steps to prevent or manage diabetes and avoid potential complications. Patients should:

- Follow their health care team's recommendations about the most appropriate plan for monitoring your blood glucose, cholesterol level and blood pressure.
- Eat healthy foods, including fruits, vegetables, whole grains, lean meats, and low-fat milk and cheese.
- If overweight, eat a healthy diet and exercise to lose weight. Obesity can lead to diabetes and other health problems.
- Exercise at least 30 minutes most days of the week.
- Brush and floss their teeth daily.
- Examine their feet daily for sores.
- Take any prescribed medications on schedule.

Small steps can make a big difference. In a large study funded by the National Institute of Diabetes and Digestive and Kidney Diseases, participants with blood sugar levels slightly above normal (prediabetes) cut their risk of developing type 2 diabetes by more than 50 percent.

Conclusions and Policy Recommendations

Diabetes is called "The Silent Killer" because its symptoms often go unnoticed. Because there is a connection between obesity and diabetes, a strategy to reduce diabetes is to get the Baltimore community to make a concerted effort to lose weight. Seniors should reduce the amount of fat and carbohydrates in their diet. On the other end of the spectrum, parents should encourage the public school system to reduce the amount of fatty and processed foods served at lunch. A change in diet that encourages eating more fresh vegetables and less meat may help swing the tide of the growing obesity epidemic in youth. Neighborhood and community associations should be encouraged to organize community walks and promote children's participation in organized youth sports programs. Employees might consider incorporating 10-minute exercise breaks at work, or hold competitions for weight loss among employees. Churches and faith-based organizations should increase their emphasis on church-organized exercise programs and encourage eating less fried foods at church events.

The African American community must get serious about preventing diabetes and its related diseases and conditions such as hypertension and obesity. In 2013, The Maryland General Assembly passed a law mandating diabetes education in all state public schools ages K-12. The Maryland State Senate and House of Delegate failed to include a fiscal note to the legislation, meaning there is no money in the state budget to implement the diabetes education bill. The public should lobby its representatives in Annapolis to fund this unfunded mandate

Families caring for seniors should be encouraged to reduce the fat content in foods served to the elderly. More fresh vegetables and fiber should be incorporated into the diets of seniors.

Public Health in the Context of the March on Washington

Stacey K. Dennis and Stacey-Ann Dyce

The Baltimore City Health Department (BCHD) is the oldest continually operating health department in the United States. By 1963, the health department had grown to accommodate a city with nearly 1 million residents (Baltimore City Health Department, 1963). There were four health department clinics: Eastern, Western, Druid, Southern and Southeastern Districts. Its first public health efforts in the early 19th century involved the constant fight to stop the spread of small pox and yellow fever. In fact, until the mid 1960's communicable infections, such as tuberculosis and polio were the main concerns of the BCHD. Public heath vaccination programs initiated in the late 1950's cause an elimination of preventable diseases such a paralytic poliomyelitis, diphtheria and smallpox. However, by 1963, the health department was still combating incidences of tuberculosis, syphilis and hepatitis and major outbreaks of influenza. In the 50 years since the MoW, Baltimore City's population has decreased by 1/3 its size in the mid-1960s, due to factors such as the demise of well paying blue collar manufacturing and Port of Baltimore jobs. The health department has since followed suit and decreased the number of public health clinics to only two- the Eastern Clinic, located near the Johns Hopkins Hospital, and the Druid Health District Clinic located on the Westside of Baltimore. In addition, Baltimore City's population in 1963 was 2/3 white, but in 2010, the U.S Census proved the Baltimore City's population of about 622,000 is now 2/3 African American (U.S Census Bureau, 2014).

Has the health department continued to be effective to the needs of the community in the 50 years since the March on Washington? The original organizers of the March on Washington (MoW) did not include public health, and certainly not sexual health education and services, within their scope of social and legislative injustices. Justifiably, issues involving police brutality, voting rights and segregation took center stage in the media and in communities across the country. However, when the wide differences in the incidence of STDs between white Americans and minorities in Baltimore City are examined, a case for making health disparities a civil rights issue may be made. Of the many health disparities that can be analyzed, Chlamydia, gonorrhea and HIV rates among Baltimore City's adolescent and young adults will be analyzed.

Chlamydia and Gonorrhea among Adolescents

In the 1963 Health Commissioner's report, the BCHD noted that the city's syphilis rate was far above that of the nation with a primary and secondary syphilis rate of 45.5/100,000 compared to 11.5/100,000 for the U.S. The health commissioner notes that the increased rates in primary and secondary syphilis rates were due to the promiscuity of Baltimore's teenagers, whose syphilis rates for those ages 0-19 were higher than the national average (22.3/100,000 compared to 5.8/100,000 respectively) (Baltimore City Health Department, 1963). The majority of the syphilis cases in Baltimore were a result of diagnosis made at one of the Baltimore City clinics.

Another pervasive STD in 1963 was gonorrhea. The 1963 health commissioner's report stated that 5,256 cases of gonorrhea were reported to the health department, 4,532 of which were diagnosed within health department clinics. Please note, the diagnosis of "Chlamydia" was not made at the time. Instead, there was diagnosis of Lymphogranuloma venereum, a chronic long term infection of the lymphatic system caused by Chlamydia trachomatis bacteria. The overwhelming majority of health department patients were "colored" based on the clinic visit data (1,266 white client visits vs. 16,658 "colored" clinic visits) (Baltimore City Health Department, 1963).

Baltimore City's population of 929,000 was 2/3 white and 1/3 "non-white". The majority of the people who visited the venereal disease clinics in 1963 were non-white, according to the health commissioner report. There were a total of 17,926 admissions to the veneral disease clinics in 1963. "Colored" clients accounted for 16,568 of those visits. Dr. Robert Farber, Baltimore City Health Commissioner, listed promiscuity, low income and "socially distressed conditions", and a "need to change the morale climate among the residents of the city living in socially distressed conditions" as the causes for the increase in diseases (Baltimore City Health Department, 1963, p. 27). He also noted that lack of education, overconfidence in available treatment regimens and lack of access to care may also be important factors in the city's venereal disease epidemic.

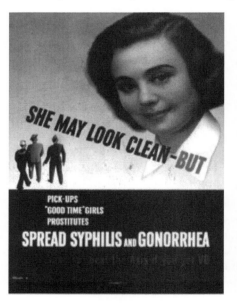

The concept of sex education during the turbulence of the 1960's was challenging, at best. Medical and public health professionals tried their best to safely place the concept of sex in the realms of morality and marriage. Short classroom films detailed human body functions during puberty in a scholarly manner while emphasizing that changes in the body are preparing young adults for procreation within marriage. Public health campaigns in the era during and following WWII were aimed at keeping soldiers and other young men "healthy" and clean of venereal diseases (National Institutes of Health- National Library of Medicine, 2011).

Source: She May Look Clean- But Pick-ups "Good Time Girls" Prostitutes Spread Syphilis and Gonorrhea. Poster Courtesy of the National Institutes of Health. 1940.

However, the socially rebellious times leading up to the Vietnam War and the approval of the birth control pill in 1960 helped to usher in changes in regards to sex. The advantages of contraception outside of marriage were still controversial topics, abortion was illegal and homosexuality was a mental problem best left to therapists to "cure". Drug stores often refused to sell condoms to unmarried men and it was not inappropriate to ask an unmarried woman about any pre-marital sexual activity (Lord, 2011). The Supreme Court ruled in favor of the rights of unmarried couples to access contraceptives only in 1972 (The American Voice 2004: A Pocket Guide to Issues and Allegations, 2004). However, many national groups, including the U.S Public Health Service and the Sexuality Information and Education Council of the United States, formed in 1964, called for the expansion of sex education standards to become up to date with the expanded views on sex and the expanded sexual activity of U.S residents.

Adolescent Sexual Health in Baltimore Today

The epidemiological data available today is more precise. Today, young people under the age of 18 years of age total 133,818, or roughly 21.5%, of Baltimore City's 622,410 residents, according to the 2010 census (United States Census Bureau, 2014). Yet, this age group also experiences the highest rates of Chlamydia and gonorrhea infection, compared to other age groups in the entire state. According to data compiled by Maryland's Infectious Disease and Environmental Health Administration (IDEHA), Baltimore City's adolescents aged 15-19 have Chlamydia and gonorrhea rates that far exceed any other age group's morbidity rate in the state.

TABLE 1: *Morbidity rates are per 100,000 people

Age Group	Maryland Counties Chlamydia		Baltimore City Chlamydia		Maryland Counties Gonorrhea		Baltimore City Gonorrhea	
	Cases	Rates	Cases	Rates	Cases	Rates	Cases	Rates
0-4	6	1.8	0	0	0	0	1	2.4
5-9	5	1.5	1	2.8	1	0.3	5	5.5
10-14	172	49.5	221	638.2	20	5.8	46	132.8
15-19	**5745**	**1593.2**	**3052**	**7399.5**	**922**	**255.7**	**538**	**1304.4**
20-24	7539	2169.2	2716	4853.6	1337	384.7	635	1134.8
25-29	2951	852.3	953	1621.3	640	184.9	313	532.5
30-34	1164	344.8	377	787.4	333	98.6	168	350.9
40-44	329	8602	96	250.7	127	33.3	54	141.0
45-54	266	32.3	98	113.8	146	17.7	79	91.7
55-64	52	7.9	31	43.3	30	4.5	19	26.5
65+	16	2.4	4	5.5	14	2.1	2	2.7
Total	18819	357.6	7715	1239.1	3742	71.1	1944	312.2

SOURCE: Maryland Infectious Disease and Environmental Health Administration website. Annual STD Ranking County Sex Age. June 10, 2014.

Baltimore City's 15-19 year olds had a Chlamydia rate of 7,399.5/100,000 people compared to 1,593.2/100,000 for all of Maryland's combined. The rate of gonorrhea for the city's 15-19 year olds measured 1,304.4/100,000 compared to 255.7/100,000 for all Maryland counties combined.

A closer look into the health of individual neighborhoods may give some insight into the youth behavior. The majority of these cases are located in neighborhoods characterized by lower income housing. A Chlamydia rate incidence map, or "Hot Spot" map, developed by the Baltimore City Health Department (BCHD) gives a visual representation, by zip code, of where chlamydia cases are clustered. The map shows that a majority of the city's zip codes have rates of at least 860/100,000, with the exception of a few low morbidity areas along the Baltimore City-Baltimore County line and in the higher economic status neighborhoods. On the West side of the city, residents living in zip codes 21217, 21216, 21223, and 21207 have the highest number of Chlamydia cases. Residents living in the East side zip codes of 21205, 21213 and 21222 have case rates higher than 1308/100,000.

MAP 1: Newly Diagnosed Chlamydia Cases

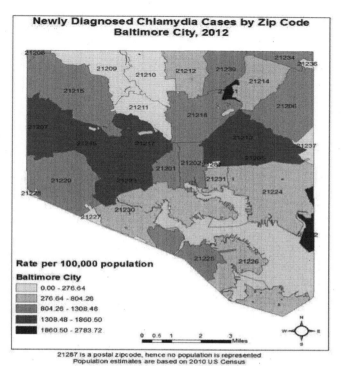

Source: Baltimore City Health Department, Sexually Transmitted Disease Program, 2013

The heaviest concentrations of cases, oddly, are clustered around the locations of the city's two STI clinics. In fairness, one of the reasons for the high incidence in these areas could be that access to clinic services may be easier for the adolescents in these areas. The West side clinic, located in zip code 21217, contains the Upton, Bolton Hill, Reservoir Hill, Forest Park and Druid Heights neighborhoods. The area around the East side clinic, located near the extensive Johns Hopkins Medical campus, contains the Belair/Edison, Greenmount East and Perkins neighborhoods. In addition, the populations in these areas are offered free testing, from various sources, frequently. So it may not be that there are new cases, just that the cases that are available are being found. In stark contrast are neighborhoods, such as Guilford, Bolton Hill and Lauraville, whose residents have, on average, a higher socioeconomic status and live in stable communities. Outreach vehicles rarely, if ever, go into those neighborhoods and offer testing.

According to the 2011 Neighborhood Health Profile conducted by the Baltimore City Hill Department, these neighborhoods are characterized by many families living at or below the poverty rate, elevated school absenteeism, violence, vacant houses and an unemployment rate greater than the city rate (chart 2). These areas are overwhelmingly

African American and, on average, one third of the households are led by a single parent.

TABLE 2: Data from 2011 Baltimore City Neighborhood Health Profile. Baltimore City Health Department.

Neighbor-hoods	Percentage of Median Household Income Less than $25,000	Percentage of Families in Poverty	Percentage of High School Students Missing 20+ Days	Non-Fatal Shooting Rate/ Homicide Incidence Rate per 10,000 Residents	Vacant Building Density per 10,000 housing Units
Baltimore City	33.3%	11.1%	39.2%	46.5/20.9	567.2
Upton	67.1%	48.8%	49.0%	108.7/37.9	1380.5
Forest Park/ Walbrook	40.9%	12.4%	44.3%	46.7/27.4	321.2
Penn-North/ Reservoir Hill	41.4%	19.0%	47.8%	53.8/27.9	935.0
Greater Mondawmin	36.5%	10.2%	39.4%	77.1/ 31.1	844.9
Greenmount East	57.3%	19.7%	45.3%	115.5/39.9	3515.7
Belair-Edison	21.5%	14.0%	42.1%	42.5/24.1	152.1
Perkins/ Middle East	56.7%	17.5%	47.2%	117.7/46.5	2265.3
Madison/East End	40.5%	40.5%	52.6%	169.6/46.3	2697.1

SOURCE: Baltimore City Neighborhood Profile Snapshot

The high incidence of Chlamydia and gonorrhea among Baltimore's young people runs counter to the decrease in their self-reported sexual risk activity. According to the 2007 and 2013 High School Youth Behavior Risk Survey, conducted by the Centers for Disease Control and Prevention (CDC), there has been a 12% decrease in the number of high school teens who report ever having sex (Centers for Disease Control and Prevention, 2014). The percentage of high school males who admitted to having sex for the first time, before the age of 13, decreased from 31.5% to 26.6% while the percentage of high school females who admitted to sex, before age 13, dropped from 7.5% to 3.4%. Likewise, both groups reported a decrease in the percentage of males and females who have had more than four sex partners in their lifetime, 45.1% to 36.9% for males and 17.0% to 10.5% for females.

Sexual Health Education…Again

If Baltimore's high school student population, as a group, is decreasing the rate of their high risk sexual behavior, what is causing the high Chlamydia and gonorrhea infection rates in this cohort? The answer may be found in their use of barrier methods. When asked about condom use during the last sexual act in the 2013 survey, 35% of Baltimore City high school students stated that they did not use a condom. This is an increase of 10% from the 2007 survey. The survey does not explore the reasons adolescents chose not to use condoms, information that could be helpful to education and public health leaders in developing HIV/STI prevention programs. However, the survey does ask students if they were ever taught about HIV or AIDS infections in school. In the 2007 survey, 11% of students stated that they were never taught about HIV/AIDS in school while in 2013, 22.7% of students denied being taught about HIV/AIDS in school.

Evidence based, timely, and well communicated information by a trained sexual health education professional is essential to providing an opportunity for adolescents to explore their attitudes and values about sexuality, develop relationship skills and to, ultimately, help them exercise personal responsibility in their sexual relationships (Sexuality Information and Education Council of the United States, 2005). In addition, although HIV has a successful treatment regime, it is still a deadly virus if left untreated or if the treatment is mismanaged. The number of students who deny that basic disease prevention and sexual health information is provided in schools is alarming and may explain the disease incidence rates among that group.

Although a significant portion of Baltimore City students deny receiving information about HIV/AIDS in school, the Maryland State Department of Education's Comprehensive Health Education Curriculum states that students are introduced to the subject of HIV/AIDS beginning in the 5th grade, around age 10. The curriculum requires that students learn the modes of disease transmission, identify the risk behaviors that lead to disease transmission, and identify prevention methods (Maryland State Department of Education). In grade 8, students delve deeper into the subject by learning the specific symptoms of HIV/AIDS, describing the diseases effects on the body, treatment methods and, again, prevention methods.

The Maryland state curricula for high school students takes a significant pro-abstinence stance with class discussions centered on the limits, consequences, and influences on sexual activity. There are also discussions on contraception, healthy and unhealthy relationships, and pregnancy prevention.

Maryland education code requires that the sex education course be designed by the school board, working with the local health department and an appointed citizen advisory committee. Parents can opt their child out of the classes. The Chlamydia and gonorrhea surveillance data suggests that the current courses are not sufficient to meet the needs of Baltimore's adolescents.

Comprehensive sexual health education is as essential to adolescent health as are vaccinations and nutrition. An effective sex education curriculum gives students knowledge "and skills to make responsible choices in their lives, particularly in a context where they have greater exposure to sexually explicit material through the internet and other media" (UNESCO, 2009, p. 2). The goals of sexuality education are simple: to increase an adolescent's understanding and knowledge about sexual health, promote healthy behaviors, explore and clarify their feelings and attitudes about their own sexuality and explore their own cultural beliefs. The role schools play in providing that education is critical given that teens spend a considerable amount of time in primary education until about the age of 18 and many adolescents have their first sexual experiences before leaving high school.

HIV/AIDS in Baltimore
According to the Center for Disease Control (CDC) the Baltimore metropolitan area (includes Baltimore City, Baltimore, Anne Arundel, Harford, Howard, Carroll Counties) has the sixth highest rate of HIV diagnoses in the nation (Maryland Department of Health and Mental Hygiene, 2014).[1] This is actually an improvement from the rates in 2008 when Baltimore was ranked third.

TABLE 3: Estimated HIV Diagnoses during 2011, Ranked by Rates

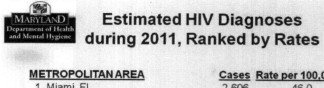

Estimated HIV Diagnoses during 2011, Ranked by Rates

METROPOLITAN AREA	Cases	Rate per 100,000
1. Miami, FL	2,606	46.0
2. New Orleans-Metairie-Kenner, LA	513	43.0
3. Baton Rouge, LA	336	41.6
4. Jackson, MS	200	36.7
5. Washington, DC-VA-MD-WV	1,969	34.5
6. Baltimore-Towson, MD	922	33.8
7. Memphis, TN-MS-AR	433	32.6
8. Atlanta-Sandy Springs-Marietta, GA	1,626	30.3
9. New York, NY-NJ-PA	5,344	28.1
10. Jacksonville, FL	382	28.1
United States	50,161	15.9

CDC. HIV Surveillance Report, 2011. Vol. 23. Table 23.

Maryland Prevention and Health Promotion Administration April 28, 2014

SOURCE: Maryland Department of Health and Mental Hygiene Prevention and Health Promotion Administration (DHMH). HIV in the Central Region: An Epidemiological Profile. 2014, slide 7

As a region, of the 28,978 people living with HIV, 41% live in Baltimore City.[2] Even more alarming, while African Americans only make up 28% of the population of Maryland, we make up close to 80% of all new HIV diagnoses.[3]

FIGURE 1: Maryland Adult/Adolescent Living HIV Cases by Region

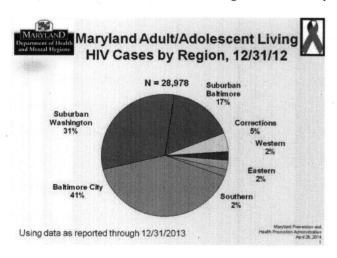

SOURCE: Maryland Department of Health and Mental Hygiene Prevention and Health Promotion Administration (DHMH). HIV in the Central Region: An Epidemiological Profile. 2014, slide 12

FIGURE 2: Adult/Adolescent Population and Living HIV Cases by Race

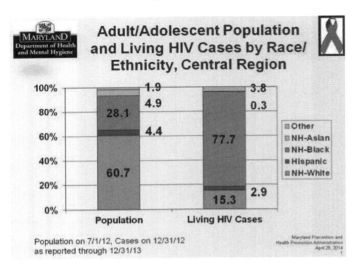

SOURCE: *Maryland Department of Health and Mental Hygiene Prevention and Health Promotion Administration (DHMH). HIV in the Central Region: An Epidemiological Profile. 2014, slide 23*

Of the 80% of new diagnoses of HIV, African American men who have sex with men between the ages 20-29 account for approximately 60% of those new diagnoses.

FIGURE 3: Reported Adult/Adolescent HIV Diagnosis Exposure Trends

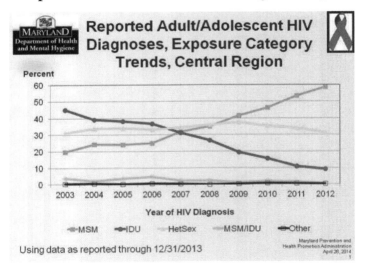

SOURCE: *Maryland Department of Health and Mental Hygiene Prevention and Health Promotion Administration (DHMH). HIV in the Central Region: An Epidemiological Profile. 2014, slide 28*

Before the landmark advent of the Affordable Healthcare Act, HIV/AIDS was the only disease for which the U.S. provides universal health care through a discretionary government programs,[5] the Ryan White Comprehensive AIDS Resources Emergency (CARE) Act in 1990. Despite the efforts of public health providers, retention in specialized infectious disease health care for people living with HIV/AIDS continues to be an issue. Of the 19,723 people living with HIV in the Baltimore metropolitan area, only 9,754 are retained in adequate medical care.[6]

FIGURE 4: Continuum of Care

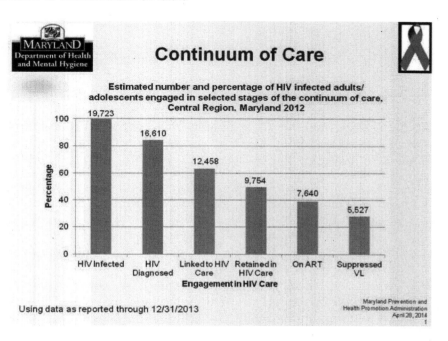

SOURCE: Maryland Department of Health and Mental Hygiene Prevention and Health Promotion Administration (DHMH). HIV in the Central Region: An Epidemiological Profile. 2014, slide 28

It is redundant to say that there is an HIV epidemic in the Greater Baltimore area. Baltimoreans have been witness to the effects of the disease on our communities and families since the beginning of the epidemic close to 30 years ago. It is still a disease of the marginalized members of our communities, the poor, people of color and sexual minorities, and the face of the epidemic has shifted yet again evidenced by the numbers and has a brown face. This shifting shows the influence of social and cultural factors on the transmission of HIV. Health disparities in marginal populations of the United States are not a new phenomenon and health disparities do not happen randomly, the range of causal factors do have a common thread, their roots are in denied social justice. Disparities in health status among different population groups are unjust and inequitable because they resulted from preventable, avoidable, systemic conditions and policies. They are not primarily the result of accidents of nature or through individual pathology, but result from patterned, long-standing historical social conditions generated by social and economic inequality.[7] There are numerous examples of historically based systematic inequalities including the GI Bill, red-lining practices, urban renewal policies, education funding policies and practices, drug use and incarceration policies, welfare policy, affordable housing policies and health insurance policies that continue to create conditions under which health disparities are created and exacerbated. The decades of discriminatory practices could only be understood through the lens of "institutionalized racism". According to Dr. Camara Jones, institutionalized racism is "differential access to the goods, services, and opportunities of society by race…it is normative, sometimes legalized, and often manifests as an inherited disadvantage. It is structural, having been codified in our institutions of custom, practice, and law, so there need not be an identifiable perpetrator. Indeed, institutionalized racism is often evident as inaction in the face of need."[8] Systemically starving neighborhoods of access to key social goods such as education, Health care, adequate housing, recreational amenities, etc., causes adverse social and physical environments within the larger community.[9] The accumulative effect of discriminatory practices and social policies creates an environment devoid of vision for the future and of hope. A sense of futurelessness adds to negative self-image, self-destructive behaviors and risk-taking.

Public health interventions generally focus on four levels: 1) individual, 2) group, 3) neighborhood/community, and 4) the larger society/policy arena. These interventions are characterized by the use of a medical model focusing on clinical and preventive services, but often do not address the other determinants that cause and fuel health disparities. The possible solutions lay in a targeted neighborhood level holistic approach that simultaneously works on other levels that counters the policies, politics and practices that fuel health disparities, working though the practice of social justice. A holistic, just approach includes interventions that address the physical environment, the social environment, and counter persistent discriminatory social policies and practices in addition to the medical model of treatment and prevention.[10]

According to the National Association of County and City Health Officials (NA-CCHO) *Tackling Health Inequities Through Public Health Practice,* a social justice practice in public health requires:

- Sustained action on the underlying injustice rather than treating symptoms or consequences. Identify social and physical environmental needs, and address the need on each level.

- Increasing the voice and influence of affected communities by building community capacity and capital. Using the power of the vote.

- Convening relevant parties and institutions that can change social conditions by partnering with advocates and systems supportive of increasing and sustaining access to critical social goods.

- Support health equity as a social right.[11]

Several authors have noted that the passage of the American Care Act (ACA) will work towards reducing health disparities because it will give minorities access to better medical care (Cohen, 2013). African American communities are resilient and have strengths that have ensured our survival for centuries. We have fought and continue to fight for parity, reframing the concept of health improvement from an entirely medical model to that of social justice and health as a right, may be a key to begin the work needed to eliminate health disparities amongst African Americans. The mission of the Urban League movement is to enable African Americans to secure economic self-reliance, parity, power and civil rights, improvements in these four areas means improvements in health.

References

Aspen Institute Roundtable on Community Change. (2006). *Community Change: Theories, Practice and Evidence.* Washingotn, D.C: Aspen Institute.

Baltimore City Health Department. (1963). One hundred and Forty-Ninth Annual Report of the Department of Health. Baltimore: Baltimore City Health Department.

Centers for Disease Control and Prevention. (2007 March). A Heightened National Response to the HIV/AIDS Crisis Among African Americans. Retrieved 2014 йил 11-June from http://www.cdc.gov/hiv/topics/aa/resources/reports/heightenedresponse.htm

Centers for Disease Control and Prevention. (2006 10-February). Racial/Ethnic Disparities in the Diagnosis of HIV/AIDS:33 States 2001-2004. MMWR, pp. 121-125.

Centers for Disease Control and Prevention. (2014, June 16). Youth Online: High School YRBS Baltimore 2013. Retrieved from Centers for Diisease Control and Prevention: http://nccd.cdc.gov/youthonline/App/Results.aspx?TT=A&OUT=0&SID=HS&QID=QQ&LID=BA&YID=2013&LID2=&YID2=&COL=S&ROW1=N&ROW2=N&HT=C4&LCT=LL&FS=S1&FR=R1&FG=G1&FSL=S1&FRL=R1&FGL=G1&PV=&TST=False&C1=&C2=&QP=G&DP=1&VA=CI&CS=Y&SYID=&EYID=&SC=DEFAULT&SO=ASC&pf=1

Chambers, S. M. (2006). *Fighting for our Lives: AIDS Community and the Politics of Disease.* New Brunswick: Rutgers University.

Cohen, R. (2013 23-August). Racial Disparities in Healthcare: A New Frontier for Civil Rights. *USA Today.*

Collins-Hill, P. (2004). *Black Sexual Politics, African Americans, Gender and the New Racism.* New York: Rutledge.

Jones, C. (2000). Levels of Racism: A Theoretic Framework and a Gardener's Tale. *American Journal of Public Health,* 1212-1215.

Lord, A. (2011). *Condom Nation: The U.S Government's Sex Eduacation Campaign from World War I to the Internet.* Baltimore: Johns Hopkins University Press.

Maryland Department of Health and Mental Hygiene. (2014 28-April). HIV in the central region: An Epidemiolgical Profile.

Maryland Department of Health and Metal Hygiene. (2014 28-April). HIV in Central Maryland: An Epidemiologic Profile. Retrieved 2014 11-June from Maryland Department of Health and Mental Hygiene: http://phpa.dhmh.maryland.gov/OIDEOR/CHSE/SiteAssets/SitePages/statistics/Central%20RAC%20Epi%20Presentation%202014.pdf

Maryland State Department of Education. (n.d.). Teaching and Learning Health. Retrieved from School Improvement in Maryland: http://www.mdk12.org/instruction/curriculum/health/index.html

National Association of County and City Health Officials. (2006). Tackling Health Inequities Through Public Health Practice. Retrieved 2014 йил 11-June from National Association of County and City Health Officials: http://www.naccho.org/topics/justice/upload/naccho_handbook_hyperlinks_000.pdf

National Institutes of Health- National Library of Medicine. (2011 8-September). Visual Culture and Public Health Posters. Retrieved 2014 6-July from http://www.nlm.nih.gov/exhibition/visualculture/infectious21.html

Padamsee, T. J. (2008). An Integrated Account of HIV/AIDS Policy Making: Health Care Institutions, Discourses of Risk and Political Action. Retrieved 2014 11-June from All Academic: http://www.allacademic.com/meta/p242318.index.html

Sexuality Information and Education Council of the United States. (2005). *Guidelines for Comprehensive Sexuality Education,* 3rd Ed. New York, NY: SEICUS.

The American Voice 2004: A Pocket Guide to Issues and Allegations. (2004 26-April). Issues and Allegations: Sex Education. Retrieved 2014 6-July from http://static.ilsr.org/voice2004/health/sexeducation.html

U.S Census Bureau. (2014 11-June). State and county Quick Facts: Baltimore City. Retrieved July 2014-6 from http://quickfacts.census.gov/qfd/states/24/24510.html

UNESCO. (2009). *International Technical Guidance on Sexuality Education.* Paris: UNESCO.

United States Census Bureau. (2014, March 27). State and County Quick Facts. Retrieved from United States Census Bureau: http://quickfacts.census.gov/qfd/states/24/24510.html

Van Ryn, M., & Fu, S. S. (2003). Paved with Good Intentions: Do Public Health and Human Service Providers Contribute to Racial/ Ethnic Disparities in Health? *American Journal of Public Health,* 248-255.

Notes

[1] Maryland Department of Health and Mental Hygiene Prevention and Health Promotion Administration (DHMH). HIV in the Central Region: An Epidemiological Profile. 2014, slide 7

[2] DHMH, HIV in the Central Region, slide12.

[3] DHMH, HIV in the Central Region, slide 23

[4] DHMH, HIV in the Central Region, slide 28

[5] DHMH, HIV in the Central Region, slide 31

[6] The National Association of County and City Health Officials (NACCHO).

Tackling Health Inequities Through Public Health Practice: A handbook for Action. Edited by Richard Hofrichter. Pg 5

7   C. P. Jones, "Levels of Racism: A Theoretic Framework and a Gardener's Tale," American Journal of Public Health 90 (2000): 1212-1215.

8   (NACCHO). Tackling Health Inequities Pg. 11

9   (NACCHO). Tackling Health Inequities Pg. 14

10   (NACCHO). Tackling Health Inequities Pg. 32

Part Two
Resources for Education and Change

In addition to the strategies and resources in the chapter in Part Two, some resources that give more information about the chapters in this section include:

National Clinical Trials Database

- http://www.clinicaltrials.gov/
- National Institutes of Health - Clinical Center (The National Institutes of Health (NIH) Clinical Center in Bethesda, Maryland, is the nation's largest hospital devoted entirely to clinical research.) http://clinicalcenter.nih.gov/

Local Institutions:

- University of Maryland: http://umm.edu/research
- Johns Hopkins School of Public Health Center for Clinical Trials: http://www.jhsph.edu/research/centers-and-institutes/johns-hopkins-center-for-clinical-trials/
- MedStar Health Research Institute: https://www.medstarhealth.org/research/Pages/Research-Areas.aspx

Cultural Competency in Health:

- Enhancing Minority Participation in Clinical Trials (EMPACT) Consortium -http://www.empactconsortium.com/training-course/cultural-competency/
- Cultural Competency and Health -http://www.nih.gov/clearcommunication/culturalcompetency.htm
- NIH "Think Cultural Health" Initiative -https://www.thinkculturalhealth.hhs.gov/cloudsearch/KeywordSearch_RightNav.asp?id=4
- HHS Office of Minority Health - http://minorityhealth.hhs.gov/

Diabetes:

- Diabetes Awareness Project
  www.diabetesawarenessproject.org
- Physicians for Responsible Medicine Diabetes Project
  http://www.pcrm.org/health/diabetes-resources/
- Diabetes and Weight control
  www.NutritionMD.org
- Diabetes Research institute
  http://www.diabetesresearch.org/diabetes-research-institute
- International Diabetes Federation
  http://www.idf.org/
- Centers for Disease Control and Prevention
  http://www.cdc.gov/diabetes/
- National Institute of Diabetes and Kidney Disease
  http://www.nih.gov/about/almanac/organization/NIDDK.htm
- Diabetes Clinical Trials Mayo Clinic
  http://www.mayoclinic.org/diseases-conditions/diabetes/care-at-mayo-clinic/clinical-trials/con-20033091

Sexual Health:

- Sexuality Information and Education Council of the United States
  http://www.siecus.org/
- Baltimore City Health Department
  http://health.baltimorecity.gov/
- Maryland Department of Health and Mental Hygiene
  http://phpa.dhmh.maryland.gov/SitePages/phpa.aspx
- World Health Organization
  http://www.who.int/topics/sexual_health/en/

Part Three:
Leadership: Reclaiming Black Power and Looking Forward

Editor's Introduction

The right to vote was a core issue of the U.S. civil rights platform. And, the movement's civil rights leadership emerged organically from youth, civic and labor groups. Built upon a foundation of organizations, the Congress of Racial Equality (CORE), Council of Federated Organizations (COFO), Student Nonviolent Coordination Committee (SNCC), Southern Christian Leadership Conference (SCLC), Mississippi Freedom Democratic Party (MFDP), National Association for the Advancement of Colored People (NAACP) and the National Urban League (NUL) educated, organized and mobilized the masses into a galvanizing force of social change. Locally, the architects of the movement emerged from some of these national organizations, as well as from churches, and student groups from local colleges including what was then Morgan State College. These early protestors set the scene by staging one of the first sit-ins in the country at a Read's store in downtown Baltimore. Baltimore's noted Goon Squad and local leaders also played a role in national leadership and local change. Authors in this section of the volume examine issues including leadership; voting; elections; the need to re-envision practices, policies and laws; and the role afforded by social media, and virtual, real-time tools in mobilizing the masses for social justice. The volume closes with a call to Black Baltimore to be mindful that the mission for justice, equal access and equality has historically been one of science, law, and faith.

The War on African American Men: The Case for Drug Legalization

William H. "Billy" Murphy, Jr.

The United States has the highest rate of incarceration in the world and keeps 7.2 million men and women under correctional supervision. More than 2.2 million are in prison or jail while nearly five million are monitored in the community on probation or parole." **The Sentencing Project, The State of Sentencing 2013: Developments in Policy and Practice**

"It's clear ... that too many Americans go to too many prisons for far too long and for no good law enforcement reason. ...Although incarceration has a role to play in our justice system, widespread incarceration at the federal, state and local levels is both ineffective and unsustainable." **Attorney General Eric Holder, in a speech at the American Bar Association 2013 Annual Meeting**

The mass incarceration of Black people is the most urgent crisis facing Black America today. It has become the apocalyptic new normal of old racism that systemically uses the 43-year-long War on Drugs to single out and routinely criminalize Black men and disappear them behind prison walls for terms out of proportion to the charges and out of balance with sentences meted out to white men even though government statistics consistently show whites use at least the same amount of illegal drugs as Blacks and in far higher numbers in proportion to their population.

Just seven years after the passage of the landmark Civil Rights Act of 1964, Black men have lost more of their economic, social and political rights, making them no better off today than they were 50 years ago. They have been disenfranchised and criminalized for behavior recognized as addictions driven by medical and psychological dependence. And Black women, traditionally the bedrock of families and communities, have not been immune. From 1977 to 2004, Maryland saw an astounding 353 percent increase in the population of women prisoners, according to data from the Women's Prison Association.

The solution is clear: Decriminalize drugs. Their use is driven by medical and psychological dependency. Redirect money misspent on mass incarcerations to providing medical treatment, education and meaningful employment training.

Black Codes Redux

In Baltimore, as in other major cities with high Black populations, government practices of zero-tolerance, mandatory minimums, and War on Drugs became code for a familiar behavior Black folks recognize as Jim Crow. Under the zero-tolerance policing in Baltimore, thousands of Black people have been routinely arrested without probable cause by Baltimore City Police officers trying to make arrest quotas. The practice made Baltimore, a city with a 63% African American population, a major driver of prison admissions in the state, responsible for 47% of them. A study by the Pew Charitable Trust of incarceration rates in 2008, showed Baltimore as having the second highest incarceration rate in the nation at 6.28 percent per 1,000 residents.

In 2006, zero-tolerance policing and its mass arrests provoked a lawsuit against the city brought on behalf of 13 plaintiffs by the American Civil Liberties Union, the Maryland State Conference and the Baltimore City Branch of the NAACP. The lawsuit laid out what the plaintiffs saw as a broad pattern of abuse in the arrest practices in the Baltimore Police Department (BPD) endorsed and enforced under the leadership of then-Mayor Martin O'Malley. The lawsuit contended that a third of people arrested in the city in 2005 were held, some for weeks, then released without charges and that officers had an incentive to make frivolous arrests since those with the lowest volume of arrests were subject to reassignment.

A settlement agreement came four years later in 2010 requiring that the Police Department be audited to determine its compliance with the suit. In 2012, the First Status Report of Independent Auditor Charles Wellford revealed that the police "did not or could not justify arrests for quality of life offenses in at least 35 percent of the cases examined; that the BPD is almost one and half years late in creating a database to allow it to effectively monitor officer and supervisor behavior; and that the BPD is improperly refusing to give the auditor records of arrests that resulted in persons being released without charge, the very arrests most likely to be improper, and the ones that led to the lawsuit in the first place," the ACLU found in its follow-up.

With the two mayors that followed Mr. O'Malley in office, some things changed for the better. Arrests in the city fell by the tens of thousands but the problems at the overcrowded City Jail and the Detention Center remained practically intact. A 2013 audit conducted by the National Institute of Corrections showed that the facilities were rife with crime, disorder and incompetent, bent staff and administrators. "No standard structure is in place at the city jail for security checks or for how often they are conducted," the audit found. "Many security gates are operated manually and have no electronic controls. Officers have a poor understanding of inmates' civil rights, and holding cells are 'uniformly dirty.'"

The audit also found that walls in some cells were dense with overlapping street-art taggings. Hand-written signs and outdated staff memos littered other walls and toilet paper was stuffed into nearly all the air vents at the central booking facility. No one could explain why. Record-keeping was unreliable; correctional officers in the male and female detention centers, central booking and other jail facilities kept hand-written records of critical inmate movements, "sometimes in erasable pencil."

The City Jail complex includes Central Booking and the Detention Center and holds an average of 4,000 people daily. Now, the jail is not to be confused with the state's prisons. The Jail is the place where the arrested and accused are held pretrial, awaiting their day in court or some kind of adjudication. The people there have been accused of crimes as capital as murder to as ridiculous as a teenager talking back to a cop. They are held there for days, weeks and sometimes months.

Still, silence from the City's leadership. Baltimore is yet to have a mayor to speak out about the unconscionable mass arrests and incarceration practices in forceful terms nor deal with the problems systemically to fix it, prevent abuse and establish balance. Baltimore's mayors have the power of office to make a difference but have been reluctant to use it.

But the City's elected officials are not the only ones failing to utilize the power of their positions. In Baltimore's courts, judges also have squandered leverage. They can use their judicial roles to speak out against injustice, fashion their prison sentences well below the sentencing guidelines to reflect what they know is Black over prosecution and incarceration, document the demographics of cases that come before them, and keep their own statistics collectively in real time rather than rely on what others choose to measure and count.

This action is especially urgent in the matter of the tens of thousands of Black Baltimore citizens languishing in Maryland prisons convicted under the War on Drugs policy and sentenced to mandatory minimums. Many are serving the same punishment for possession of 5 grams of crack as those convicted of possessing 500 grams of cocaine.

Numerous public and private studies of arrest and incarceration policies and practices conducted since the 1970's have shown that racial bias throughout the Criminal Justice System has been influencing arrest, prosecution, and sentencing decisions to the economic, social and political peril of cities like Baltimore with large African American populations. Even though solutions are in plain view, they have escaped the courage or interest of a succession of public officials and the judiciary – Black and White, men and women - who failed to use the powers of their office to make a difference. In 1995, The Center for Institutions and Alternatives studied Baltimore and first realized that 95% of people prosecuted for drugs in Baltimore were Black even though figures showed there is as much use among whites.

The War on Drugs – the numbers

The numbers talk and they say that the so-called War on Drugs is a war against black and brown people who sell and use drugs. By all accounts, this war has been a tragic failure and the key contributor to a second holocaust for Black America. Half of inmates are incarcerated for drug crimes, yet drug usage has risen an astounding 2,800 percent. That's two thousand eight hundred percent.

Like too many other cities around the country, Baltimore City has been plagued with drug crime and usage. Data from the FBI and the U.S. Census between 2001 – 2010 analyzed by the ACLU show that:

1. The drug arrest rate in Baltimore is 11.4 per 1,000 people, the worst in the state.

2. Nearly 30% of all arrests for marijuana possession in the state were in Baltimore City.

3. Blacks in Baltimore City are 5.6 times more likely to be arrested for marijuana possession than whites.

4. Blacks accounted for 92% of all arrests for marijuana possession.

5. 98% of youth arrests for marijuana are Black

6. Blacks were being arrested at a rate of 18 a day compared to the one to two whites a day. Baltimore City spent about $32 million on marijuana enforcement and $10.6 million on recreation centers.

7. Between 2001 and 2010, Black arrests increased by 5,614 compared to the increase by 371 for whites.

Nationally, prosecution of the War on Drugs created overcrowded prisons at an annual cost of $80 billion in 2010. The cost to Maryland that year was $836.2 million or $38,373 per inmate. In FY 2011, the state spent an additional $97 million on the Baltimore City Detention Center and another $53 million on Central Booking and Intake. While the numbers on the balance sheet are easy to add up, the human and moral costs are impossible to calculate, easy to overlook and certain to underestimate.

During the 1980's at least a dozen government, private and nonprofit analysts reviewed the criminal justice system and the impact of the War on Black people. Reports showed that during the prosecution of the initiative, incarceration rates for African American men exploded 700 percent between 1985 and 1995. Nationally, their imprisonment was at a rate six times higher than for white men. In Maryland, the rate was eight times that of whites. Nationally, Blacks served sentences that were 20 percent longer than for white men convicted of similar crimes. Upon release from prison, as with the general ex-prisoner population, they continued to be punished, unable to get work because of a lack of marketplace skills, job training and the onerous stigma of a felony conviction.

In 2010, African American men constituted nearly half of the total 2.4 million incarcerated population; the Maryland prison population was 22,009. A further breakdown of the numbers studied that year showed 1 in 9 black men age 20-34 was imprisoned and 1 in 11 black adults was under correctional supervision. Screen shots of the incarcerated population of African American men in Maryland showed that between 1987 and 2013, the rate fluctuated between a low of 71.9% to a high of 77.2 percent. In its analysis of data on incarceration trends, the ACLU projects that 1 in 3 African American males born today can expect to spend time imprisoned in his lifetime. Disturbing.

Even more unsettling are the statistics on Black youth who represent 26% of juvenile arrests, 44% of youth who are detained, 46% of the youth who are judicially waived to criminal court, and 58% of the youth admitted to state prisons, according to the Center on Juvenile and Criminal Justice.

What's going on?

The over-subscription of African American males in federal and state prisons is neither coincidental nor because Black males are more inclined to a criminal pathology than anyone else. The fact is the mass incarceration of African American males is the direct result of pernicious systemic policies and practices in the Criminal Justice System that target and disenfranchise racial and ethnic minorities. Many independent studies done since early 2000 support this finding. In her 2012 book on mass incarceration, Michelle Alexander appropriately calls it "The New Jim Crow."

In 2003, the numbers of African Americans in prison was so jarringly out of proportion it prompted U. S. Supreme Court Justice Anthony M. Kennedy to comment in a keynote address to the American Bar Association (ABA):

> We must confront another reality. Nationwide, more than 40% of the prison population consists of African-American inmates. About 10% of African-American men in their mid-to-late 20's are behind bars. In some cities, more than 50% of young African-American men are under the supervision of the criminal justice system...Our resources are misspent, our punishments too severe, our sentences too long.

Ten years later U.S. Attorney General Eric Holder was very direct in his conclusions about the numbers. In an address to the 2013 ABA conference and again in commencement remarks at Morgan State University in May 2014, he said plainly, "In our criminal justice system, systemic and unwarranted racial disparities remain disturbingly common."

As a former Circuit Court Judge in Baltimore City and a practicing defense attorney for more than 43 years, I am very familiar with the underlying causes and effects of policies and practices in our system of crime and punishment, justice and injustice and am especially aware of and sensitive to the impact on African American men, their families and their communities. In looking back over the 50 years since the historic March on Washington for Social and Economic Justice, one can see a frustrating pattern of victories and set backs in the law and public policy. The setbacks outweigh the victories when it comes to alleged crime and punishment. Many factors driven by official policies compound to push up incarceration numbers with Black families and communities the collateral damage. Expressions of moral outrage are insufficient. We know the problem: the punitive mass imprisonment of African American males.

The task at hand is to uniformly work up and down the Criminal Justice System with the urgency of a house on fire to end the bigoted practices that target and strip African American men of their liberties. There are a few significant signs of hope. In just 2014, the White House and Attorney General's office announced easing the pressure points in the system at the federal level. A few years ago, Maryland abolished the death penalty as a sentencing option and made other adjustments to ease sentencing practices. Baltimore City is slow to get on board at the earliest point in the process that matters, arrest and charging. Keeping people out of the system who really don't belong there is a pivotal point in alleviating a host of problems troubling Black communities and society at large.

The War on Drugs: Background

The War on Drugs has known no political party bias. It has been prosecuted with escalating enmity by Republican and Democratic Presidents alike from Richard Nixon to William Jefferson Clinton. Jimmy Carter remains the exception. In fact, the largest expansion of the War on Drugs occurred under the "Black friendly" Clinton Administration. Although Clinton advocated for treatment instead of incarceration during his 1992 presidential campaign, once elected he built upon the policies and practices of his predecessors. During his administration, The U.S. Sentencing Commission recommended eliminating the disparity between sentences for crack and powder cocaine and his own Secretary of Health and Human Services, Donna Shalala, proposed ending the federal ban on funding syringe programs. He rejected both recommendations. When Bill Clinton swore the oath to the Presidency, the prison population stood at 1.3 million. It had grown to over 2 million by the time he left office.

The groundwork for bad things happening to Black folks at Draconian levels in the Criminal Justice System was laid by Richard Nixon with his 1971 declaration of a "War on Drugs" that dramatically increased the size and presence of federal drug control. Suddenly, mandatory minimum sentencing and no-knock warrants were the rule of law that expanded prosecutorial and policing practices to an extreme. Even marijuana, which was regarded as the most benign of drugs, was kicked up to the onerous Schedule One category reserved for hard core drugs like heroin.

In 1977, it seemed there would be a return to humanity and common sense with the election of President Jimmy Carter who ran on a platform that included decriminalization of marijuana. His position found gradual support later in 1977 when the Senate Judiciary Committee voted to decriminalize possession of up to an ounce of marijuana for personal use. Then came another election. It delivered to the nation President Reagan and his aggressive, intolerant version of the War on Drugs. He created a drug task force and put Vice President George H. W. Bush in charge. It meant all agencies were pulled into a coordinated assault exercising more powers than they ever had before. More judges, more prosecutors and more law enforcement personnel were conscripted into the effort. New legislation was created to remove barriers to using military radar and intelligence to detect traffickers. Mandatory minimum sentences for low-level offenses were added to the legislative mix. Words like drug lords, continuing criminal enterprise, kilos of cocaine, and crack heightened the courtroom theater for an uninquisitive media who influenced a growing public appetite for punishment which became more influential in a deliberation for a defendant's freedom than the actual circumstances surrounding the charges for the crime.

Under the vice president's leadership, drug-related arrests shot up over 40 percent, the amount of marijuana seized was over 80 percent and, the amount of cocaine seized had doubled. President Reagan proudly declared that all of those numbers amounted to "hurting the traffickers." Unfortunately, tangled in that dragnet were tens of thousands of low-level dealers and no-level drug addicts in a dependent cycle of buying, selling and using. Now they were sent to prison for long stretches. Those who needed treatment for their addictions got none. The War on Drugs was a priority-one criminal justice initiative with catastrophic results for African Americans. The kind of sentence you received didn't matter whether you were caught selling or possessing heroin, marijuana, cocaine, crack, or pain killers. Get caught and one devastating residual effect was your family could be out on the street if you lived with them in public housing thanks to zero tolerance housing policies.

Not a Drug War; a Public Health Dilemma
The War on Drugs quickly began costing state budgets and communities astronomical amounts in fiscal and human capital. Agencies and prisoner advocacy organizations began looking at the economics and studying the impact of the program and recommending ways to rollback the harm being done in a program that was neither sustainable nor effective. The request to end it came from many corners including bi-partisan coalitions in the U.S. Congress. In May 2014, five Nobel prize winning economists joined in a report urging the world's governments to shift the focus from mass incarceration to public health and human rights.

Their recommendations brought to mind the events of 1988 when Kurt L. Schmoke, Baltimore's newly elected Mayor argued for drug decriminalization. He recommended treating the drug abuse issue as a medical rather than criminal problem. The City was in the grips of a drug and medical epidemic with the presence of HIV/Aids. Evidence was emerging that medical treatment for drug addiction was a feasible alternative to wholesale prosecution and incarceration.

The City Health Department had already begun a needle exchange program in the 1980's issuing free syringes to addicts to mitigate dirty needle usage believed to be what was passing along the Aids virus. As a former federal prosecutor and former City State's Attorney, Mr. Schmoke was uniquely familiar with the Criminal Justice System and the prosecution of drug cases. Despite his expertise, his presentation at his first meeting of the National Conference of Mayors was met with a wall of resistance and ultimately national derision. He was ahead of his time. In an interview with the Baltimore Sun in early 2014, Mr. Schmoke, now President of the University of Baltimore, made it clear that he still stands by the recommendation he made 25 years earlier. "My firm belief is, and was during my tenure as mayor, that there should be a war on drugs, but it should be primarily a public health war not a criminal justice war. And it should be a war led by the Surgeon General not the Attorney General."

Had Baltimore adapted a health rather than criminal approach to dealing with drug use we might be further ahead in creating solutions with fewer costs to humanity. Lexington Market and its surrounding streets might not today be the staging area of hundreds of Baltimore's drug addicted walking dead. Maryland's General Assembly came to its senses in 2014 and decriminalized possession of Marijuana. Still, even while federal and state legislators are siding with legalizing marijuana and Nobel Prize winners are making a case for medicalization and decriminalization, Baltimore's Mayor Stephanie Rawlings-Blake remains rigidly against decriminalization. "I don't think it serves anybody's purpose to clog up the system with this type of offense," she told the Baltimore Sun, "but I'm not going to be waving the Schmoke flag of legalization." The mayor did concede that she believes in diversion programs to get people off of drugs before it becomes a criminal justice issue but no city facing the economic and social fallout of its drug prosecution practices has the luxury of ignoring legalization.

Sentencing and Probation Opportunities for Change

Though Circuit Court judges typically adhere to guidelines set by the Maryland State Commission on Criminal Sentencing Policy, (MSCCSP) for sentencing persons convicted of crimes in the state, they don't have to. Maryland Judges are not locked into handing out mandatory minimum sentences. They may impose lower sentences outside the prescribed guidelines and document their reasons.

States that have experienced recent drops in the crime rate also have taken substantial steps to rein in the size and cost of their corrections systems. With the support of their elected officials, leaders in these states have shortened prison terms for lower-level offenders or diverted them from prison altogether. They have reinvested the savings to improve public safety and reduce recidivism.

In August 2010, President Barack Obama signed the Fair Sentencing Act into law, which reduced the discriminatory sentencing disparity between crack cocaine and powder cocaine offenses. Prior to passage of the Fair Sentencing Act, a person charged with possession of just five grams of crack cocaine received the same five-year mandatory minimum sentence as someone caught with 500 grams. The Fair Sentencing law reduced the sentencing disparity from a ratio of 100-to-1 to 18-to-1 and eliminated mandatory minimum sentences for simple possession of crack cocaine.

In 2013, Attorney General Eric Holder urged the U.S. Sentencing Commission, the independent federal agency that sets sentencing policies for federal crimes, to approve a measure that would make potentially thousands of non-violent drug offenders now serving time in federal prison eligible for reduced sentences. In July 2014, the Commission unanimously agreed. Last spring, President Obama announced he would extend clemency to nonviolent drug offenders.

In a move toward bipartisan teamwork Senators Dick Durbin, D. Ill., and Mike Lee, R. Utah, introduced the Smarter Sentencing Act of 2013, a bill to reduce mandatory minimum sentences for some drug offenses and would give judges more flexibility to impose sentences below the mandatory minimum requirement. The bill would also allow judges to retroactively apply the new crack/powder cocaine sentencing policies under the Fair Sentencing Act of 2010 to offenders currently incarcerated under the old law. So, what are we waiting for?

Crime Rates Dropping, But...

Statistics show crime rates falling. In the five-year period from 2007 – 2012 Maryland's crime rates fell 21 percent and its incarceration rate declined 11 percent. According to a study done by the Pew Charitable Trust, states that have worked to contain corrections populations are proving that less crime can occur without jeopardizing public safety.

To ease the growing overcrowded situation at Baltimore City jail, there were plans to expand and build additional facilities to accommodate youths charged as adults, women and additional programs. But as other states have concluded, building their way out of the overcrowded situation only means spending more money and never addressing the root cause of the congestion. Baltimore is realizing it has to look at ways to more effectively deal with its criminal justice needs other than lock up. In its 2012 study entitled "Baltimore Behind Bars," the Justice Policy Institute found that out of the top 20 largest jail systems in the country, Baltimore locks up the highest percentage of its population. There are more enlightened remedies to consider including interventions in lieu of jail.

Recidivism, Education – Zero Tolerance in Schools and Suspicion of Black Boys

A high concentration of inmates in the prison system is mostly uneducated and lacking in skills to gain meaningful employment. Back on the streets without survival tools to make a legitimate living means a return to prison. The Criminal Justice System has a critical role to play in aggressively addressing this failing with those in their custody. Developing more effective rehabilitation and intervention programs that include education elevation, job training, substance abuse treatment, and addressing anti-social behavior are common sense approaches to reducing the number of repeat offenders and the cost of keeping them behind bars. Once free, getting employment also is instantly blocked by having to check the box on applications inquiring about convictions for crime. In a move that has promise if enforced by the city and regarded by employers, the City Council passed legislation in 2014 to "ban the box," forcing employers to refrain from asking the question about an applicant's criminal history until a conditional job offer has been made.

Staying in school and completing at least a high school education with a diploma remains a critical factor. In 2003, the Justice Policy Institute reported that half of all African American male dropouts had prison records by their early 30's and that 22 percent of African American men in their early 30s had prison records compared to 12 percent with college degrees.

Behavior that once got a student sent to the principal's office increasingly lands them in police custody under arrest, suspended or expelled under a school system's zero tolerance policy. Even four and five year olds were being suspended from pre-K and Kindergarten. There is an increasing number of little children arriving at school with serious problems that need the intervention of a team of professionals who could recommend handling behavior issues in more constructive ways. Applying inflexible approaches with children in school settings begs for a pitched battle and a poisoned atmosphere for learning. And, too often the target of harsh discipline are Black boys.

A February 2014 study by the Kirwin Institute for the Study of Race and Ethnicity at Ohio State University showed that African American students, particularly boys, are disciplined more often and receive more out-of-school suspensions and expulsions than White students.

Another study reported in Education Week 2013 found that over 70% of the students involved in school-related arrests or referred to law enforcement were Hispanic or Black. A 2009–2010 survey of 72,000 schools in kindergarten through high school shows that while Black students made up only 18 percent of those enrolled in the schools sampled, they accounted for 35 percent of those suspended once, 46 percent of those suspended more than once and 39 percent of all expulsions. Over all, Black students were three and a half times more likely to be suspended or expelled than their White peers.

Early in 2014, U.S. Attorney General Eric Holder and U.S. Department of Education Secretary Arne Duncan acknowledged those findings when they jointly released new federal recommendations for school policies. They encouraged limited use of out-of-school suspensions, warning of their inappropriate use against Black children.

"Too often, so-called zero-tolerance policies, however well intentioned they might be, make students feel unwelcome in their own schools," Mr. Holder said. "They disrupt the learning process, and they can have significant and lasting negative effects on the long-term well-being of our young people." In 2003, out-of-school suspensions in the Baltimore City Public School System was at a high of 26,300. Changes in suspension and discipline practices have brought suspensions down to 9,000.

For now, the numbers of students completing high school in Baltimore City have been improving. The four-year graduation rate for the class of 2013 was 68.5 percent, an improvement over the class of 2010, which was 61.5 percent. The graduation rate among African American students improved to 78.26 percent compared to the previous year of 76.50 percent. The dropout rate for Baltimore City schools fell from 23.8 percent for the class of 2010 to 12.1 percent for the class of 2013. This is good news but what's next? Where are the jobs?

Caution Ahead
In Summer 2014 Baltimore City imposed one of the strictest curfews in the country. The Mayor and Council members said the rule was designed to curb violence. Children under 14 would need to be home by 9 p.m. year-round, among the earliest curfews nationally. Teens 14 to 16-years-old would have a curfew of 10 p.m. on weeknights during the school year and 11 p.m. on weekends. The problem is it also establishes an earlier stage for tagging kids in the Criminal Justice Systems and positioning them

for a seat in the penitentiary. Parents and local authorities must engage as partners to keep children involved in meaningful activities that help them grow into responsible citizens. The punitive approach from the start invites conflict and push back.

Solutions to Consider

Moving forward to fix what remains broken are 10 key areas worth pointing out for concentrated attention:

- The Mayor and City Council and state elected officials must use the power of their positions to set a tone and make changes they are empowered to make through leadership

- Judges should use their discretion and end mandatory minimum sentences. The State's Attorney should more closely scrutinize police charges and lessen the severity of drug charges for possession and distribution

- The State's Attorney should bring only the most serious crimes to trial. The Police Commissioner should eliminate the department's policies and practices that results in mass arrests without charges. The City Council should regularly monitor the department's arrest records for patterns of recklessness and abuse

- The State's Attorney should develop an effective tracking system to reduce and or eliminate the length of time the accused is held in the City Jail pending trial

- The Office of the Mayor in concert with the State's Attorney and the Police Department should work out a plan for ending overcrowding at the City Jail

- The Office of the Mayor should direct that drug usage be treated as a medical issue

- Maryland Department of Education and Baltimore City Schools should end the zero tolerance polices and practices in schools that fuel a school-to-jail pipeline for black youths. Resources such as conflict mediation, parenting courses, behavioral services and other interventions should be made available to keep children in school as much as possible

- The public, private and non-profit sector should work collaboratively to reverse the elevation of recidivism rates by providing job training, employment referrals, early drug and mental health treatment and a better support system to transition ex-offenders back into society as productive citizens

Action Steps to Take

1. Develop a positive attitude of helpfulness, constructive thinking and participation in your neighborhood.

2. Visit the school in your neighborhood; introduce yourself to the school leadership including, the principal, guidance counselor, and president of the Parent Teacher Association. Ask where you can be of help as a volunteer, keep your word and show up.

3. Lobby your local, state and federal elected officials about ending zero tolerance arrest policies. Urge them to speak out against mass incarceration.

4. Learn what non-profit and political organizations are working on issues concerning incarceration, school suspensions, zero tolerance policies. Get involved.

5. Knowledge is power. Get curious and learn more about the policies, practices and habits impacting your community and the economy and well-being of the city at large.

6. Do something with what you learn.

Baltimore Elections in the 21st Century

John T. Bullock

Introduction

The promise of the Civil Rights Movement was that it would not only break down social barriers predicated upon race, but more importantly, that it would allow for greater political access and inclusion for African Americans. The Civil Rights Act of 1964 and the Voting Rights Act of 1965 would prohibit discrimination in public accommodations as well as protect the electoral participation of Black Americans, which had been prevented for a century after the Civil War Amendments (13th, 14th, and 15th) were passed by Congress. As many activists fought, protested, and died to have Black citizenship rights respected, the degree of participation following such gains was significant. Specifically, the promise of electing Black politicians at the state and local level provided the semblance of community control and policy change.

However, electoral participation has not solved many of problems endemic to urban centers. Just as the Kerner Commission determined in aftermath of the 1960s riots, in the urban North – the so-called "promise land" – conditions were not equal as it related to race:

> Our nation is moving toward two societies, one black, one white—separate and unequal…Segregation and poverty have created in the racial ghetto a destructive environment totally unknown to most white Americans. What white Americans have never fully understood but what the Negro can never forget—is that white society is deeply implicated in the ghetto. White institutions created it, white institutions maintain it, and white society condones it.[1]

While African Americans in Northern and Midwestern U.S. cities have historically exercised the right to vote for far longer than their disenfranchised counterparts in the Jim Crow South, this participation has often be co-opted and manipulated. Nonetheless, in light of the demographic changes among the urban electorate in cities such as Baltimore due to White (and Black middle-class) flight over the past several decades, there continue to be racial and economic disparities that influence politics and elections.

Given the social and economic conditions in American cities such as Baltimore, it is important to understand past and current circumstances in order to make future predictions. While this analysis uncovers a host of challenging indicators and trends, there are some potential solutions. Whereas the prescribed methods for weakening the entrenched incumbency related to political machines include term limits and at-large elections, Baltimore stands as the epitome of a non-reform city as it lacks these, as well as other elements found in more progressive cities. Regardless of the outcome of specific elections, the stage is also being set for electoral contests to be shaped by a relatively recent set of occurrences. The waning of civil rights activism, the rise in black professionalism, and the flight of whites back to urban centers is resulting in a seeming evolution of city politics.

Before going any further, it is necessary to present a working definition of machine politics and describe how current operations may be similar in some ways and different in other ways than an earlier generation. "The word 'machine' connotes an organization capable of delivering a vote with mechanical regularity."[2] Machines personalized politics, and by becoming friendly with the electorate, they engendered popular support in exchange for favors.[3] Political machines were rooted in neighborhoods, and a combination of material incentives (i.e., patronage) and ethnic loyalty held them together. In most large American cities, a "friends and neighbors" or "local followings" style of politics evolved that reflected the decentralized nature of their political systems."[4] Machine interaction with voters was mainly about personal obligations and the exchange of favors such as jobs, contracts and favorable administration of the law.[5] Close attention to the personal needs of individual voters provided a loyal constituency.[6] Conversely, policies that benefit everyone and cannot be allocated on the basis of favoritism do not generate individual obligations to the machine.[7] Thus, policies that provided universal benefits had little attraction to machine politicians.

Although political machines no longer have as much ability to control jobs and services, this does not mean that the electorate does not remember the days when they could; it also does not preclude voters from continuing to believe that local politicians still retain that power. This is especially true in jurisdictions where the electorate is dominated by an elderly age bracket familiar with the past. In this regard, perception does become reality among some voters:

> With the decline of ward organizations and big-city machines they coalesced to form, concern with the material advantages of office-holding has not disappeared. Favors to constituents also remain as a major strategy of officeholders in search of electoral support. While reciprocal favors and personal obligations do not undergird the kind of elaborate ward-based organization once so common in the urban communities of the nation, they remain a formidable force in contemporary politics.[8]

This is particularly pronounced in Baltimore as there are a very high percentage of people (22.4%) living in poverty, or barely above the poverty level that are in dire need of material assistance.

Historically, it has been difficult for independent voices in Baltimore (not affiliated with a machine) advocating for change to be heard or elected. With plenty of patronage – opportunities to dole out rewards or punishment – political incumbents had the ability to pacify individuals and small groups, thereby preventing broad systemic issues from coming to the fore. The patronage system, though involving a number of African Americans, was challenged in the 1960s and 1970s by civil rights figures seeking more comprehensive attention to problems in the city; but such challenges were limited and not particularly effective.[9]

In Baltimore, relations between African American and white leaders centered around patronage politics. However, one of the problems with machine and patronage politics is that it undercut discussions of broad issues, such as housing, employment, and public education. "Black machine politicians' preconceptions with the control and distribution of material and personal benefits encouraged them to accept the desires of White civic and political leaders; Black political cooperation was secured at a relatively low price, thus forsaking any real inroads on communitywide concerns."[10]

Despite the fact that Baltimore now has a majority Black population and Black elected officials hold top leadership positions, this has not appreciably changed how business is conducted. As Orr describes, "Where urban machines have dominated, competing views have been ignored and new actors discouraged from participating."[11] As a result, Black voters who had been initially excited by the election of Black elected officials have become increasingly disenchanted. This created, in turn, incentives for Black officials to demobilize the Black poor or to allow demobilization to occur.[12] Consequently, incumbent public officials who are driven by the goals of reelection and consolidation of power tend to have an interest in dampening the possibilities for new or widespread mobilization. These electoral considerations translate into a preference for a brokered "politics as usual" that limits the number and claims on the policy agenda.[13] In this vein, it has been found that people tend be apathetic about politics when they are not consulted about decisions that affect their lives.[14] Moreover, people who are disadvantaged by the status quo often lack the capital to be heard and are thus unable to make their demands known. While this phenomenon may be welcomed by entrenched incumbents, as low turnout tends to result in reelection success, it portends disastrous results for the city's political future.

Subsequently, the remnants of the machine system are a fixture in the city's political culture. However, one significant element of the machine structure – the political clubs – have vanished in recent years. While being somewhat of an insider establishment, it served the purpose of creating a pipeline of future political candidates. In their absence (and with no entity filling this void), the political development and engagement of younger citizens has seemingly halted. Moreover, past political machines were instrumental in voter turnout; however, the current lack of effectiveness among elected officials – embodied in long-standing problems and complaints – has contributed to diminishing electoral participation. In the absence of significant systemic change, scores of previously active registered voters have made the calculated decision to tune out. Also troubling is the fact that many younger potential voters have never been acclimated to the electoral system and see little reason to do so. While this phenomenon may be welcomed by long-term officeholders, as low turnout tends to result in reelection success, it portends disastrous results for the city's political future.

Despite the demise of a centralized machine, what the author describes as "mini-machines" have survived. There are several "mini-machines" currently operating in Baltimore that focus on smaller geographic areas and tend to be family-based. Having multiple family members in elected office at the same, as well as having family members serve for extended periods of time, boosts name recognition and organizational support. However, there are some significant differences from the machines of the past. Most critically, there are currently not the same types of patronage to be doled out. However, there still remain some token gestures which inculcate loyalty (e.g. promises of low-level jobs, speculative property transfers, legal assistance, etc.). Additionally, the potential retribution for disloyalty remains a strong incentive for supporting or appearing to support incumbents.

Candidacy

One of the most instructive ways to understand politics and elections is to be a candidate. In the 2011 Baltimore City Primary Election, the author was also a candidate for City Council. This specific district, which occupies a large swath of West and Southwest Baltimore, is the most populous in the city. According to 2010 Census data, 88% of the nearly 47,000 residents are African American and 9% are white. The district includes many of the city's poorest neighborhoods, as well as gentrifying areas with middle-class pockets. Nearly half of Baltimore's approximately 16,000 vacant properties are in the district, and more than one-sixth of the city's residents currently in prison are from this district which comprises less than 8% of the total population.[15] Even though this piece focuses on one specific district, the political and social conditions – as ominous as they may be – are also reflected in other in areas throughout Baltimore City.

As a candidate, one is exposed to experiences that are unparalleled. Through participant observation, I have been able to develop a typology of candidates – differentiated by generation, race, and class – that emerges in such a system. This full representation of characters is instructive for civic observers as they represent reoccurring themes in an urban political drama. While they may not be exhaustive of all possibilities, they comprise a broad cross section. Arguably, this typology may apply to urban areas across America, given similar contextual conditions. Although there were nine candidates in the race, this typology includes the top six who garnered close to ten percent or more of the vote total. These six are then divided into two divisions: the 'Old Guard' – native Baltimoreans over the age of 55; and the 'New Guard' – non-native Baltimoreans under the age of 45. The Old guard consists of insiders, activists, and administrators. The New guard consists of liberals, entrepreneurs, and professionals.

Insiders can be defined as the heirs to political dynasties or candidates supported by incumbent administrations. Insiders benefit from political connections within the machine structure; as a consequence, they are often times insulated from incompetence and/or scandal. The insider candidate raised over $33,350 (25% from individuals, 39% from businesses, 34% from other candidates and elected officials – including $4,000 from a former councilmember and $3,000 each from the city council president and a current councilmember. Activists can be seen as an extension of the civil rights tradition both in generation and tactics. Activists push for the inclusion of the economically and socially marginalized; considering the intersection of race and class, they tend to operate in a highly racialized manner. The activist candidate raised

$3,399 (48% from individuals, 50% miscellaneous). Administrators represent those who have held supervisory positions in government/educational institutions. Administrators are somewhat connected to the existing system; in light of their positions, some are perceived to be part of long standing problems. Additionally, they compose a significant percentage of the older black middle class. The administrator candidate raised approximately $9,358 (64% from individuals, 2% from businesses, 2% from other candidates, 2% from political action committees, 28% miscellaneous).

Liberals can be defined as being slightly more affluent and exhibiting marked socioeconomic distinctions. Liberals are likely to be white and employed in a "helping" occupation such as a teacher or social worker; while embraced by some, they may be viewed as paternalistic by others. The liberal candidate raised $25,530 (90% from individuals, 6% from businesses). Consistent with expectations, the liberal candidate won in the two precincts with the highest concentration of white voters. Entrepreneurs are those whose experience lies largely in business ventures. Entrepreneurs may be of any race (white in this case) and their vested interest is based primarily on the viability of business in the area and the related potential for economic development. The entrepreneur candidate raised $23,589 (61% from individuals, 16% from businesses, 23% miscellaneous). Professionals are those with higher levels of education employed in white collar/highly skilled capacities. Typically, these professionals represent younger black middle class residents ("buppies") who are identifiable along racial lines but diverge upon class dimensions. The professional candidate raised approximately $13,555 (93% from individuals, 7% miscellaneous).

Leading up to elections, a number of media outlets, interest groups, and labor unions issue questionnaires and conduct interviews as a part of the endorsement process. Traditionally, these endorsements go to incumbents or those candidates who are most likely to win. In this city council contest, two media endorsements – Baltimore City Paper and Baltimore Afro American – went to the activist and one—Baltimore Sun— went to the liberal; one environmental endorsement—Clean Water Action—went to the professional. Additionally, the union endorsement process was quite an insightful experience. The AFL-CIO comprises most of the local unions who jointly make endorsements of political candidates. These endorsements are important as they often relate to money and ground support (i.e., mailings, campaign workers) for candidates. This level of support can be instrumental in the outcome of elections. Not only is there a detailed questionnaire, but there is also an interview. For one meeting, the head of the labor council came out and personally welcomed the former incumbent (who consistently received union endorsements and support) along with the insider candidate and ushered them both into the interview room. The interviews are closed to other candidates, so there is no way to definitely know what occurred.

The interviews are fairly straightforward as there is a review of the previously submitted answers. However, one of the major questions asked is how candidates plan to win the election. This is significant because unions tend to support candidates who they think will win or candidates that they would like to win. In other words, unions tend to support incumbents, unless the incumbent has done something to upset the unions, in which case they will support a challenger. From the perspective of the unions, this method is somewhat effective. If they support the incumbent and he or she wins, this means continued access and influence. Even if the incumbent loses, they can reach out to the successful challenger and provide assistance in the General Election. Nevertheless, there are also times when the unions decide to make no recommendation; this effectively means that the various unions either cannot agree on a candidate or chose not support one at all. This district was the only city race where the unions decided to make no endorsement. This seems to be a culmination of the sheer number of candidates combined with the relatively low approval of the incumbent. With such a split field and problematic incumbent it may have seemed politically prudent to remain neutral. However, from the perspective a relatively weak incumbent, a no recommendation is more favorable than the unions endorsing a challenger.

Campaigning

Additionally, knocking on doors is a well-established way to connect with voters and answer questions on a one-on-one basis. However, in this process, citizen apathy as well as low political knowledge and efficacy were apparent. Many regular voters had no idea what district they lived in or how many candidates they could vote for. Some had no idea of when the election would take place, who the other candidates were, or who currently represented them. While part of this may stem from the recent redistricting which occurred several months prior, most voters have been in the same district for several elections. Granted there have been slight changes in the electoral districts, but the lack of knowledge went much further. Additionally, there seemed to be confusion between the roles of state delegates versus city council members; and while state legislative districts have three seats, council districts only have one (they were three-member districts until 1999). This relative ignorance of voters impedes electoral prospects, as there seems to be a tendency for candidates to exploit this lack of information. However, it also demonstrates a failure on the part of the electorate.

Walking neighborhoods and knocking on doors provides an opportunity to not only see conditions, but to also have conversations with voters (and non-voters). A number of potential voters indicated their support for the incumbent based upon the promise of a job. This made it especially difficult for non-incumbent candidates who were asked "can you get me a job". While employment is important, it is not necessarily the main role of a city councilmember. However, this harkens back to patronage jobs which were the lifeblood of machines. But it also indicates the dire needs of residents that can be manipulated for their votes. In the most challenged sections of the district, some blocks had an extraordinary amount of vacant homes. However, even in areas with less vacancy, there were relatively low numbers of registered voters. And even among a number of registered voters—some of whom had participated in recent elections —there was a sense of apathy and frustration with the political system. Additionally, the conversations with potential voters revealed some themes that were repeated time and again. One of those themes was the allegiance of voters (and contributors) to particular candidates, which was largely related to personal relationships as opposed to policies and platforms.

Some may argue that people vote with machines out of a practical rationality. But this is only true when people actually receive some material benefits. In this particular case, there is no evidence of any substantive assistance provided by the vestiges of the machine. Even in years past, the number of jobs that could be doled out was limited. Therefore, much of what party activists could offer were "social benefits" including friendship, token gestures and assistance with parochial issues. Nonetheless, it seems that there still remains a faith in the machine and reliance upon it for city services. Although citizens are already entitled to these services, they are often not provided. The low level of service provision and belief that this is controlled by the councilmember leads to continued support. In reality, one of the reasons that service provision is low undoubtedly has some connection to inattention from the incumbent for years. While some would likely argue that poor conditions and inadequate services would increase the chances of defeat, in some ways the opposite is true. By keeping a very low level of service, the slightest improvements or unsubstantiated promises are welcomed by residents who are accustomed to nothing more.

One of the main criticisms of machine politics has been the attendant corruption—real or perceived. In Baltimore, this is represented not only by back room deals and cronyism (e.g., hand-picked candidates), but also the blatant flouting of the law (e.g., ghost addresses, whereby representatives live outside of the district and/or city). Additionally, alliances with businesses—legal or illicit—have also proven to be valuable to politicians. Before and after the elections, many of the neighborhood liquor stores —the most numerous type of business in the immediate area – posted large campaign signs emblazoned with the incumbent's name.

Election

In Baltimore, it is a well-known phenomenon that super-voters – senior black women who vote in every election – tend to dominate the electorate. The fact that the long-term incumbent is a member of this electorally powerful demographic had a significant impact. As seniors had been the former incumbent's primary constituency, they proved to be loyal supporters election after election (as well as for her son). Moreover, the support for the insider candidate, despite well-publicized shortcomings, lends credence to the perceived willingness of some urban voters to forgive politicians who had previously been accused of misbehavior.

Furthermore, non-Baltimore City/non-district residents continue to play a significant—if yet, not fully understood—role in shaping elections. Generally, campaign contributions and volunteer efforts are the most common mechanisms that can help sway elections. One somewhat prominent figure in Baltimore who also supported the incumbent/insider loyally is the mother of a late multimillionaire and business tycoon whose name is quite well-known in Baltimore as the city's African American history museum as well as a high school are named in his honor. For years she has lived in the relatively wealthy suburb of Randallstown. When approached about a donation to a challenger, she indicated that she had promised her support (and several thousand dollars) to her best friend's son, the insider. In addition, on Election Day the octogenarian campaigned vigorously for the insider candidate, even intercepting a conversation another candidate was having with a voter. In talking with the younger candidate following the exchange, the older woman said that "…your time will come".

This violates any understanding of the concept of intergenerational equity. Not only does the octogenarian not have to live with the consequences of this outcome in the present, she will not be around in years to come to see future conditions. Unfortunately, this means those who have the most to gain (young adults) tend to have a smaller voice—due to low turnout, while those who have the least to gain (senior citizens) are likely to have a louder voice—due to high turnout. While seniors clearly have tangible interests, theirs are more temporal, as opposed to younger voters who will be around for many more years and will continue to be affected by suboptimal conditions. There does seem to be an element of generational warfare embodied in the resistance from an elder generation; older voters support well-known names regardless of long-term ineffectiveness. This has the potential effect of dooming future generations to incompetent leadership for the sake of personal relationships. This is not only a manifestation of low political knowledge, but also a holdover from machine politics which stresses loyalty over competence. Another local phenomenon is the maintenance of Baltimore City voting registration, despite residential migration into suburban areas of Baltimore County. This means that many of those selecting local elected officials, have no tangible stake in the outcome. While there may be a personal relationship, these individuals are removed from the day-to-day realities and do not have to live with the consequences of their electoral decisions.

Additionally, with more money than all the other candidates, the insider could afford to pay an army of campaign workers. Regardless of the relative quality of the workers, it is always helpful to have steady shifts of multiple people in campaign shirts handing out literature. There were a number of workers who were destitute and the appeal of money for the day was quite attractive. Hence, the intense poverty and dysfunction in many parts of the district makes machine-style politics even more attractive. The focus on material needs rather than policy issues has a significant impact and is a key issue in local campaigns. Candidates attempting to undercut the incumbent engaged in a number of tactics to gain supporters and votes – from offering free beer and pizza, to mowing lawns.

Election Day also provided an opportunity to see the advantages of incumbency. The mayoral ticket (unified slate of candidates) also seems to be a holdover from machine politics. This is particularly important among a low-information electorate. Uninformed voters are most likely to vote for the name that they see the most and/or the name that they saw last. At polling locations, campaign workers hand out literature with the mayor's ticket—including most incumbents and the challengers that he or she supports. For an incumbent, it solidifies one's position; for a challenger, it validates their candidacy. Being on the mayor's ticket can also have financial benefits. In the case of a neighboring district, mayoral (and union) support was integral to the success of a challenger over a multi-term incumbent from a family-based "mini-machine" who ran afoul of the mayor. The successful challenger received $4,144.44 from the mayor and $4,000 from another councilmember.

Dysfunction and Reform

As far as civic participation, many neighborhood associations are largely ineffective as their meetings are sparsely attended. For the most part, this further demonstrates the lack of political efficacy in economically disadvantaged communities. In economically challenged communities, the associations tend to operate in a less professional and structured manner; because of infrequent turnover and the close connection to individual personalities, there is limited age diversity as they are comprised mostly seniors. However, in gentrifying areas, the associations are much more functional which demonstrates greater social and political capital—reflecting the class dimensions. They operate in a more professional and structured manner, with greater participation and turnover, along with age diversity.

In Baltimore, the main institutions that would encourage participation (i.e. churches and neighborhood organizations) are largely broken and dysfunctional. While many may worship in Baltimore on Sundays, their actual residence is outside of the city, thereby weakening the civic role of religious institutions with middle-class congregants. Also, in many instances community associations and their members fear being on the outside by supporting a candidate other than the incumbent/expected winner. While many of them may personally dislike the incumbent, the fear of retribution keeps them in line. This is very much in the tradition of machine politics which places a premium on loyalty. Also, homeowners vote at higher rates than renters; and in a city where almost half of residents rent, this has a significant impact on the voting demographic.

Moreover, scholars have noted differences among cities depending on the degree to which they have "reformed" characteristics such as a nonpartisan ballot, at-large elections, and city-manager form of government.[17] Reformers of the late early 20th century sought to remove power from the machine politicians who they viewed as corrupt and inefficient. As ward-based elections were easily dominated by machines, reformers sought to institute at-large elections.[18] With no term limits or at-large elections, Baltimore is the epitome of a non-reform city. I argue that in somewhat of a parallel to the reform movement of the early 20th century, former industrial/machine cities such as Baltimore may be primed for a similar political change in the early 21st century. But what would such a movement look like in today's times? Reform recommendations would naturally include term limits and at-large elections, as well as special elections rather than appointments in the case of death or retirement.

"Urban regimes persist, enjoying long periods where incumbency advantage increases and turnover and turnout are reduced."[19] Despite significant voter registration and outreach attempts, advocacy/organizing groups have been unable to increase turnout and/or achieve significant policy promises from candidates and elected officials. Additionally, low-turnout elections are more predictable. Political leaders have an easier time ensuring that voters will cast ballots for their candidates if there are fewer voters to consider.[20] On Election Day 2011 there was a historically low turnout as only 23% of registered voters participated in Baltimore City; the turnout in this particular district was even lower at 19%. This initiated a citywide discussion on the causes of this low turnout and possible ways to increase it. Interestingly, there have been suggestions to schedule municipal elections in conjunction with state elections.

Following the dismal participation in the primary, the Baltimore Election Change Coalition was formed by several organizations whose aim was to hold city elections at the same time as state elections to increase turnout. This would also have brought the city into compliance with every other jurisdiction in Maryland. The coalition included the League of Women Voters of Baltimore City, American Civil Liberties Union of Maryland, Baltimore City Branch of the NAACP and other groups. In the 2012 session of the Maryland General Assembly, the coalition had bills sponsored by Baltimore legislators in both the House and Senate. However, many elected city officials—including the Mayor and City Council—favored legislation that would combine local elections with the presidential cycle, thus allowing them to run for state office without having to give up their positions if they are unsuccessful. In the end, the bill joining presidential and municipal elections was successfully passed in the state legislature. As a result, the current terms of the Mayor and City Council are extended for an additional year until 2016.

Conclusion and Predictions

This is largely an analysis about what is broken in urban politics. While patronage—the lifeblood of machines—may not exist as it once did, there are still opportunities to dole out favors to supporters. This different type of patronage provides influence rather than jobs; however, in largely impoverished districts, the promise of jobs (real or unreal) has salience among the electorate. At this juncture, younger politicians are quite frustrated by an older generation's seeming complacency with current conditions, reflecting sentiments of 1960s and 1970s. As in the past, emergent urban political candidates will likely need liberal White and middle-class Black support to defeat entrenched machine power; this requires a platform of Black progress without White alienation, notwithstanding the sometimes inconsistent nature of White allies.[21] It is important to note that the district in question—and much of Baltimore—lacks a sizable Black middle-class. At the same time, gentrification has changed the nature of urban politics. Rising property/real estate values have attracted a new, more affluent, increasingly White population. The incoming Whites tend to have less (or no) tolerance for incompetent/ineffective Black politicians than African Americans who remember the days of segregation and relish the novelty of Black incorporation.

Accordingly, higher degrees of education and political efficacy – social capital and the ability to raise money – correspond to this segment's interests being increasingly likely to be heard. With the money to finance campaigns, they pose a formidable threat to inexperienced/unorganized/poorly-financed Black candidates. Calculating White candidates will see a quite unsophisticated electorate and a field with multiple Black candidates as an opportunity to win an election without necessarily commanding a majority of the vote. Generally, scholars have attributed the victories of White candidates over Black candidates in majority Black cities/districts to united White support in the absence of a large turnout among Black voters.[22] Others contend that the presence of multiple Black candidates effectively splits the Black vote, thus allowing for a White candidate to emerge successfully.[23] Nevertheless, in many cases this new collective arrives with a disconnection from the historically Black community and attempts to restructure neighborhoods in ways that are more congruent to their vision. Unfortunately, in the eyes of many long-term residents it seems that African Americans have to be removed/priced out from neighborhoods for them to improve, rather than benefitting from changes such as new shops, restaurants, and increased safety.

Meanwhile, in a number of historically healthy parts of the city, the Black middle-class has been diminishing, along with long-established community institutions (churches, neighborhood organizations, etc.). Following years of outward migration and social distance, middle-class/professional Black candidates may be seen with air of distrust/suspicion and curiosity in high poverty areas/districts. "The "ethnic group model" often used to describe political mobilization and group cohesion among Black Americans has its limitations. While embracing ethnic solidarity, the model undermines the internal differences among Blacks that dilute collective political behavior. For example, one finds that contrary to popular belief, Black voters do not always support Black candidates when they face White opposition."[24] This is also consistent with the assertion that differences in ideological positions make it difficult to mount unified political movements.[25]

The election results tell most of the tale, as contenders finished in the order of money raised. The candidates from gentrified communities had more resources on hand which undeniably helps with organization and public promotion. The candidates from non-gentrified neighborhoods had considerably less resources on hand, which undoubtedly affected organizational and promotional capabilities. There are also a number of ways to interpret the results. One interpretation is that the (White) candidates in gentrified communities paid more per vote than (Black) candidates in non-gentrified communities. A useful example is the distribution of campaign mailings; mailings are one of the most effective ways to broaden name recognition and persuade voters. However, mailings can be relatively expensive at a cost of approximately three to five thousand dollars apiece. The incumbent was able to send out several mailings as was the second place finisher. The third and fourth place finishers each got out only one mailing. The fifth place candidate did not have resources for a mailing, and the 6th place candidate paid for a mailing, however, the piece was delivered after the election.

Another interpretation is that the White candidates finished second and third (with a combined total of 27% of the vote), while the top Black candidates—excluding the incumbent – finished fourth, fifth and sixth (with a combined total of 31% of the vote). This suggests that neither a single leading white challenger, nor a single leading black challenger would automatically defeat the incumbent without broader support. What this further intimates is that a new guard candidate would be the most viable option as a challenger. Perhaps only a candidate from the new guard—which received a combined total of 39% of the vote—may have the ability to defeat the incumbent—who received 35% of the vote. While there is no guarantee that all of these votes are transferrable, individually and collectively, the new guard candidates outperformed their older counterparts; and there appears to be significant overlap among the respective bases of support for the younger candidates.

In some ways these demographic and electoral shifts are fitting given that urban politics has always been about change and flux. Decades of White flight have now been reversed by a recent trickle of young White professionals who desire an urban experience with proximity and access to downtown, unlike their suburban upbringings. Additionally, young Black professionals may be more willing to remain in central cities given certain amenities and housing options sought by the middle-class. Under such a scenario, the urban political landscape may set for the next generation of successful candidates in Baltimore if new guard elements can unify and garner broader support.

Current Opportunities for Change

As 2014 is a gubernatorial election year (with no major statewide candidate hailing from Baltimore) and the primary election being three months earlier than in past years, observations following the election showed relatively low turnout at about 22% of registered voters in the city. Nevertheless, there are some opportunities to improve the electoral process and voter participation. If Blacks in Baltimore are to achieve true progress in the 21st century, significant changes must occur with regard to city elections. However, many of the changes would have to be approved by local elected officials who have little motivation to vote against their own interest of maintaining power. For instance, term limits can be effective at creating turnover in public office as well as increasing the number of truly competitive elections. Also, having some at-large (citywide) seats on the City Council as well as elected School Board seats (currently they are appointed), would broaden the types of political actors at the local level.

Moreover, political education coupled with voter registration would also be a key mechanism; academics and activists could partner to highlight systemic disparities and the implications of electoral participation. One of the ways such training sessions could be accomplished is by partnering with high schools to reach younger voters and with neighborhood associations to reach older voters. Additionally, with a significant population of ex-offenders, there must be wider awareness of the fact that once probation or parole is complete, their voting rights can be restored. As far as groups informing people and getting voters to the polls, a small subset of churches discussed the upcoming election and made coordinated efforts to get people to polls for early voting. This eight-day period produced an all-time high for early voting, even though overall turnout including Election Day was so low.

Lastly, youth-based political organizations would go a long way in cultivating a new crop of leaders. Just as there was a need for young political organizers in the 1960s, the same need exists in 2014. But the troubling reality is that in many ways the baton has not been passed to the next generation. The older entrenched incumbents who were once the activists of the past are now graying. It should be noted that much of their success came not only from asserting their youthful perspective, but also being encouraged by an older generation. Unfortunately, many have been reluctant to share —and jealously guard—the prize garnered in their relative youth. Regardless, there are some indications that such youth-oriented political and social activism is burgeoning in Baltimore City. Time will tell how successful such movements will be, but intergenerational support would only increase the likelihood of change.

Stop O'Malley's Jail: A Coming of Age Account of The Grassroots Campaign Against a Multi-Million Dollar Youth Jail in Baltimore

Heber Brown, III with Chabria Thomas and Adam Jackson

"…Social circumstances transform and popular attitudes shift, in part in response to organized social movements."
—Angela Davis, "Are Prisons Obsolete?", p. 25

During the fall of 2010, young American African leaders and activists in Baltimore staged direct action demonstrations to protest the construction of what was termed, "Governor Martin O'Malley's Youth Jail" in East Baltimore, tapping into a schema of active resistance reflective of past local history. A part of this history draws on energies reminiscent of a period of racial violence that was both lawful and distinguished by behaviors from Law Enforcement. The proposal to build another jail targeted at juvenile offenders would resurrect the spirit of everyday people who decided to push back against a more sophisticated model of philosopher, Jeremy Bentham's eighteenth century panopticon, an 'all-seeing' prison system concept.[1] The idea of an all-seeing system of correction, is demonstrated currently by the Baltimore City Police Department's (BCPD) use of the "blue light" surveillance system throughout the City – a controversial Homeland Security funded public safety project initiated by then Mayor Martin O'Malley in 2005, which purported to address crime by wiring a network of cameras, marked with flashing blue lights, throughout the city with images transmitted to a centralized monitoring system. The "blue light cameras," which were reserved for the Black and poorer neighborhoods of Baltimore City were a lightning rod at their introduction and invited much disgust by many Baltimoreans who saw the measure as an invasion of privacy that would do more to "move" crime to a different block in the same neighborhood as opposed to engage systemic factors that foster criminal activity in impoverished communities. To understand the significance of the momentum garnered in 2010 by grassroots American Africans[2] in Baltimore, we must view the call-to-action through the lens of Baltimore's history fifty years ago.

Freedom Expressed in Community

Before the 1963 March on Washington For Freedom and Jobs, Black Baltimore had long been restless in its wait to be acknowledged as co-existing human beings among their white counterparts. Twenty years before "The March" where Dr. King shared his "dream," 2,000 Blacks from Baltimore participated in a march on Annapolis organized by the Citizens Committee for Justice, which was led by former Baltimore Afro-American Newspaper Editor, Carl Murphy. Before then-Governor Herbert O'Conor, State Comptroller, Millard Tawes, and Secretary of State, Thomas E. Jones, the massive group submitted petitions and raised concerns on a range of issues prevalent in the Black community at the time including, but not limited to police brutality, discrimination in

Defense Industries, and the desire to control institutions within their own community.[3] A little more than a decade later the fight for freedom was still evident in Baltimore. In 1955, students from Morgan State College [now Morgan State University] with students from Howard University worked together to demand public accommodations at Read's drugstore in downtown Baltimore and at the northeast Baltimore Northwood Theatre which was adjacent to Morgan State. Morgan State students formed the Baltimore Civic Interest Group (CIG), partnered with the local chapter of Congress of Racial Equality (CORE), and strategically planned two different sit-in actions: at Read's drugstore demanding public accommodations at the lunch counter and Northwood Theatre. Shortly after the demonstration at Read's drugstore, the manager caved under pressure and desegregated the lunch counter in 1955. It would take another eight years before the Northwood Theatre would follow suit.[4]

Distinction should be made concerning the direct action activities of CIG and CORE. The activities coming out of these civil rights groups should be recognized as a movement to go beyond exchanging currency for goods purchased at white establishments. Black Baltimoreans began to recognize the "Black dollar" as an important leveraging tool in the struggle for equity and against institutional discrimination. As we scale back on the historical context related to the community's organizing against the youth jail, it is important to make clear that these actions indicate consciousness-raising among the Black citizenry of Baltimore to organize toward self-preservation and community sustainability.

Another example of this occurred in September 1962, when thirty-five American African youth decided to go for a swim at the Riverside Park pool in South Baltimore. White protestors rallied together to dissuade their recreation. Word about the rally got around to other communities and a noted one thousand persons came to witness the assault. One of the individuals who came out to be an eye-witness of this racially motivated assault was Reverend Frank Green, a Black pastor that ironically received a fine of $25 dollars due to a fight which broke out within the crowd.[5]

Jobs, Jobs, Jobs!

At this same juncture in 1962, Maryland Delegates Irma George Dixon and Alexander Stark drafted a fair employment bill and asserted the bill before the Judiciary Committee of the Legislative Council with Delegate Irma George Dixon stating: "We can't wait for education and persuasion to accomplish the aims of the bill." And, Delegate Alexander Stark followed her lead with: "It would take too many years. Must [sic] social progress is the result of legislation."[6]

These arguments culminated from grassroots activities launched by concerned citizens from the Black community, in general, expressing the impatience on the part of the Black collective to sit idly by, awaiting the moral shift of the White Power Structure to bend the psychic underpinning of popular thought. There was a political boldness to represent respect for American Africans by demanding the right to work.

Education As A Right

The County Citizens' Education Committee, a citizens' group designed to put pressure on the Prince George's County School Board regarding school integration, posed these assumptions before the State Board of Education on December 18, 1962:

1. Is segregation perpetuated by reliance on school attendance districts adopted long ago for a dual system?

2. Are school bus routes assigned in order to keep Negro children attending predominately Negro schools?

3. Are teaching staffs really being desegregated or only in a [token] manner?

The Citizens' group of Prince George's County, Maryland sought redress through the legal counsel of attorney, David B. Isbell of Washington D.C., declaring that the goal was "to get a new and specific plan for full desegregation by a certain date". For the 1962-1963 school year, Prince George's County expected 38,000 more students to enroll in the public school system.[7]

Subsequently following the events spearheaded by the Citizens' group of Prince George's County, Maryland, Mrs. Juanita Jackson Mitchell, secretary [and emerging lawyer] of the redress committee of the Baltimore branch of the National Association for the Advancement of Colored People (NAACP), led pickets in the streets of Baltimore accusing the Board of School Commissioners of "deliberate perpetuation of school segregation". Mrs. Jackson Mitchell was analyzing the immediate and long-term implications of an overwhelming number of Black students on a part-time school schedule and the new plan adopted by the Board to end part-time schooling with the remedy of creating portable classrooms instead of transporting students to "under-utilized white schools". Doing so, Mrs. Jackson Mitchell believed, would further block integration, because of the psychological and visceral fear of race-mixing among whites. The contention raised in the demonstration of pickets spoke to the need to escalate direct action activities to breakdown political barriers to accommodating all of the public –the Black public in particular. At this time in 1963, Baltimore City projected an additional student enrollment of 31,000; 7000 less when compared to the influx expected in Prince George's County the year before.[8]

Those who played prominent roles overseeing the management of race relations through policy formation in Baltimore's City Hall also sought to stymie the progress of Black inclusion in public spaces. Twenty-five days after the NAACP led pickets, Baltimore City Solicitor, Joseph Allen held that the Board of School Commissioners were not legally obligated under the constitution to move forward with instituting policies of integration. The Board agreed with the solicitor's ruling.

With a growing number of over 50% of Black children scheduled to enroll in Baltimore's public schools in 1963 and with millions of dollars being approved by both school Boards in Prince George's County and Baltimore, the White Power Structure, with their own legal interpretations of the intent of the 1954 Brown v. Board of

Education decision, determined further discrimination through policy use to suppress the educational aspirations of Black children by overcrowding all Black schools and building portable classrooms. Currently, portable classrooms are still being used to address overcrowding in predominately Black schools. Schools operating from the "feeder" system require investigation as this was and still is a sure way of maintaining consistency in the racial makeup of most of Baltimore's independent schools such as The Gilman School for Boys and The Bryn Mawr School for Girls in the Roland Park neighborhood in Baltimore, where there is a history of racially regulating housing access through *restrictive covenants.*[9]

Baltimore, A Ripened Social Justice Environment and 1963

The 1963 March On Washington For Jobs and Freedom, was a national call for a year of direct action and voter registration. Baltimore, with its history of recent protests and victories, was already in line with this call and continued being trailblazers for social justice. With the work of people like Juanita Jackson Mitchell, Parren J. Mitchell, Walter P. Carter, the Interdenominational Ministerial Alliance and a whole host of other individuals and organizations, Baltimore activism roots run deep. The 2010 Youth Jail campaign then was little more than a continuation of a legacy of grassroots activism and direct action

Stop O'Malley's Jail!

The plan to build a new youth jail facility in Baltimore dated back to a 2000 Department of Justice Report criticizing the city for its lack of adequate resources and confinement issues related to juveniles detained at the Baltimore City Detention Center.[10] While the report was issued under Maryland democratic governor, Parris Glendening, the plan to build a youth jail in Baltimore started to move forward under Glendening's successor, republican governor, Robert Ehrlich. The 2000 Justice Report left it up to the state to determine how it would address the inadequacies of the juvenile justice system and it was under the Ehrlich Administration that funds were approved for planning and population surveys for a suggested remedy – the building of a new youth jail. However, despite the report being issued and planning funds being spent prior to his becoming governor, real momentum for the construction of the proposed youth jail occurred under the gubernatorial administration of democrat, Martin O'Malley who began serving his first term as Maryland state governor in 2007.

By 2008, groups like the Baltimore Algebra Project were actively protesting against the proposed youth jail, however, the following year is when real, broad-based grassroots organizing against the project began. Community members were incredulous upon learning about what was now deemed "O'Malley's Youth Jail." So many basic services for adults and youth in Baltimore City were being cut or altogether eliminated with a justification given that the state and city were under financial strain. This helped feed the longstanding perception in Baltimore that when it comes to Black people generally and Black youth specifically, the proclivity of the White Power Structure is to advance the kinds of policies that profile, criminalize, marginalize, and incarcerate. More and more, American Africans in Baltimore appear to be a tolerated majority and not citizens of the city deserving of the same rights, services, and respect as white, well-to-do, and more economically affluent groups that reside here.

Thankfully, and at least on this issue, Black people in Baltimore rose up and organized in mass to decry Governor Martin O'Malley's plan to build this youth jail. Large segments of the community were united in its voice and effort to fight back against powerful political actors who were attempting to continue the centuries long legacy of the commodification of Black bodies to the benefit of the White Power Structure. It was a historic campaign infused by grassroots "people power." It could be said that the inauguration of the grassroots Black-led campaign against O'Malley's Youth Jail was October 31, 2010 – the date of Youth Justice Sunday, a community rally organized near the site of the proposed youth jail. Jamye Wooten, the Baltimore Algebra Project, Leaders of a Beautiful Struggle, and I planned this event which was intentionally held just 48 hours before Maryland's statewide elections which included the gubernatorial election. The goal was to force this issue to the center of public discourse and perhaps even impact elections at a time when the electoral fervor had reached fevered pitch in the state.

Youth Justice Sunday featured a diverse segment of Baltimore's Black Community. With the Marcus Garvey-inspired, red, black, and green flag waving high, the event began with a collective singing of the Black National Anthem. I mc'd the event and invited a number of people to participate including, but not limited to Mashica Winslow of the musical group, Winslow Dynasty, Student Minister Carlos Muhammad of Muhammad Mosque #6, Pastor Eric King of what is now St. Matthews New Life United Methodist Church, State Delegate Jill P. Carter (D-41), daughter of Baltimore civil rights icon, Walter P. Carter, Brother Jabari and Sista Yaa of Solvivaz Nation, the Baltimore Algebra Project and members of Leaders of a Beautiful Struggle. After the rally, which was held on Dunbar High School's football field, members of the grassroots campaign along with supporter Rev. Kinji Scott led the group of a few hundred people to the actual site of the proposed jail which the state had fenced off and leveled. Members of the group chanted and cheered as various persons participated in civil disobedience, cutting the chain of the gate which fenced off the designated land. Various persons placed books and other symbols on the "youth jail grounds" as signs of our displeasure and articulations of our hopes.

After 4 years of relentless opposition, Governor Martin O'Malley yielded and surrendered to the will of the people. In January 2013, the Governor and state officials announced that the funding for the new construction of a multi-million dollar youth jail in East Baltimore had been removed from the state budget.[11] Though the fight against the prison pipeline continues, this represents a significant victory and chapter in the "People's History" of Baltimore.[12] The ingredients that contributed to the qualified success of this campaign center on the Team, the Tools, and the Timing.

THE TEAM

Already established community organizations partnered with particularly invested and passionate organizers and activists to create a formidable force. The main youth and young adult-led organizations involved in the fight against the Youth Jail were The Baltimore Algebra Project and Leaders of a Beautiful Struggle. The Baltimore

Algebra Project, which has been in Baltimore since the early 1990s has been known to help mold a cadre of youth whose training program in times past has helped point youth toward a particular inclination toward direct, non-violent civil disobedience. Former Student Nonviolent Coordinating Committee (SNCC) activist, Bob Moses founded the National Algebra Project and established chapters all over the country including in Baltimore. Leaders Of A Beautiful Struggle, is a for-profit young adult-led think tank and political action committee (PAC). This organization, founded by a group of friends who are past collegiate debate champions from Towson University, brought a focus on policy research and legislative advocacy that proved invaluable to the campaign against the Youth Jail.

In addition to these main groups, other individuals also brought particular gifts to the table. Jamye Wooten is a skilled strategist, business owner and independent media maven who was instrumental in helping to organize "Youth Justice Sunday" on October 31, 2010. Chabria Thomas, is an experienced community organizer and labor activist whose passion for self-determination for Black people has manifested itself on issues of housing, gentrification, and worker's rights. Tanay Lynn Harris, an organizer who was then with the NAACP Leadership Defense Fund, supported the campaign against the Youth Jail in its final stages helping to bring a national perspective. State Delegate Jill P. Carter, daughter of the late Baltimore Civil Rights icon, Walter P. Carter, was the lone legislator in the early stages who lent her name and submitted legislation to halt the construction of the jail.[13] Finally, as pastor of Pleasant Hope Baptist Church in Baltimore, Maryland; I was afforded the privilege of helping to lead a congregation to the frontlines of this fight as well while preaching sermons, conducting "teach-ins," and inviting clergy colleagues to join the effort.

There were many others who at different times and in different ways helped to spur this effort forward, but this "young, gifted, and Black" eclectic mix of activists and organizers brought just the right combination of gifts, insight, resources, and abilities to the core of the movement that helped thwart state plans to build another jail for youth in Baltimore. A lesser-recognized aspect of this grouping of strategists, activists, and organizers is that they had already established friendships prior to the start of this campaign. The relationships, which existed before the fight against the Youth Jail, helped set the stage for a campaign with a low to negligible degree of internal power struggles, friction, or misunderstandings. It also created a framework where members were already familiar with one another's sharpest gifts and were comfortable deferring to members of the team who we felt were best suited to the task at hand. It was by no means a panacea, but the combination of gifts and accountable relationships at the core of this unit helped hold the usual divisive and counterproductive "spirits" of fear, insecurity, jealousy, and envy at bay. This aspect of the campaign should not be minimized.

THE TOOLS

The tools and strategy employed by the grassroots and youth and young adult-led protests against the youth jail were varied and creative. Instead of just relying upon conventional and familiar avenues of protest; technology and social media were employed in a way that helped frame the popular narrative around the issue. The diverse members of this loosely allied, but strategically organized campaign used technology to fight the Youth Jail like Civil Rights Era activists used "spirituals" to fight Jim Crow.

Starting out, youth and young adult activists were told that there was no way that the Youth Jail plan would be sidelined. It was already too late. In the largely democratic state of Maryland with a very powerful and popular Governor with national aspirations, there were few openings that would allow these young activists' voices to be heard. So in turn, they amplified their voices using that which was readily available – cell phones and social networking sites. They created a stage that demanded an audience using their Facebook, Twitter, and YouTube pages. Facebook status updates were coordinated across various team members' pages. Twitter discussions and debates were held online using hashtags like: #StopOMalleysJail. YouTube videos made by cell phones and consumer model camcorders helped give the local community and the world a "street-level" view of the community's response to the plan to incarcerate more Black youth. This became more than just independent media reporting – it became a highly effective art form that ultimately shifted public opinion.

Leading up to Youth Justice Sunday, Deverick Murray, the current Director of Youth Development at LBS and independent rap and spoken word artist, created an anthem to help popularize the day's event and the larger movement. He penned and produced a song entitled, "I Be Damned" which went viral on YouTube. The song states defiantly:

> Baltimore City! Stand Up!
> Youth Justice Sunday
> Democrat This
> Republican That
> Read This
> Read That
> Don't none of them care about Black!
> Be there on Sunday or be affected by it one day
> I be damned if I'm goin' let O'Malley lock me
> I be damned if I'm goin' let Ehrlich lock me[14]
> I be damned if I'm goin' let O'Malley lock me
> lock me lock me

Other videos were also made that framed the issue of O'Malley's Youth Jail in the context of the historical oppression of Black people in America. Songs by popular artists such as The Last Poets, Dead Presidents, and Chicago-born rapper, Common were used to provide the soundtrack for the street interviews and confrontations that members of the alliance initiated. For example, I produced a video which simply showed the land where Governor O'Malley planned to build the Youth Jail, as the camera panned over the site, I edited in the African drums and popular chant, "Black People What Ya'll Goin Do?" – a revolutionary poem and work from The Last Poets, a group of poets and musicians who became popular in the 1960's for their socially conscious and Black nationalist raps, rhythms, and messages. These videos produced by young activists involved in the campaign to stop O'Malley's Youth Jail were uploaded to YouTube, linked to Facebook and Twitter and viewed by thousands of Maryland residents – including those outside of the State as well.

THE TIMING

The allied campaign against the O'Malley's Youth Jail picked up real steam in 2010 – a Maryland State election year. During campaign season, it is widely known that political incumbents and their challengers are engaged in a number of activities all designed to get them elected or re-elected to their respective office. Politicians are in some respects "creatures" of self-preservation and are less likely to be non-responsive to the concerns and expressed needs of constituents because during an election year it is believed that their political future hangs in the balance. Therefore, politicians are more vulnerable during campaign season and during election years than at any other time. What this means for community activists and organizers is that a number of opportunities are available during campaign season to get the "people's agenda" in the streams of popular and public discourse. It also means that political candidates who tend to be particularly careful about their public image are more apt to act predictably in the face of any framing that would associate them with unpopular policies and plans. Politicians and "wanna be" politicians were swarming all over the state of Maryland in 2010 imploring voters to give them the gift of their confidence in the voting booth on election day – chief among them was Governor Martin O'Malley.

Since before his start in elected office in Maryland, Governor Martin O'Malley has had a swirl of sometimes frenzied discussion surround him as a presidential aspirant.[15] In 2010, the swirl had almost reached tornadic proportions as O'Malley was elected as the Chair of the Democratic Governor's Association – giving him a national platform.[16] With such a long political track record in Maryland, his political and behavioral proclivities became calculating and predictable.[17] This proved to be beneficial to the campaign against the planned youth jail as O'Malley and his machine weren't just running to be reelected in Maryland, but working to preserve his national standing as well. Knowing this, organizers and activists in the Stop The Youth Jail Campaign made the most of this window of opportunity to challenge O'Malley and other democratic politicians on the issue while they were most vulnerable and protective of their political profiles and legacies.

Strategists in the campaign partnered primarily with the youth of the Baltimore Algebra Project to show up at Governor O'Malley's planned campaign stops in the Baltimore area. They marched, rallied, chanted, and interrupted Governor O'Malley's events in attempts to force him and his operatives to speak on the issue of the Youth Jail and commit to halt construction and redirect jail funds to capital projects and programs approved by community members. On one such occasion, activists interrupted an event on September 25, 2010 where the Maryland chapter of American Federation of State, County and Municipal Employees (AFSCME) – one of the nation's largest public service employees unions was endorsing Martin O'Malley for governor. With bullhorn, camcorders and rousing chants of "Stop O'Malley's Jail!" the small handful of Baltimore youth and young adult activists made a crowd of more than a hundred union members and campaign staff pay attention to their concerns. O'Malley and all political candidates in attendance were pressed to speak to the unpopular issue of the planned Youth Jail and commit to stand against it. Not taking the interruption too kindly, union members confronted the youth and young adult activists and bordering on a physical confrontation expelled them from the premises.[18] It should be noted that in addition to the more direct street level protests, members of the Stop The Youth Jail campaign were also writing opinion editorials, testifying at legislative hearings, gathering the endorsements of Faith leaders and meeting with community members to educate them on the issue and request their support. This was a multi-faceted effort that studied the local Prison Industrial Complex and applied unrelenting force to every available "pressure point."[19]

THE TENSION

In addition to possessing the team, tools, and timing to successfully thwart state plans to build the multi-million dollar youth jail, the way that the grassroots campaign engaged the TENSION and internal pressure was also an interesting feature of the campaign. While existing relationships between the various members of the campaign helped to minimize destabilizing friction, dissension was not altogether eliminated. Much of the friction experienced arose when the grassroots element of the campaign was invited to partner with nonprofit organizations and foundations such as OSI-Baltimore, Advocates For Children and Youth, Community Law In Action and Safe and Sound, who were working in their respective lanes to stop the jail as well. While much has been written concerning the potentially disastrous and deliberately debilitating dynamics invited by community partnership with nonprofit organizations and foundations, members of the Stop The Youth Jail Campaign experienced it first-hand. In our engagement with nonprofit structures and foundations, we were reminded of how the imbalance of power and conflicts of interest found within nonprofit organizations can slow and stall the work of the people when it comes to social justice activism. In fact, some make the case that this is by design.

The Industry of Black Suffering:
Breaking Down the Non-Profit Industrial Complex

Incite! is a national activist organization of radical feminists of color who edited a book in 2007 entitled The Revolution Will Not Be Funded: Beyond The Non-profit Industrial Complex. In the edited book, they embrace a definition of the Nonprofit Industrial Complex (NPIC) which describes it as "a set of symbiotic relationships that link political and financial technologies of state and owning class control with surveillance over public political ideology, including and especially emergent progressive and leftist social movements."[20] Using this definition, the management of political movements becomes either the goal or the natural byproduct of such a cozy relationship between grassroots activists and those that could be called "career advocates." For those employed by the Nonprofit Industrial Complex, comfortable salaries are provided along with prestige to an entire class of people many of whom are not most directly affected by the problems that their organization directs them to address.

There are millions of dollars in grant money that flow through Baltimore. That money is typically in the hands of affluent white people who shape and mold the services that non-profits provide. This is true especially when we're talking about programs that serve Black people in Baltimore City. This arrangement is predicated on the notion of charity work toward American Africans rather than justice-oriented work to aid in abolishing the root causes of Black suffering.

This is best exemplified by the idea that many non-profits geared at empowering Black people will use phases like "anti poverty" instead of terms like "wealth development". Many would agree that social justice and economic equity are preferred goals for Black people. However, these goals require white people to renounce their loyalty to a social arrangement that maintains White power and control. Justice and self-determination for Black people would mean that the Black community would control its own political and economic resources – a move that has long been considered taboo in the non-profit sector because it requires sacrifices from white executives and Board members that many of them are just not willing to give up. This conclusion can be surmised from the findings of reports like that of The Urban Institute. In their March 2010 survey entitled, "Measuring Racial-Ethnic Diversity In The Baltimore-Washington Region's Nonprofit Sector," they found that despite the growing racial and ethnic diversity of the Baltimore-Washington region, American Africans, Latinos, Asians, Pacific Islanders and other People of Color are largely underrepresented in nonprofit executive leadership. More specifically, they write, "Although nearly half (49 percent) the population in the Baltimore-Washington region is people of color, 22 percent of nonprofit organizations in the region have executive directors of color.[21] The implications of this on grassroots organizing and activism in majority Black cities like Baltimore is profound. The cadre of activists working in their local neighborhoods to affect social change on a number of fronts are overwhelmingly Black while the overseers and funders of the work being done tend to be white. Hence, the reach of the White Power Structure's surveillance of Black bodies does not just include the penal system, law enforcement, or even the "blue cameras" that decorate Black and poor neighborhoods, but includes the activist and organizer communities as well. White people – even and perhaps especially benevolent and social justice-inclined whites, must be confronted with the white privilege afforded them by this dynamic and challenged to use said privilege responsibly toward the goal of upsetting the social arrangement that gifted them with the privilege in the first place.

The aforementioned dynamics were present for the duration of the organizing against O'Malley's Youth Jail. This manifested itself in the form of the "Stop The Jail" coalition – an alliance between primarily American African grassroots activists and white nonprofit executives. While the grassroots campaign was marshaled by local, indigenous leadership living closer to the reality of the ever expanding prison industrial complex, the "Stop The Jail" coalition, a later development in the march against the Youth Jail, had white-led nonprofit organization's as its chief architects. The sentiments expressed by the non-profits involved would often characterize the organizing as a project they were consulting on – not a reality that touched them personally. Mass mobilizations, like Youth Justice Sunday in 2010 were the major engines of the resistance to construction of the youth jail. These mass demonstrations were organized and carried out by Black organizations and activists. However, with the launch of the "Stop The Jail" coalition, those energies were redirected to numerous meetings with preference given to more subtle and less controversial actions against Governor O'Malley's juvenile justice plans.

In the coalition, many meetings (which took place at downtown nonprofit and foundation headquarters) were convened around the structure of the coalition's leadership and clarity about decision-making. Increasingly, the Black youth activists were growing uncomfortable at the table with nonprofit and foundation executives who by the very nature of their positions wielded considerable power at the point of negotiation and planning. These coalition meetings where leadership and decision-making desires were expressed by Black activists would typically appear to cause anxiety in the white people present and would lead to tense moments throughout the process. There was general discomfort with the idea of the coalition being expressly led by Black activists and organizations. After a series of discussions, an environment was created where the non-profit executives would apprehensively defer to the expertise of the grassroots Black leaders. There were several disagreements along the way, which led to some individuals rescinding their participation in the coalition and others pulling their organizations out as well. Hathaway Ferebee, the Executive Director of The Safe and Sound Campaign, expressed consistent concern and frustration with the coalition, its goals, and positions on policy related to the proposed Youth Jail. She, mistakenly believing that the coalition was considering agreeing with the administration on the construction of a smaller jail, decided it was best to remove Safe and Sound from the coalition altogether. From that point on the relationship between Safe and Sound and the Stop The Youth Jail Coalition including Black grassroots activists effectively dissolved and became contentious. The tipping point of the friction, however, came at a November 2012 rally hosted by Safe and Sound. It was called the "Affirmative Opportunity Rally" at the War Memorial building in downtown Baltimore. The event featured national Civil Rights leader, Rev. Jesse Jackson and a host of other Black politicians and clergy members many of whom to that point had been virtually silent on the issue of the youth jail. To an uniformed observer of the "Affirmative Opportunity Rally," it appeared that Hathaway Ferebee was the leader or at least chief engineer of the advocacy against the construction of the youth jail. The broad and popular appeal of Rev. Jesse Jackson helped solidify Ferebee's standing as a credible leader of the movement. The Youth Ambassadors of Safe and Sound who were Black youth from Baltimore, were trotted out to the podium at the rally with prepared speeches that gave further credibility to Ferebee and her organization.

This dynamic posed a problem to Leaders of a Beautiful Struggle (LBS). The issue was not public recognition, rather it centered on activism with integrity. There was no coordination and hardly any communication between Safe and Sound and local Black grassroots activists who had been essential in the resistance of the youth jail to that point. The concern was that the Affirmative Opportunities Rally was a misrepresentation of the true nature of the fight against the youth jail.

LBS' conclusion was that this was an attempt to co-opt the genuine movement around improving the quality of life for Black youth in Baltimore. There was great dismay expressed at the possibility that years of hard work and struggle against O'Malley's

Youth Jail on the part of Baltimore's grassroots activists would devolve into just another win and "pay day" for some in the city's Non-Profit Industrial Complex who already had social standing, economic power, and a history of access to political power. The threat to the convictions and ideals of the grassroots Black activists seemed very real. The driving energy of our street-level activism – that sustainable fuel that has been present in many of the world's most inspiring social movements – was seemingly being co-opted and re-routed for private gain with the Black masses being left out in the end. For the goal of the original grassroots campaign to stop "O'Malley's Youth Jail" was not only to halt the construction, but to redistribute the dedicated financial resources toward programs, plans, and capital projects that American Africans in East Baltimore defined as their priorities. The closer we appeared to get to winning on the front of stopping the youth jail, the more uncertain we were that we would actually win the big prize of securing the redirection of state funds for community priorities. In fact, to date that goal has not been realized and the relentless nature of the prison industrial complex is on display as rumors of other jails and so-called treatment centers persist.

One would be mistaken to conclude that our position is that all non-profit organizations and Foundations are inherently evil and work against the community. Furthermore, the takeaway should not be that white people have no role in the fight for justice. However, it is clearer today to those of us who worked on the front lines of the Stop O'Malley's Jail campaign, that non-profit organizations can play a supportive role in helping to empower communities in their quest for self-determination, justice and equity. Nevertheless, nonprofit executives should regularly examine their privilege and the privilege afforded their organizations, analyze candidly their relationship with state power (confessing when it conflicts with community goals) and submit to a process of accountability where the populations they profess to serve oversee their decisions and actions in local communities.

Concerning Baltimore, the Black community should not be forced to remain in a position where we are dependent on the benevolence of white people or the illusory mercies of the white power structure to provide community services and resources. We also argue that white-led non-profit organizations operating and active in Black communities must be essentially led by affected Black people and defer to their direction and vision when engaging issues that most directly impact them.

These distinctions are important because the priority for Black people in these instances should be building independent Black institutions. Oftentimes, the Non-Profit Industrial Complex frames out the capacity for us to have conversations about how we build institutions for Black people that accurately respond to the forces present in our community. If the priority is not building Black institutions, it offers an opportunity for white led non-profits to usurp the resources and social capital of the Black leaders and organizations. This has the impact of destabilizing Black organizing while dually increasing the wealth, prestige and status of non-profit organizations. This effect, while insidious, can easily go unnoticed by whites and Blacks alike. Explicit challenges to the institutional arrangement of the Non-Profit Industrial Complex must be made on non-profit executives of all racial and ethnic backgrounds – for the features of the system of oversight, management and even derailment of social movements are reinforced regardless of who is at the helm of the organization. There are too many Black children's lives at stake to play polite parlor games for grant money, prestige and status with white liberals or the Non-profit Industrial Complex.

Closing Thoughts

The Stop The Youth Jail Campaign should not be understood in isolation from Black people's continuous struggle for self-determination, justice, and freedom. Since, and long before, the March on Washington, American Africans have been fighting for their God-given right to determine their own future, define their own reality, and defend those principles, ethics, and values that are deemed communal priorities. Stopping O'Malley's Jail was just one of the latest chapters in this ongoing saga. The grassroots campaign was an effort inspired by the audacity, idealism, and energy of youth and young adults of Baltimore. The Governor of the state of Maryland was made to pay attention to Black youth and heed their demands. The campaign was historic in the sense that it honored the tradition of Baltimore freedom fighters from years gone by and hopefully will leave some clues for activism and organizing to the rising generation of youth who will be called upon to fight the battles that will be theirs. The youth and young adults who led the effort to stop the construction of a multi-million dollar youth jail in East Baltimore did not ask for permission to take a stand, however, with the guidance of The Ancestors, true Elders, and allies, dared to leave a mark in the sand of Baltimore's activism history.

Notes

[1]   Report of the National Advisory Commission on Civil Disorders, New York: E.P. Dunton, 1968, p. 2

[2]   Clarence N. Stone "Urban Political Machines: Taking Stock." *PS: Political Science and Politics,* Vol. 29, (Sep. 1996): 446-450.

[3]   Robert Kerstein, "Political Machine" in *Encyclopedia of Urban Studies,* Ray Hutchison ed. (Thousand Oaks, CA: Sage Publications, 2010).

[4]   Dennis R. Judd and Todd Swanstrom, *City Politics: The Political Economy of Urban America* (New York: Longman, 2004), p. 48.

[5]   Alan DiGaetano, "The Rise and Development of Urban Political Machines." *Urban Affairs Quarterly* 4 (1998): 243-267.

[6]   Milton Rakove, *Don't Make No Waves, Don't Back No Losers* (Bloomington: Indiana University Press, 1979).

[7]   William Foote Whyte, *Street Corner Society* (Chicago: University of Chicago Press, 1995).

[8]   Clarence N. Stone "Urban Political Machines: Taking Stock." *PS: Political Science and Politics,* Vol. 29, (Sep. 1996): 446-450.

[9]   Marion Orr, *Black Social Capital: The Politics of School Reform in Baltimore.* (University of Kansas Press, 1999).

[10]   Orr, *Black Social Capital,* 62.

[11]   Christopher Howard, Michael Lipsky, and Dale Rogers Marshall, "Citizen

Participation in Urban Politics: Rise and Routinization" in Big City Politics, Governance, and Fiscal Constraints, ed. George E. Peterson (Washington: Urban Institute Press, 1994), 181.

12 Adolph Reed, *Stirrings in the Jug: Black Politics in the Post-Segregation Era* (University of Minnesota Press, 1999).

13 Reed, *Stirrings in the Jug*.

14 Floyd Hunter, *Community Power Structure: A Study of Decision Makers* (Chapel Hill: University of North Carolina Press, 1953).

15 Appleton, Andrea, "Nine in the 9th: Challengers line up to take on the 9th District's appointed incumbent," *Baltimore City Paper*, July 27, 2011.

16 Robert Kerstein, "Political Machine" in *Encyclopedia of Urban Studies*, Ray Hutchison ed. (Thousand Oaks, CA: Sage Publications, 2010).

17 Arnold Fleishmann and Lana Stein. 1998. "Campaign Contributions in Local Elections." *Political Research Quarterly*, Vol. 51 (Sep. 1998): 673-689.

18 Swanstrom, "Machine Politics and Political Bosses."

19 Trounstine, "Dominant Regimes and the Demise of Urban Democracy," 879.

20 Dianne Pinderhughes, *Race and Ethnicity in Chicago Politics: A Reexamination of Pluralist Theory* (Chicago: University of Illinois Press, 1987).

21 Stokely Carmichael and Charles V. Hamilton, *Black Power: The Politics of Liberation*. (New York: Random House, 1967).

22 John Mollenkopf, "New York: Still the Great Anomaly." In Racial Politics in American Cities, 3rd Edition, ed. Rufus P. Browning, Dale Rogers Marshall, and David H. Tabb (New York: Longman, 2003)

23 Canon, David T. Canon, *Race, Redistricting, and Representation* (Chicago, IL: University of Chicago Press, 1999).

24 Bryan O. Jackson, "The Effects of Racial Group Consciousness on Political Mobilization in American Cities." *The Western Political Quarterly*, Vol. 40, (Dec. 1987): 644.

25 William Nelson and Philip J. Meranto, *Electing Black Mayors: Political Association in the Black Community*. (Columbus: Ohio State University Press, 1977).

"It's Both/And, Not Either/Or: Black Power AND Black Love for Black Baltimore"

S. Todd Yeary

The Remembrance

On July 2, 1964, President Lyndon B. Johnson signed the Civil Rights Act of 1964 into law. The passage of the CRA was an earnest attempt to move the conversation around racial disenfranchisement forward, and an effort to take the next steps toward dismantling the lingering effects of the legal construction of race, most notably articulated in the Plessy decision of 1896, and later repealed in the Brown decision of 1954. As we approach the 50-year anniversary of the enactment of the Civil Rights Act of 1964, and mark the 60-year anniversary of the Supreme Court decision in Brown, we also must reexamine what role the faith community (the Black Church) plays in impacting the political benefit of Black communities. It is recognized that Black churches played a significant role (at least at the local level) in the organizing and strategizing, supporting and sustaining the civil rights movement in all its phases. It was later that more cohesive national support for the movement was expressed within the faith community. However, there is much debate about the extent to which the church has played (or ought to) in the affirmative outcomes for Black people specifically, and the entire society overall.

August 2013 marked the beginning of new season of milestones in the historical racial memory of the United States. The semi-centennial remembrance of the historic March on Washington for Jobs and Freedom has allowed for mental and spiritual returns to the events of that day in August 1963, which was highlighted by a sequence of coordinated speeches that culminated with Dr. Martin Luther King, Jr.'s epic oration, "I Have a Dream." It is this season of remembrance that forces us to go beyond nostalgic replays to real-time assessment of Black progress in the areas for which the significant milestones of the 1960's have been marked, and the original events were initially purposed. This analysis and assessment must be completed at all levels, recognizing that national movements have local consequences and local movements have national potential.

When one considers the need for jobs and freedom in 2014 in Baltimore City, one must recognize that there still exists a deep cynicism amongst constituencies of color, and a dismissiveness of the needs of the oppressed on the part of the largely white power elite. This reality warrants a renewed consideration of the future political and economic course within the Black community primarily, as well as other affected communities of poor, disenfranchised people. As we examine the state of Black Baltimore, when the focus shifts from the national influence and impact of Black activism, there must be a consideration whether there is a concerted, committed, and coordinated political agenda that advances the causes of the Black electorate in Baltimore City. Or, is there a significant vacuum that continues to suck the life out of the displaced, dispossessed, and marginalized among us? The recent loss of key faith leaders and activists in Baltimore - Rev. Marion Bascom, Rev. Vernon Dobson, Dr. Homer Favor —forces us to remember the significance of coordinated struggle, and to assess if the Black community is achieving maximum results for the level of political engagement that is observed within/from the faith community.

The other plausible consideration in this analysis is also more disconcerting. Namely, whether the perceived lack of demonstrated political empowerment is an indication of the declining role of the Black faith community in helping to shape public policy and advance a sustainable political agenda. This essay attempts to focus our attention on the potential value of faith-based engagement on the electoral process. As we are now firmly situated in the 21st century, we are also witnessing the Supreme Court's overt subversion of the civil rights advances achieved at the height of the civil rights movement, and which we commemorate this year and in years that will follow.

Politics and Faith

Just prior to Dr. King's assassination in April 1968, and in the aftermath of a series of protest uprisings in cities across the country, the U.S. Riot Commission (known as the Kerner Commission) was established to identify and assess the contributing factors that led to such volatile responses to racial inequality. Oddly enough, the breadth of the Riot Commission's report extended to the critique and evaluation of various aspects of the civil rights movement. The Commission assessed a variety of considerations, including the historical sketch of the protest movement from the colonial period to that time. The scope of that appraisal included the establishment of the Niagra movement, and later the NAACP (whose founding has significant ties to the Black Church in Baltimore), the influence of the Black Muslim movement, and the freedom movements of the 1960's. There was also a critique of the failures of direct action, the anemia of Black Power, and the notion of "old wine in new bottles."[1]

The Riot Commission report noted that the most effective demonstration of direct action was present in areas where Black political engagement and voting was concentrated sufficiently to impact election outcomes. The Commission noted, "The demonstrations of the early 1960's had been successful principally in places like Atlanta, Nashville, Durham, Winston-Salem, Louisville, Savannah, New Orleans, Charleston, and Dallas —where Negroes voted and could swing elections." (Emphasis mine.)[2]

Black Baltimore has the potential to affect the outcomes of citywide elections, and to greatly influence statewide election outcomes only to the degree that there is optimum participation in the electoral process. The hinging of political outcomes on a voting block that is engaged and invested forces all potential players (candidates) in the political arena to advance an agenda that speaks to the needs of affected Black people as a key component of any populist political agenda. When reviewing the voter participation in the 2011 city-wide election by elected office, one recognizes that voter turnout was approximately 13% of the potential number of voters overall, and was as low as 6% in some council districts. From the board of election data on the 2011 general election, it is noted verbatim:

- For the General Election there were **372,888** registered voters.
- **49,463** voters went out to cast their vote on Election Day, early voting and by absentee ballots.
- Total percentage was **13.28%**. (Emphasis mine.)[3]

When considering the demographics in each council district, one recognizes that, in many instances, there was a much lower participation among eligible Black voters than amongst their white counterparts. If this trend continues, especially in light of the difficulty in generating excitement around local and state elections, there will be little incentive for any political constituency (regardless of party or appearance) to take seriously the issues and concerns of Black people in a majority-minority city. Without any political will or moral imperative to drive voter engagement and participation, the aspirations of underserved communities and communities of color will be left to chance and coincidence.

Political Will as a Demonstration of Revolutionary Faith

"…Martin Luther King, Jr. was not simply a churchman who happened to be caught up in a revolutionary moment. Rather, he was one who, while caught up in a moment much larger than himself, came to see revolution as central to the church's primary reason for being."[4]
                    —*Rev. Dr. Raphael G. Warnock*

"The revolution will not be televised, will not be televised, will not be televised, will not be televised. The revolution will be no re-run brothers; the revolution will be live."[5]

                    —*Gil Scott-Heron*

The mean and the manner through which one attempts to change the political and economic realities of Black Baltimore continues to hinge on political engagement, political empowerment AND political will. Without these key ingredients, one is left with a default position of dependence on a political system that is not designed to advance the causes of Black people in any arena, whether in education, economic empowerment, access to employment, wealth building, and the like. The faith community's role in advancing a comprehensive political agenda is essential in that the self-interest of these institutions is intertwined with the political reality of its constituents. For example, Black churches make more bank deposits and own more real assets than almost any other industry in the Black community. Some estimate that Black congregations deposit an average of $50 million in banks each Monday.[6] At over 2.5 billion dollars in deposits, these FBO's should be able to leverage capital to support community development activities. However, we know this is not the case. As a matter of fact, lending to Black faith-based organizations is down since 2008, and major banks are proving to be reluctant to address the capital needs of churches in general, and Black churches particularly.

The Black Church's engagement in the political infrastructure, and the forming of strategic alliances with other communities that face similar concerns around disenfranchisement will be necessary if the decline in political influence is to be altered. Although the Riot Commission's diagnosis of anemia in the Black power agenda seems to give rise to a dismissive attitude toward any Black electorate, the recognition that concentrated political participation sufficient to affect election outcomes presents an opportunity to re-engage in the electoral process in all phases. Furthermore, recent voting opportunities as those presented with early voting allow for the faith community to influence greater participation in every election, regardless of level of government. Faith based organizations, particularly in the Black community, have the ability to influence more votes than any other organization in the community, and therefore must advance a vested effort in helping to "swing" political outcomes that advance causes in the Black community's self-interest, though not necessarily exclusive interests.

An Empowerment Agenda

There must be a concerted effort around the setting/updating of a comprehensive, long-term urban reconstruction agenda for Black Baltimore. This agenda begins with exercising political influence in supporting representatives who will advance a holistic empowerment agenda. This agenda must include urban reconstruction of neighborhoods that have been disrupted by the public policy of the past, and remain neglected by underinvestment and lack of needed access to capital to facilitate urgent revitalization. This revitalization is necessary to altering the fortunes and futures of underserved communities.

Faith based organizations (FBO's), as holders of significant real property, must be partners in the development strategy and implementation. Stegman argues, "While structural changes in the national economy having contributed to the growth of an urban underclass, and continuing problems with out educational, health care, housing, and welfare systems, one might conclude that all cities and most African Americans are worse off today than they were when the [riots] broke out in the late 1960's."[7] The conditions of many communities across the country, and particularly in Baltimore City, continue to lag behind more affluent communities in economic progress, as well as other key indicators of overall community health.

Two of the areas in which there is continued cause for concern is community development and high Black unemployment. The correlation between rebuilding communities and creating employment and other economic opportunities is significant. FBO's who have capacity potential must be developed to support community economic development, and should embrace a collaborative economic model of partnership in order to leverage capacity in order to achieve a larger scale of development impact. Community Development Financial Institutions (CDFI's) such as Enterprise Community Partners and The Reinvestment Fund can be significant partners in this capacity building effort.[8] It is through partnerships with organizations that have development capacity that the Black Church will be able to actively participate in the development profile of the communities they serve. Billingsley argues, "The idea of black churches using their enormous economic and financial resources as leverage for building programs that benefit not just individuals and families but the entire community is an idea whose time has come."[9] Indeed, for many communities, it is well past time.

Additionally, there must be an affirmative political strategy that does not leave to chance the advocacy of concerns that are germane to all communities, especially communities of color. This includes leveraging a fully engaged Black electorate that cannot only impact outcomes, but can also establish political succession in key positions that will address a sustainable economic and political agenda that benefits everyone, and not just a few. Finally, there must be a new strategy for participating in the political process. With the erosion of limits for campaign contributions in recent SCOTUS decisions, it is now more incumbent that political action committees that advocate for a comprehensive urban agenda be formed AND funded. Mutual self-interest on behalf of the communities that face similar challenges can only be advanced as each community assumes an assertive posture within the political process.

It's About Power AND Love

"Black Power rhetoric and ideology actually express a lack of power."[10]
—*U.S. Riot Commission*

"Power, properly understood, is the ability to achieve purpose. It is the strength required to bring about social, political or economic changes. In this sense power is not only desirable but necessary in order to implement the demands of love and justice."[11]
—*Dr. Martin Luther King, Jr.*

In December 1964, John Coltrane recorded his epic four-part masterpiece, "A Love Supreme." There are four progressions of the project, thematic shifts that rise to a high finale. The four parts are "Acknowledgement", "Resolution", "Pursuance", and "Psalm."[12] "A Love Supreme" represents the metaphorical progression of Black Power, from recognizing our unique identity and contribution to the whole of society, to the resolve and pursuit of the highest ideals and, ultimately, to the acknowledgement of the divine imperative. Black Baltimore's political future must continue to follow the trajectory of a supreme love that affirms the best of who we are, and fully engages (without compromise or apology) within power conversations at all levels.

According to the Mayor's Office of Neighborhoods, there are at least 2,400 churches in Baltimore City.[13] Within this collection of churches is a significant number of African American Christian congregations. The "Black Church" must assume and accept its responsibility in advancing the human rights causes of its community AND the broader community of which it is a part. In The Politics of God, Joseph Washington proposes, "Religion as central to the black community in the past may be vital in the present to the extent it is relevant to the problems of power and politics."[14] Accepting this responsibility requires that the faith community continue to assert an ethic of power AND love. The two are inextricably connected.

Although the Kerner Commission was quite dismissive of many of the political tactics and strategies of the 1960's, the notion of Black empowerment (or Black Power) must continue to be an essential part of any and all power discussions about the future of Baltimore City. There can be no assumption that passive engagement is sufficient to counter the erosion of the economic and political fabric of the Black community. Additionally, there must be a renewed commitment to organize and mobilize Black people to engage and participate in the electoral process. Until the potential of the Black community's vote is leveraged to determine election outcomes on a consistent basis, Black people will continue to be manipulated and dismissed in the larger conversation about power, education, economic empowerment, and wealth building.

To assert the political strength of the Black community about issues that affect the Black community is not a sign of weakness, it is the beginning of establishing and re-establishing credible conversations and potential strategic relationships that accrue to the benefit of all people. In Where Do We Go From Here, Dr. King reminds us that there is no dichotomy between power and love – you can't have one without the other: "What is needed is a realization that power without love is reckless and abusive, and that love without power is sentimental and anemic. Power at its best is love implementing the demands of justice. Justice at its best is love correcting everything that stands against love."[15] Kwame Ture (Stokely Carmichael) noted, "Black people in the United States must raise hard questions, questions which challenge the very nature of the society itself: its long-standing values, beliefs, and institutions."[16] This is the justification and necessity for Black Power and Black Love in Black Baltimore.

Here's to the revolution going LIVE…

Notes

1 National Advisory Commission on Civil Disorders. *"Report of the National Advisory Commission of Civil Disorders."* Bantam Books, 1968. xxii. This word play on a well-known biblical text indicates the degree to which the analysis was dismissive and critical of the role of the church in advancing the causes of Black people.

2 Ibid., 231.

3 Baltimore City Elections Board. "November 2011 General Election Results." p. 11/28/2011. Web. 04/08/2014. http://www.baltimorecity.gov/Government/BoardsandCommissions/ElectionsBoard/PastElectionResults.aspx

4 Warnock, Raphael G. *The Divided Mind of the Black Church: Theology, Piety & Public Witness.* New York University Press, 2014. 176.

5 Gil Scott-Heron. "The Revolution will not be Televised." Pieces of a Man. RCA, 1972. Album.

6 May, Lucy. "Cincinnati's black churches organize to gain business bargaining muscle." Cincinnati Business Courier p. Feb. 25, 2011. Web. April 9, 2014. http://www.bizjournals.com/cincinnati/print-edition/2011/02/25/cincinnatis-black-churches-organize.html?

7 Stegman, Michael A. "National Urban Policy Revisited." *Race, Poverty and American Cities.* Ed. John Charles Boger and Judith Welch Wegner. Univ. of North Carolina Press, 1996. 230.

8 Community Development Financial Institutions (CDFI's) are financial institutions that specialize in providing financial products and services in underserved and distressed markets and communities. A variety of banks, credit unions, and special lenders serve as CDFI's. For more information, see http://www.cdfifund.gov/what_we_do/programs_id.asp?programID=9

9 Billingsley, Andrew. *Mighty Like a River: The Black Church and Social Reform.* Oxford University Press, 1999. 144.

10 National Advisory Commission on Civil Disorders. "Report", 234.

11 King, Jr. Martin Luther King. *Where Do We Go From Here? Chaos or Community?* (King Legacy) (Kindle Locations 526-528). Kindle Edition.

12 John Coltrane. "A Love Supreme." *A Love Supreme.* Impulse Records, 1965. CD.

13 The number of churches is an anecdotal estimate from a representative in the Mayor's Office of Neighborhoods in Baltimore City.

14 Washington, James. *The Politics of God.* Beacon Press, 1969. xiii.

15 King, *Where Do We Go From Here?* (King Legacy) (Kindle Location 531). Kindle Edition.

16 Ture, Kwame and Charles V. Hamilton. *Black Power: The Politics of Liberation.* Vintage Books, 1992. 34.

The State Of Black Baltimore: Where Do We Go From Here?

Diane Bell McKoy

When people hear the name Associated Black Charities, they assume—and dismiss—ABC's agenda as being "just" for African Americans.

But that is like saying that the social ills of Maryland "just" impact African Americans or that negative health outcomes "just" impact African Americans when we know that quite the opposite is true.

THE STATE OF BLACK BALTIMORE and the agenda of Associated Black Charities impact ALL citizens who live, work, go to school, and have businesses in Baltimore City and Maryland. It impacts all of us because race-based health and wealth disparities rob our city and state of its economic and health prosperity. And while the comfortable and/or short-sighted amongst us will not see or will deny that, the following attests to its reality: by (an estimated) 2020, not only the city of Baltimore but the state of Maryland will be "majority-minority." (Currently, Maryland is "majority-minority:" people of color comprise 50% of the populations for every age group 40 and under, with the exceptions of ages 24 [in which people of color comprise 49.7% of the population], and 25 [in which people of color comprise 49.8% of the population]).[1]

And as an increasing percentage of Baltimore City and Maryland's populations of color are locked out of opportunities for advancement—such as workforce trainings and college access—the city and state will eventually pay the price: in a workforce that is unprepared for 21st Century jobs and in the shared costs of lost tax bases; revenue; discretionary spending; and incarceration and other social program costs.

Our collective economic future is dependent upon our ability to move as many people as possible to tax-base contributors rather than tax-base dependents.

Our ability to do this critical 21st Century work is dependent upon our ability to see that although neither our progress nor our pathways to opportunity have been "color-blind," we have an opportunity now to build our collective future upon a promising agenda that offers an economic equity approach to transformative change.

In Baltimore City, Maryland, and all of America, while there has been progress, the past has left legacies of color-coded access to opportunities inside of our systems and institutions. The data clearly surfaces the outcomes of these legacies in color-coded economic, educational, criminalization, and health disparities. But this data does not answer the most important question facing us in this 21st Century: WHERE DO WE GO FROM HERE?

Do we continue to pretend that the impact of our current societal path is not color-coded? Do we continue to pretend that it does not give automatic, unearned advantages based on race- and class- (operating within the context of race) privilege?

Do we continue to advocate for and enforce policies that—while seemingly race-neutral—disproportionately impact communities of color by criminalizing, further marginalizing, and creating even more barriers for those who are already criminalized, marginalized, and facing race-based structural and institutional barriers?

Do white Baltimoreans and Marylanders, in general, stay trapped in guilt, entitlement, willful blindness, ignorance, or hopelessness about these issues?

Will African Americans and other people of color who have successfully negotiated the system despite race-based barriers opt out of these critical conversations in order to protect their accomplishments, their positions, their opportunities, their families?

WHERE DO WE GO FROM HERE?

Associated Black Charities' More in the Middle—an initiative to grow the number of African American and other citizens of color with increased financial assets who are securely-positioned members of the economic middle-class—is a roadmap for eliminating racialized disparities and strengthening the economic futures of our children and our communities. This initiative addresses six areas of racialized disparities: Higher Education (College Readiness, Access, and Completion); Workforce and Career Advancement (for low-skilled and higher-skilled, and career-professional workers); Business and Economic Development (inclusion for high-growth, people of color-owned businesses); Health; Homeownership and Foreclosure Prevention; and Financial Literacy and Wealth-Building (a component in each of our other five intervention areas).

Of these six, we focus upon four for deeper implementation—Higher Education; Workforce; Business and Economic Development; and Health. We have chosen to focus on these four based on the dire need for addressing them, their potential for increased traction and partnership opportunities, and in acknowledgement that there are many other partner-groups doing good work around the remaining two. (And while there are also groups doing good work around the four we've targeted for deeper implementation, our specific lens, research, framework, and strategic collaborative partnerships positively add to the good work being done and to the approaches, solutions, interventions, and policies being proposed and implemented.)

We have also chosen these four understanding their critical impact on the future of both Baltimore City and Maryland. Studies show that African American-owned businesses are willing to hire and give African American workers more of a chance than white-owned businesses. Higher Education increases opportunities for both wealth-building and community stability, as well as fosters civic engagement and leadership. A ready and skilled Workforce attracts and keeps businesses in our city and state. And more successful Health outcomes lowers healthcare and social programs costs for us all.

Just as importantly, the success of these intervention areas creates a "win-win" for our city and state regardless of race. Focus upon these areas offers us opportunities to work collaboratively in ways that cross race and resource lines, and our "wins" – both transactional (direct interventions) and transformative (public and institutional policy shifts) positively and ultimately impact ALL of our families and ALL of our communities.

YES, we STILL have to be honest about the impact of race-based structural and institutional barriers; we cannot run away from that conversation. But we can understand that WE DO NOT have to continue the racialized legacies of the past; that WE CAN use our areas of privilege to change them; and that WE MUST if we care about changing the outcomes for thousands of children in our city; in our state; and in our region.

The States of Black Baltimore—and Brown Baltimore—and Yellow Baltimore—and Red Baltimore—the whole racial mosaic of Maryland—are in our hands, permanently linked. White Baltimore—as well as the state and region—can no longer deny or pretend that this is not so.

The numbers for our state and region speak otherwise.

And because of that, so must we.

To find out more about Associated Black Charities' More in the Middle Initiative, visit www.abc-md.org. We welcome your feedback and your participation.

Additional Reading: More in the Middle Initiative Dashboard Report: An Overview of Economic Gaps in Black and White; Associated Black Charities' Framework Report: An Economic Equity Approach to Transformative Change; and other readings can be found at www.abc-md.org.

Notes

[1]   The Data Mine, Maryland Department of Planning MD State Data Center 2011

"A NEW VISION"
For Baltimore
2014

Douglas Miles

1963 was a watershed year for the Civil Rights Movement because it marked a significant shift in how America viewed the racial divide. That year saw the historic March on Washington which was viewed in diametrically opposed perspectives by African Americans and White Liberals. The event was the launching pad for eventual passage of the Civil Rights Bill of 1964 and the point of separation between what up until then had been partners in the struggle. Most White Americans viewed the March as a sign that "the race problem had been solved". Most African Americans viewed it as a beginning point for the nation to move toward real equality. From that date the ominous signs that the racial divide would persist despite progress towards equality begun in the 1950s and pushed further through the 1960s. The 1970s saw the erosion of the Movement as rival camps in the African American community could not come to agreement on a strategy to meet objectives and as White allies slowly began to distance themselves from what they began to view as unrealistic expectations given the political climate in America post Viet Nam.

It was at that point that organizers of the Industrial Areas Foundation and African American clergy in various cities began to look for ways to institutionalize the strongest aspects of the Civil Rights Movement so that progress grinding to a halt could be continued especially in urban centers. It was this thinking that led such giants of Baltimore's Civil Rights community as Reverends Vernon Dobson, Wendell Philips, Marion Bascom and Monsignor Claire O'Dwyer to invite the Industrial Areas Foundation to come into Baltimore to create a faith community response to the urban decay and loss of employment that were rapidly destroying communities and riveting down the horizons for many. Most urban communities were undergoing re-development but it was largely limited to gentrification and revitalization of downtown areas. Neighborhoods, schools and many mediating institutions were left to fend for themselves in ever increasingly hostile environment of downsizing corporations and middle class flight to the suburbs. Abandonment became the new watchword in neighborhoods as one generation of homeowners left the stage of history and their children who had moved to more upwardly mobile communities refused to occupy the old "homestead".

As African Americans began to gain political control of major cities, they discovered that a once supportive federal government was losing interest in urban renewal and the support services necessary to help struggling families survive in economies soon bereft of "living wage" employment. Public schools which had once been the backbone of quality education and thus the key to upward mobility were abandoned by Whites and middle class African American. Quality teachers began to look for more lucrative employment in private and charter schools. Bank red-lining persisted as those left in the cities found it increasingly more difficult to purchase home or acquire decent insurance rates for homes and automobiles. Black churches increasingly became mesmerized by neo-Pentecostal religion that sapped them of interest in and resources for social engagement as a "health, wealth and prosperity" brand of religion captured the imagination of the Baby Boom generation returning to church after a prolonged absence.

It was into this void of effective leadership, failing neighborhood community association responses and an often impotent elected leadership that Baltimoreans United In Leadership Development began organizing in the strongest remaining mediating institution in the African American community. IN 1978 the organization held its founding assembly convinced it could be the vehicle to effectively organize families and community to fend off the assault coming from both right wing politics and economic neglect of the corporate community.

"The Tent of Presence" and "The Vision Glorious" are documents developed by Baltimoreans United in Leadership Development to cast a vision for Baltimore that looked beyond downtown re-development to address the needs of the "other Baltimore"- that Baltimore not seen in glossy promotion brochures nor talked about when the city is trying to win convention business. Out of the vision of those two documents, BUILD crafted, fought for and won campaigns to secure affordable car insurance for Baltimoreans, competitive financing for home purchases and dramatic improvements in nursing homes throughout the city. Such times of reflection and prophetic insight gave BUILD the spiritual under-girding and the practical expression that brought into being the Commonwealth Agreements (which still finds expression through the College Bound program), Nehemiah housing, a ban on "Saturday Night Specials", the Living Wage Campaign and Child First Authority – the largest after school initiative in the state.

Dr. Cornel West in Prophetic Reflections reminds us that there are three basic components in "Prophetic Theology" - religious vision, historical and social analysis and action.[1] West states, that one dimension of the "religious vision has to do with the coming of the kingdom, with the empowerment that flows from the inbreaking and invading of a kingdom that on the one hand is beyond our power and on the other is inseparable from what we can do."[2]

It's that vision of the coming kingdom that both empowers us and sustains me at times when our organizational best efforts seem woefully lacking to correct the injustices which abound in our neighborhoods, our schools, our city, state and nation. Such a vision of the Beloved Community as lifted up in "The Vision Glorious" is what has kept my hands to the plow and my eyes focused on what must be done.

Yet there comes those times when I find myself feeling like and responding as did the prophet Habakkuk in his generation. Unlike most of the prophets of the Old Testament canon, who spoke for God to troubled situations, Habakkuk raises his complaint to God because of what he perceived to be God's inaction in the face of the violence and injustice overwhelming his people. Hear Habakkuk's complaint raised in prayer,

> "O Lord, how long shall I cry for help
> and you will not listen?
> Or cry to you, 'Violence.'
> And you will not save?
> Why do you make me see wrongdoing
> And look at trouble?
> Destruction and violence are before me,
> Strife and contention arise
> So the law becomes slack
> And justice never prevails.
> The wicked surround the righteous-
> Therefore judgment comes forth perverted.
> (Habakkuk 1:5-11)

In recent days I have asked, "O Lord, how long shall I cry for help?"

How long must I witness the violence done to our children by blighted housing that exacerbates asthma and triggers Hanta Virus? How long must I witness the wrongdoing wrought upon our children and teachers by inadequate and disparate funding of our schools? How long must I look at the trouble in our neighborhoods brought on by benign and malignant neglect? How long must I endure the violence and destruction that wreak havoc on our families through poverty wages and lack of wealth?

Habakkuk witnessed Assyrian domination followed by Babylonian domination. As Habakkuk came to know, I have come to know - that often calamity follows calamity. I see the pain of neighborhoods drowning in a sea of drugs, of families threatened by drug dealers and ignored by brutalized by rogue police officers. I know the despair of a failing school system that continues to be a political football kicked about by state and local politicians. I know the agony of decaying communities in which the church stands as the sole viable institution.

As a leader of BUILD I have given much time and effort in the attempt to save and revitalize failing communities through our "Blight Removal Campaign" begun in the East Oliver Community in response to the 2002 Dawson Family firebombing. Through that effort the neighborhood is being revitalized through the construction of new homes, the renovation of others, through the purchase of a liquor license to eliminate a drug attracting liquor establishment and through joint efforts with the Mayor's office and Police Department to reduce the drug trafficking in the community. That effort was led by the local BUILD churches that put up the first $2 million in property and assets and raised $10 million in public and philanthropic money to keep construction cost and thus home prices reasonable. Through Child First Authority and BUILD much has been done to organize parents to advocate for their children with that advocacy resulting in nearly a billion dollars for new school construction and renovation of others. The Living Wage Campaign which was conducted by BUILD in an attempt to save families doomed to poverty only to be preached to about the need for "competitive wages" was won and gave impetus to the new effort that will raise the minimum wage in Maryland to over $10/hour in a few years.

Walter Brueggeman tells us that it is our task- the task of prophetic leadership- "to bring to public expression the fears and terrors that have been denied so long and suppressed so deeply that we do not know they are there."[3]   He says, "Thus the prophet must speak evocatively to bring to the community the fear and the pain that individual persons wait so desperately to share and to own but are not permitted to do so."[4]

The prophet is challenged "to speak metaphorically but concisely about the real deathliness that hovers over us and gnaws within us, and to speak neither in rage nor in cheap grace, but with the candor born of anguish and passion."[5]   Brueggemann reminds us that,

> "It is the task of the prophet to invite the king [the political and economic leadership] to experience what he must experience, what he most needs to experience and most fears to experience, namely, that the end of the royal fantasy is very near."[6]

Our survey in 2003 of Baltimore's neighborhoods as we launched the "Blight Campaign" and our research through The Reinvestment Fund revealed the anguish of a city at the crossroads. We saw that Baltimore will become a ghost town unless there is dramatic intervention to save existing communities and to rebuild blighted communities.

Our 2012 survey of many of the schools of Baltimore revealed a school system in chaos. We encountered administrators too frighten to talk to parents, teachers demoralized by endless layoffs and re-assignments and students angry because they are the pawns in adult games. And we have publicly grieved the loss of school we had experienced in our youth and neighborhoods knew in their glory days. "O Lord, how long shall [we] cry for help?" We found buildings unfit for human habitation housing our children infested by mole and rodents, too cold in the winter and too sweltering in the spring.

Our 2011 survey of employment opportunities for African Americans in management and ownership in business revealed the same dismal findings of the 1980s- less than 5% African American. Drop- out rates and graduation rates were just as discouraging as many African American males sought employment in the only growth industry in the African American community- illegal drugs.

Grief without hope devolves to despair and inaction. Grief anchored by hope leads to renewed energy and action. In the darkest nights of grieving, in the loneliest moments of anguish there is always a "word from the Lord" to people of faith. Habakkuk found such to be true as God spoke to him in answer to his complaint,

"Write the vision,
make it plain on tablets,
so that a runner may read it.
For the vision is still a vision for the appointed time;
It speaks of the end, and does not lie.
If it seems to tarry, wait for it;
It will surely come, it will not delay.
Look at the proud!
Their spirit is not right in them;
But the righteous live by their faith."
(Habakkuk 2:2a - 4)

That is the challenge we face - to write anew vision for Baltimore, for our neighborhoods and our schools. It will be a vision birthed through the labor pains of our grief and our communion with God. This vision must be an alternative to the prevailing vision for Baltimore that sees gentrification of our neighborhoods, displacement of long-time residents, the persistent effects of redlining, profound health disparities, astonishing gaps in life expectancy by decades, marginalization of the poor, incarceration of our sons and daughters, lowering wages in the service industry by underpaying our newest immigrant population and continued feeding from the public trough by Baltimore's leading medical institutions and private developers as the only viable vision.

Brueggeman states,

"It takes little imagination to see ourselves in the same royal tradition
     -Ourselves in an economic affluence in which we are so well off that pain is
     not noticed and we can eat our way around it.
     -Ourselves in a politics of oppression in which the cries of the marginal are
     not heard or are dismissed as the noises of kooks and traitors.
     -Ourselves in a religion of immanence and accessibility in which God is
     so present to us that his abrasiveness, his absence, his banishment are not
     noticed and the problem is reduced to psychology."[7]

And the question we must ask ourselves is whether or not we have been so assaulted and co-opted by the prevailing vision that we have been robbed of the courage and power to create an alternative vision. Brueggemann says,

"The prophet engages in futuring fantasy. The prophet does not ask if the
vision can be implemented...Our culture is competent to implement almost
anything and to imagine almost nothing."[8]

Our task is to imagine an alternative inclusive vision for our neighborhoods and our city. Let that vision begin with the prospect of reclaiming our neighborhoods with the intent of creating the wealth necessary to sustain our families and our future. The vision must begin with a vision of neighborhoods free of blight. We know what blight does to a neighborhood and its people- the diseases it cultivates, the crime it breeds and sustains, and the sense of hopelessness and helplessness it engenders. And we know that the answer to blight is investment in the creation of neighborhoods of affordable, decent housing for working class and middle income homeowners. Our experience in has proven that in partnership with city and state government, we are and can continue to be the largest developer of affordable housing in the city. Everyone knows that home ownership leads to equity and equity is the beginning of wealth creation for most families. It's the American dream and we must make it our neighborhood's reality. "WRITE THE VISION, AND MAKE IT PLAIN!"

Let our vision include creation of healthy, well kept schools in every neighborhood. The schools must again reclaim their place as the center of neighborhoods, as a welcomed friend rather than a dreaded foe. We know that the wealth of any family oriented neighborhood, in part, is predicated on the quality of its schools. One of the major differences in the price of townhouses in Baltimore and the same townhouse in Howard County is the quality of the local schools. We must move quickly and deliberately to organize parents to reclaim our schools. Our survey revealed that there is great disparity in funding and resources of schools in the same district in Baltimore City. That disparity in part exists because of the involvement or lack of involvement of parents in the life of the schools. Every school, every teacher deserves quality parental involvement in the life of the school. Organized and involved parents will demand more resources for our children. Organized and involved parents will hold our school board accountable. Organized and involved parents will demand that control of the school system be returned to local control. Our schools must be made whole. "WRITE THE VISION - A NEW VISION- AND MAKE IT PLAIN!"

This new vision is for an appointed time - for a people who live by faith. We know the task awaiting us is a daunting one. We understand that visioning is the front-end of the process. We are not aiming for tomorrow or next week or next month. We are writing a vision that will propel us toward November 2016. This vision is for an appointed time. It may be delayed for a season but it will surely come.

M. Craig Barnes writes,

The most important thing we do in responding to the call of God is to show up. We don't have to be certain. We don't have to the best. We don't even have to want to be there. All that would matter if [ultimately] we were responsible for making changes. But we aren't. That's the life we had to abandon when we started following God's call. Now we just are responsible to show up with a vision of what God is doing in the world.[9]

> Show up as Noah did to build the Ark.
> Show up as Moses did to confront Pharaoh.
> Show as David did in a valley to encounter Goliath.
> Show up as Jesus did on Good Friday.
> Show up as Peter did on the Day of Pentecost.
> If we show up, ready and willing to be used God will show off by bringing to pass the vision He alone has given.

"WRITE THE VISION - A NEW VISON - MAKE IT PLAIN!"

Five Action Steps:

1. Invest time, energy and resources in non-partisan political organizing around an agenda negotiated within the African American community of Baltimore. Such an agenda can be determined through what the corporate community calls focus groups but in organizing are called "house meetings". House meetings are small gatherings of interested person to discuss what they see as the major problems facing a neighborhood or city. Listed problems are then tallied among groups and the top 3-4 issues are then interpreted into winnable issues that can be measured and evaluated to determine when they have been achieved.

2. Negotiate with Baltimore's corporate community job opportunities for ex-offenders who have demonstrated their willingness to engage in lawful employment and or training opportunities that will lead to jobs. Johns Hopkins Hospital/University is the largest employer in Baltimore and also the corporation that employs the most ex-offenders. Hopkins has demonstrated that ex-offenders can be effectively re-integrated into society if given a chance for "living wage" employment. Baltimore civic employment entity —the Mayor's Office of Economic Development—must be reorganized to provide training that leads to available jobs in growth industries while offering wrap-around services to those struggling to overcome addiction and other issues encountered by ex-offenders.

3. The religious community invest in utilizing their facilities to provide out-of-school time gathering places for youth. Such houses of worship can form both the value centered backdrop and daily programming to provide tutoring, recreation and homework assistance to young people struggling in the current public school system.

4. Because Baltimore has such a high level of drug addiction, drug treatment on demand must be available 24 hours a day if the city wants to seriously address the drug problem facing the city. Religious entities should use their bully pulpits to urge the philanthropic community to join the faith community in creating a pool of resources that could then be used to leverage additional resources from both the city and state to create the facilities and hire the staff necessary to seriously address the drug problem the city faces.

5. The African American community lead the effort to re-develop communities uptown to insure that neighborhood re-development doesn't devolve into re-gentrification but will be a process that recognizes the need for affordable housing for young families.

References

1. Barnes, M. C. (2009). *When God interrupts: finding new life through unwanted change.* InterVarsity Press.
2. Brueggemann, W. (2001). *Prophetic imagination:* Revised Edition. Fortress Press.
3. Chambers, E. T., & Cowan, M. A. (2003). *Roots for radicals: Organizing for power, action, and justice.* Bloomsbury Publishing.
4. Easum, W. (1993). Dancing with dinosaurs: Ministry in a hostile and hurting world. Abingdon Press.
5. Miles, D. I. (2000). *The pastor as discipler and church planter in the urban environment* (Doctoral dissertation, Wesley Theological Seminary).
6. West, C. (1993). Prophetic reflections: Notes on race and power in America. Monroe, ME: Common Courage Press.

Notes

[1] West, Cornel <u>Prophetic Reflections</u> p.224
[2] Ibid, p.224
[3] Brueggemann, Walter <u>The Prophetic Imagination</u> p.50
[4] ibid, p.50
[5] ibid, p.50
[6] ibid, p.50
[7] Brueggemann, p.41
[8] ibid, p.45
[9] Barnes, M. Craig, p.64

Part Three
Resources for Education and Change

In addition to the strategies and resources in the chapter in Part Three, some resources that give more information about the chapters in this section include both online resources and books:

Online resources

- Justice Policy Institute (justicepolicy.org)
- The Urban Institute (urban.org)
- The Sentencing Project (sentencingproject.org)
- National Women's Prison Project (nwpp-inc.com)
- Open Society (opensocietyfoundations.org)
- U.S. Sentencing Commission (ussc.gov)
- American Civil Liberties Union (aclu.org)
- The Drug Policy Alliance (drugpolicy.org)
- Office of Juvenile Justice and Delinquency Prevention (ojjdp.gov)
- The Coalition for Juvenile Justice (juvjustice.org)
- Baltimore City Online Community Association Directory
  http://archive.baltimorecity.gov/Government/AgenciesDepartments/Planning/OnlineCommunityAssociationDirectory.aspx
- Closing Cages: People Power Helps Stop Youth Incarceration
  www.truth-out.org/news/item/15023-closing-cages-people-power-helps-stop-youth-incarceration
- Leaders of A Beautiful Struggle
  www.LBSBaltimore.com
- Just Kids Partnership
  www.JustKidsMaryland.org
- Baltimore Algebra Project
  www.BaltimoreAlgebraProject.org
- YouTube Journal of Stop The Youth Jail Campaign Videos
  http://www.youtube.com/playlist?list=PLIZWFn4di5sqBbMxP9_1wcg-zAPvvzpPHn

Books

- Alexander, M. (2012). The new Jim Crow: Mass incarceration in the age of colorblindness. The New Press.
- Miller, J. G. (1996). Search and destroy: African-American males in the criminal justice system. Cambridge University Press.

City, State, and Federal Government

- Baltimore City Council District Lookup

  http://cityservices.baltimorecity.gov/citycouncil/
- Baltimore City Elections Board

  http://archive.baltimorecity.gov/Government/BoardsandCommissions/ElectionsBoard.aspx
- Senate Judicial Proceedings Committee

  http://msa.maryland.gov/msa/mdmanual/05sen/html/com/05judp.html
- House of Delegates – Judiciary Committee

  http://msa.maryland.gov/msa/mdmanual/06hse/html/hsecom.html
- Maryland State Board of Elections

  http://www.elections.state.md.us
- Who Are Your Elected Officials?

  http://mdelect.net
- United States House of Representatives

  http://www.house.gov/representatives/find/
- United States Senate

  http://www.senate.gov/general/contact_information/senators_cfm.cfm

ABOUT THE AUTHORS

Diane Bell-McKoy is President/CEO of Associated Black Charities, Maryland's leading African-American philanthropic organization. Its signature strategy, More in the Middle, expands opportunities/access for people of color, counteracting the detrimental impact of structural racism on economic and health outcomes. She serves on a number of philanthropic and civic boards in the State of Maryland to expand the conversation about these impacts. Diane has received numerous awards among them being named the Daily Record's Top 100 Women on three occasions, placing her in their "Circle of Excellence." She has also been named one of the Daily Record's Most Influential Marylanders in two categories - Philanthropy in 2010 and just recently in 2014 for civic leadership.

Ms. Bell-McKoy attended the University of Maryland, College Park and Baltimore County, an Honors University and received a Bachelor of Arts in Social Work. She received a Master's Degree in Social Work from the School of Social Work and Community Planning at the University of Maryland. She has received Leadership/Management certifications from a number of organizations including Harvard's Kennedy School of Government. Regardless of these accomplishments, Mrs. Bell-McKoy is most proud of her role as wife, stepmother and grandmother.

Rev. Heber Brown, III is an organizer and clergy-activist who currently serves as pastor of Pleasant Hope Baptist Church in Baltimore. For more than a decade he has devoted himself to community activism, legislative advocacy, and social justice. He travels the country engaging issues of racism, white privilege, poverty, food sovereignty, the prison industrial complex, police brutality, and gentrification. Dr. Brown is also the creator of Orita's Cross - an African Centered Church School curriculum and program designed to transform Sunday Schools into Freedom Schools - giving rise to the next generation of society's change makers. He earned a B.S. in Psychology from Morgan State University, a Master of Divinity from Virginia Union University, and a Doctor of Ministry degree from Wesley Theological Seminary.

Lawrence Brown is an assistant professor at Morgan State University in the School of Community Health and Policy. He partnered with Union Baptist Head Start in the Upton neighborhood to create the men's health and wellness program entitled You're the Quarterback: Gameplan for Life. Additionally, he has collaborated with the Baltimore Redevelopment Action Coalition for Empowerment (BRACE) in the Middle East neighborhood to push for justice for displaced communities by EBDI. He frequently appears on the Marc Steiner Show as a guest commentator on racial justice and health policy topics. He earned a B.A. in African American Studies from Morehouse College, a M.A. in Public Administration from the University of Houston, and a Ph.D. in Health Outcomes and Policy Research, University of Tennessee Health Science Center.

Samuel L. Brown is an Associate Professor of Public Administration and the Director of the Master of Science in Nonprofit Management and Social Entrepreneurship at the University of Baltimore. His primary research involves studying social, economic and health disparities. His current research efforts are on developing theoretical frameworks and practical guidance to permit enhanced understandings of how American institutions continue to foster current barriers to achieving the democratic ideal of social, economic, and political equality for all Americans. He graduated magna cum laude with a bachelor's degree in Economics from Towson State University, earned a M.B.A. from the University of Baltimore, and a Ph.D. in Public Policy from the University of Maryland, Baltimore County.

John T. Bullock is an Assistant Professor in the Department of Political Science at Towson University where he teaches courses in Urban Politics and Metropolitan Studies. He is a member of the Baltimore City Democratic State Central Committee and serves on several boards of directors including the Coppin Heights Community Development Corporation, the Empowerment Academy, and the Park Heights Community Health Alliance. Professor Bullock received a Doctorate in Government and Politics from the University of Maryland, a Master's in City and Regional Planning from the University of North Carolina, and a B.A. in Political Science from Hampton University.

Jeanetta Churchill is a Research Associate in the Institute at Urban Research of Morgan State University where she uses geographic information systems (GIS) to spatially investigate issues impacting urban populations. Ms. Churchill previously directed the Baltimore City Data Collaborative, where she produced tables and maps to monitor demographic and social indicators for children, youth, and families at the neighborhood level. Ms. Churchill holds a Masters in Urban Spatial Analytics degree from The University of Pennsylvania and a Master of Science degree in Biometry from the Louisiana State University Health Sciences Center.

Stacey K. Dennis is a graduate of Capella University's Master in Public Health program, with a concentration in Social and Behavioral Health. She has worked for the Baltimore City Health Department for ten years as a Disease Intervention Specialist within the Sexually Transmitted Diseases (STD) Program. Her work for the STD program has inspired her to create a comprehensive sexual health education program for adolescents, young adults and parents which she facilitates at schools and youth groups. Ms. Dennis is the Public Health Director for the Greater Baltimore Leadership Association and an active member of the Towson, Maryland chapter of Zeta Phi Beta Sorority, Incorporated.

Stacey-Ann Dyce is an alumni of University of Maryland Baltimore County (UMBC), and is a graduate of the Lincoln University Masters of Human Services Program, with a focus on Counseling, she is also working towards a PhD in Public health. She is currently an employee of the Baltimore County Department of Health as a Public Health Investigator, and human Services Associate. Ms. Dyce has worked in HIV/AIDS, STI prevention/service and care for over 10 years. In her spare time Ms. Dyce has participated in productions of The Vagina Monologues and continues to volunteer for the V-Day campaign, she also is a member and Assistant Director of Public Health of the Greater Baltimore Leadership Association (GBLA). Ms. Dyce is a Labor and Delivery Doula and an International Childbirth Education Association Childbirth educator.

J. Wyndal Gordon, Esq., "The Warrior Lawyer," is a noted Maryland attorney with office in Baltimore located who handles a wide-range of legal issues in the areas of criminal and civil litigation. Gordon has over 19 years of experience and is licensed in Maryland State & federal courts, as well as D.C. federal court. Gordon has litigated numerous high-profile cases in Maryland that have received both local & national attention. Additionally, he is a very active community servant, and works tirelessly to help improve the lives of young people. Professionally, Gordon is a member of several state and national bar associations, and is a past President of the Monumental City Bar Association, in Baltimore, founded in 1935 in part by Hon. Thurgood Marshall. Gordon has received numerous honors, awards, and certificates, for his dedication to legal profession and the people he serves.

J. Howard Henderson, President & CEO of the Greater Baltimore Urban League, has an impressive and successful history of dedicated service to his community and the nation. He has spent his adult life working to improve the living and working conditions of African Americans, other minorities, the underprivileged and the underserved. Prior to his Urban League appointment, Mr. Henderson demonstrated his commitment to human rights and civil rights in other employment venues. From 1980 to 1993, he served the National Association for the Advancement of Colored People, he served as a principal advisor to Dr. Benjamin L. Hooks, Chief Executive Officer. Before joining the national executive leadership team of the NAACP, Mr. Henderson was appointed by Gov. John D. Rockefeller, IV to serve as Director of the West Virginia State Employment and Training Division, Governor's Office of Economic and Community Development. Mr. Henderson is recognized nationally for his expertise in the areas of human and civil rights. During the past 30 years, he has been involved in many of the major civil rights issues, including affirmative action, economic parity, political empowerment, fair housing, and education. J. Howard Henderson graduated from Marshall University with a B.S. degree in Education and a M.A. degree in Education Administration. Mr. Henderson has completed The Center on Philanthropy at Indiana University the Fund Raising School, Chevron Texaco Management Institute and the Harvard Kennedy School of Executive Education.

Maurice Hunt is the President and Founder of Diabetes Awareness Project. His near death experience of surviving a 1616 mg/dL blood glucose level drives his passion for diabetes awareness. The Diabetes Awareness Project is a state-wide initiative that has set out to test and educate 1 million persons of the symptoms, treatment, and prevention of diabetes. His collaborations within Baltimore City have included Delegate Shirley Nathan-Pulliam and John Hopkins Center to Eliminate Cardiovascular Health Disparities. For more information about the Diabetes Awareness Project please visit www.diabeteswarenessproject.org.

Adam Jackson is CEO of Leaders of a Beautiful Struggle (LBS). Adam is a West Baltimore native, and Towson University graduate. He is engaged in community service projects around Baltimore City that deal with social and economic inequality. Adam is also the Director of the Eddie Conway Leadership Institute (ECLI) hosted by Morgan State University. ECLI is currently the only policy debate camp at a Historically Black College/University in the United States. He holds a B.S. in Interdisciplinary Studies and a M.A. in Geography and Environmental Planning from Towson University.

Linda Loubert earned a doctorate in Political Economy from the University of Texas at Dallas, is an Assistant Professor in the Economics Department at Morgan State University. Dr. Loubert's primary research interests are in the areas of public policy, including education finance. She integrates spatial mapping techniques with economic analysis and uses Geographical Information Systems (GIS) for spatial analysis of urban education in public schools. Much of her work also extends to gender and inequality in the workforce, and environmental and social justice issues for underserved populations.

Nicolette A. Louissaint holds B.S. degrees from Carnegie Mellon University in Chemical Engineering and Biological Sciences. She also completed her Ph.D. and post-doctoral training at Johns Hopkins University in Pharmacology in 2010 and 2013, respectively, specializing in HIV Clinical Pharmacology. Her dissertation research focused on HIV and drug distribution in the female genital and gastrointestinal tracts, to understand the behavior of drugs for HIV prevention. This work influenced drug formulation development for activity in key targets. She worked alongside investigators to develop methods for international trials. Nicolette also completed several clinical studies as a part of this work. As a member of the Baltimore Urban League, Nicolette has focused on addressing public health issues in the Baltimore area for over 4 years. Nicolette previously maintained an adjunct faculty position at Sojourner Douglass College, designing science and biotechnology curricula for Baltimore city adult learners. Her long term career interests include integrating science with policy to improve the lives of historically underserved populations.

Bishop Douglas I. Miles is a native Baltimorean. Bishop Miles is a graduate of Johns Hopkins University (1970), St. Mary's Seminary (M.A. Theology- 1984), and Wesley Theological Seminary (D. Min. – 2000). He was awarded an honorary Doctor of Divinity from Virginia Seminary and College.Bishop Miles has been in ministry 1967. For 15 years he served as pastor of Brown's Memorial Baptist Church in Baltimore. The church established the first homeless shelter with accommodations for women and their children in the city.He served as pastor of Greenwoood C.M.E. church in Memphis, TN. from 1988-92. The membership grew from 89 active members to well over 800. He is the organizer of Koinonia Baptist Church in Baltimore. Under his leadership the church has initiated a number of innovative ministries including an after-school initiative called Project Safe Haven, a juvenile alternative sentencing program called the Neighborhood Evening Reporting Center and a program for women recovering from addiction called the House of Tabitha.

Bishop Miles has served twice as president of the Interdenominational Ministerial Alliance and as a Clergy Co-Chair of BUILD. He has served as second vice-president of Mission Baltimore He is co-founder of the Baltimore Interfaith Coalition. Bishop Miles is a national award-winning columnist with the Afro-American newspaper. He has preached and lectured throughout the world lastly serving as Jellicoe Preacher at Oxford University in England and is published in a book of sermons entitled Living in Hell. He is married to the former Rosanna White, the proud father of two sons – Harvey and Dante and grandfather of five.

Judge William H. "Billy" Murphy, Jr. is the founder and a senior partner of Murphy, Falcon & Murphy and a former judge on Baltimore City's Circuit Court. With more than 42 years of practice Judge Murphy is recognized for his case success rates of 90% in state court and over 40% in federal courts. As a law student, he challenged the admissions policy at the University of Maryland Law School and persuaded his alma mater to set targets for enrollment of African American and female students. As a litigator he established legal precedents and a winning track record in complicated criminal and civil cases from corporate to consumer. His sought-after firm has led the defense teams for a host of the largest corporations in America, winning against high profile litigators. He has earned a reputation as being "scary smart" and encourages others to be fearless leaders on the subjects of race, economic prejudice, gender bias, and the politics of incarceration.

Tracy R. Rone is a native Baltimorean. She is a linguistic and cultural anthropologist at the Institute for Urban Research at Morgan State University. She also serves as Research Co-director for the Baltimore Education Research Consortium (BERC). Her research aims to illuminate urban education issues in high-poverty, resource-poor contexts through an anthropological lens. She is especially interested in issues of narrative, identity, the interface between health and educational disparities in urban communities. Her publications explore issues in narrative, African American academic achievement, and strategies for creating civic and intellectual engagement in undergraduate classrooms. She earned a B.A. from Goucher College, a M.A. from the University of Chicago, and a Ph.D. from the University of California, Los Angeles.

Chabria Thomas is the Project Manager and Lead Community Organizer in the Department of Community Outreach at Sojourner-Douglass College in Baltimore, MD. She has experience as a union organizer and representative for AFSCME and SEIU, two of the largest international unions. She continues to volunteer her support toward regional union organizing efforts. She was the recipient of the Dr. Charles W. Simmons Scholarship Award and Grant which supported her research on urban renewal in Houston, Texas. Currently, while studying urban planning and community economic development, she uses narrative-based writing to explore the intersections between Women of Color and community organizing as they relate to relationship-building and self-love. She will be conferred with a B.A. in Urban Planning and Community Economic Development conferred in March 2015 from Sojourner-Douglass College.

Roderick C. Willis is a journalist, senior citizen, and suffers from Type II Diabetes. He has been a social activist much of his life. He is an award winning journalist and photojournalist who reported on Environmental Justice and Environmental Racism, alternative energy, global warming and pollution and health disparities. His Type two diabetes Type 2 diabetes has caused him to experience some of its medical complications, including diabetic neuropathy and skin disorders.

He formerly wrote for The AFRO Newspapers. For seven years, he served as media consultant to the Greater Baltimore Urban League and is the former radio host for the Greater Baltimore Urban league radio program, The Viewpoint and was host of Morgan State University Radio WEAA AFRO First Edition. He is executive producer of a weekly TV news magazine broadcast in Washington, DC entitled, NewsULM. He has formed a strategic partnership with Diabetes Awareness Project and has been commissioned to produce a documentary film, The Faces of Diabetes, which is scheduled to be released in November 2014 with a companion book, Faces of Diabetes. The film and companion book are designed to educate the public about ways to manage, treat, prevent and reverse diabetes.

Donn Worgs is an Associate Professor of Political Science, and director of African and African American Studies at Towson University. Dr. Worgs received his doctorate in Political Science from the University of Maryland, College Park. His research focuses on education politics, African American politics and community development.

Rev. Sheridan Todd Yeary serves as senior pastor of the Douglas Memorial Community Church, and is an adjunct professor in the College of Public Affairs at the University of Baltimore. Dr. Yeary's justice work includes serving as Political Action Chair for the Maryland State Conference NAACP, and as co-founding principal of Community Churches for Community Development, Inc. A former air traffic controller and university administrator, Dr. Yeary is often called upon to facilitate creative conversations that solve tough problems. "Pastor Todd" believes honest dialogue creates opportunities to form partnerships that strengthen families and communities. Dr. Yeary serves on the boards of Baltimore City Community College, Behavioral Health Systems Baltimore, and the Center for School Mental Health. Dr. Yeary holds a Bachelor's Degree in Management from National-Louis University, a Master of Divinity Degree from Garrett-Evangelical Theological Seminary, the Graduate Certificate in African Studies from Northwestern University, and the Doctor of Philosophy Degree (Ph.D.) in the area of Religion in Society and Personality from Northwestern.